AF646461

ISLAM
and
SCIENCE

ISLAM
and
SCIENCE

Edited by

M.H. SYED

ANMOL PUBLICATIONS PVT. LTD.
NEW DELHI - 110002 (INDIA)

ANMOL PUBLICATIONS PVT. LTD.
4374/4B, Ansari Road, Daryaganj
New Delhi - 110 002
www.anmolbooks.com

Islam and Science

©Editor

First Edition, 2003

ISBN 81-261-1345-6

[Responsibility for the facts stated, opinions expressed, conclusions reached and plagiarism, if any, in this volume is entirely that of the Editor. The publishers bear no responsibility for them, whatsoever.]

PRINTED IN INDIA

Published by J.L. Kumar for Anmol Publications Pvt. Ltd., New Delhi - 110002 and Printed at Mehra Offset Press, Delhi.

Contents

Preface 7

1. **Introduction** 9
Furthering the Cause of Science •Foundation of Physical Science •Subservience of Natural Elements •Nature's Exploration, God's Glorification •Reason, the Test of Faith •Education made Compulsory •Persecution of Scientists in the West •Western Civilization: Direct Offspring of Arab Civilization •Intellectual Achievements of Early Muslims

2. **What is Science?** 29
Branches of Science •What is Directed in Al-Quran? •Ethical Values •Quran for Studying Science •Branches of Science Mentioned in Quran •Muhammad (PBUH) on General Education and Knowledge •Muhammad (PBUH) on Practical Education •Supremacy of God and Limitations of Scientists •The Apprehensions •Opinions about Religion •Cases of Believers •Cases of Unbelievers •Golden Age of Islamic Science •Muslims' Contribution •Spread of Islamic Science •The Downfall •Indian Muslims and Science •Consequences of Negligence

3. **Religion and Science** 87
Where Science Failed?

4. **Quran and Science** 107
Authenticity of the Quran. How It Came to be Written •Creation of Heavens and Earth •Basic Process •Modern

Scientific Order •The Solar System •The Galaxies •Plurality of the Worlds •Confronting Points •Answers to Objections •Quran on Astronomy •Sun and Moon •Stars •The Planets •Lowest Heaven •Celestial Organisation •Sequence of Day and Night •Evolution of the Heavens •Expansion of Universe •Conquering Space •The Earth •General Statements •Water Cycle and Seas •The Seas •More about Earth •On Electricity •On Shadows •Animals and Vegetables •Origin of Life •Reproduction in Human Beings •On Sex Education

5. **Greek Science Transferred to Arabs** 195
Conquest of Syria •The Abbasid Revolution •Translations into Arabic

Bibliography 239

Index 245

Preface

Islam is a scientific and progressive religion. Contrary to the common belief held by most of the people—who do not have an authentic and thorough knowledge about Islam, the religion and its philosophy—all its teachings have a scientific and logical approach.

Islam directs all its followers to learn, gain knowledge and master the arts and sciences of the contemporary world. Islam, as a living faith stands for spreading light and eliminating darkness from the world. This is a well-known fact now that Muslims were leading the world of knowledge and wisdom, when Europe was still a dark continent, far behind in education and science.

In the early era of Islam, the Muslims were in full command of the science and technology of the times. They not only unearthed, adopted and preserved the lost treasure of the Greek wisdom, but also promoted it to new heights. Muslim academics and scientists were among the leading lights of that period of history. They contributed a lot to the growth of all branches of science, be that Physics, Chemistry, Mathematics or Medicine.

This is all recorded in History, but the hard facts are least known to common people, as there is no comprehensive book on the subject, with an aim to cater to general readers. This modest work is an endeavour in the same direction.

This study has been based on a painstaking research, consuming years and benefited from the original sources and the holy scriptures. Its basic approach is empirical and scientific in spirit and practice.

Hopefully, this book would be able to satisfy the urge of all those who desire to know about real Islam and also to create a new awareness, regarding this religion, as a radical discipline, based on reason and opposed to fundamentalism and dogmatism. If that much is achieved, this humble effort may be taken as successful.

Editor

ONE

Introduction

The world history bears incontestable testimony to the fact that Islam gave unprecedented impetus to the intellectual development of the human race and that the early Muslims held high the torch of light and learning at a time when the whole world was immersed in ignorance and barbarity. The impression prevalent in the West that Islam is an unprogressive religion, antagonistic to science and civilization, is absolutely incorrect. Perhaps, no religion has been so greatly misrepresented and misinterpreted by prejudiced and uninformed critics as Islam. Far from adequately appreciating the glorious scientific achievements of the early Muslims and gratefully acknowledging the immense debt the world owes to them, the designing critics have shamelessly calumniated Islam by completely distorting historical facts and wilfully perverting established truths. Hopefully, it may be proved conclusively that Islam, far from retarding the progress of science, the chief factor of civilization, immensely furthered its cause. In fact, it was Islam that gave birth to modern science, inaugurated a scientific era in the world's history and made the early Muslims precursors of modern scientists and pioneers of modern civilization. The subsequent intellectual stagnation that came upon the Muslim world, giving rise to a false impression regarding Islamic influence, was entirely due to certain historical circumstances similar to those that prevailed in Europe during the Middle Ages, before the Renaissance and the Reformation. The Islamic faith and its teachings were in no way responsible for this social degeneration and political debacle.

Furthering the Cause of Science

It is now being realised that modern science owes its origin to Islam and modern progress is the outcome of the freedom of thought and spirit of enquiry prescribed for the Muslims by the Holy Quran, and not a product of Christianity which for a long time relentlessly proscribed all free thinking and liberal reasoning and even scientific researches on original lines, and horribly persecuted all those who indulged in these. The impression that it was Christianity that advanced science and civilisation is, therefore, as erroneous as the idea that Islam hampered their progress. In fact, there can be no comparison between Islam and Christianity as civilising forces. While the Muslims rose to a pinnacle of learning within a few centuries of the promulgation of Islam, the Christians remained steeped in ignorance for more than a thousand years.

After a careful study of the history of Islam, Canon Isaac Taylor came to the definite conclusion that "Islam has done more for civilisation than Christianity."[1] If Europe's indebtedness to Islam for the extraordinary progress it has latterly made in science and civilisation were adequately known, it would have astounded the modern civilised world. "During the darkest period of European history,"writes Bosworth Smith, "the Arabs for five hundred years held up the torch of learning to humanity." Arthur Leonard has truly said, "Islam, in fact, has accomplished a great feat. It has left a mark on the pages of human history, which is so indelible that it can never be effaced............. only when the world grows wiser will that be acknowledged in full."

That the early Muslims very largely contributed to the cultural development of the world cannot but be admitted by all unprejudiced and fair-minded critics of Islamic history. It is nothing but religious prejudice and an overweening sense of racial superiority which have stood in the way of acknowledgement and appreciation by the West of the glorious achievements of the East. Draper is perfectly justified in deploring "the systematic manner in which the literature" of Europe has continued to put out of sight our scientific obligations to Mohamedans. Surely they cannot be much longer hidden. Injustice founded on religious rancour and national conceit cannot be perpetrated for ever.

Foundation of Physical Science

It is a historical fact that cannot be controverted that, before the advent of Islam, the cultivation of science was condemned as heresy. The reason for this is not far to seek. The bulk of mankind could not at that time think in the abstract, and they looked upon the elements of Nature, the subject-matter of science, as sacred objects, possessing supernatural powers. They made idols, symbolizing different elements, and worshipped them as gods and goddesses, either for protection from evil or for attainment of certain objects. Thus were the sun, the moon, the stars, air, water, animals, and even trees and stones, deified and adored. It was not unnatural that in such circumstances any deviation from the prevailing belief in their sanctity should have been branded as sacrilege, and any attempt at a critical examination of their potentiality, for good or evil, stigmatised as profanity. Thus all that was useful in the heavens and the earth remained altogether unexplored, and for thousands of years man did not realise the sublime utility of the forces of Nature. It was reserved for the untutored son of the desert to open man's eye to the wonderland of Nature by bringing down her elements from the high pedestal of divinity, on which they had been placed, to the position of servants of mankind.

Subservience of Natural Elements

> *And He has made subservient to you the night and the day and the sun and moon and the stars are made subservient by His commandment; most surely there are signs in this for people to ponder.....*
>
> *Al Quran.*

Thus were the gods of the pre-Islamic people reduced by one stroke to man's servants. For the first time in the history of the world the Holy Quran declared in unmistakable language that the main purpose for which all objects, from the mightiest sun to the most insignificant atom, were created, was to minister to man's needs. Everything in the universe being intended for his use, man has been commanded to investigate their intrinsic properties,—in other words, to cultivate every branch of science. Thus, by declaring man the lord of the universe and everything in it subservient to him, the Quran gave a tremendous impetus to the development of scientific research. In fact the foundation of modern science was thus laid by acquainting man with the real nature of the forces and laws of Nature and by teaching him how to harness them for human service. The initiation of the conquest of Nature leading to the utilisation of its forces for the good of humanity is, indeed, one of the greatest blessings Islam has conferred upon mankind.

The Quran clearly indicated the way in which to reduce Nature to human service by contemplation and observation of four kinds, viz., *Tafaqquh, Tadakkur, Tafakkur* and *Taaqqul.* By the first a correct idea of things and their different features can be arrived at, by the second the knowledge of how to utilise them properly can be acquired, the third teaches the ways by which things have come into existence, while the fourth gives the knowledge which enables man to make the right use of different things in everyday life. It was the meditations indicated by *Tafakkur* and *Taaqqul* that actuated different kinds of scientific research among the early Muslims. This is how the Quran placed in the hands of man the key to the treasure-house of Nature, and Divine Revelation came to show him the way to material progress. Everything in the universe having been intended for the use of man, it was a virtuous act for him to conduct research into the realms of Nature in order to discover the utility of its various components. Thus, the first principle of progress, — the utilisation of the forces of Nature for the needs of man —became an article of faith with the Muslims, and impelled them to engage in scientific research.

Nature's Exploration, God's Glorification

The Prophet of Islam went so far as to carry out explorations of the realms of Nature, the real glorification of God, and to place the acquisition of knowledge on an equal footing with His worship. Man was required to glorify God not by mere lip service, but by discovering and utilising the properties and potentialities of the things He created to meet the needs of His creatures. Realisation of the scattered bounties of God was to be the realisation of God Himself. A Muslim was to spiritualise, as it were, his whole material surroundings by seeing and feeling the evidence of God's power and love in every blade of grass and in every breath of air.

> *Truly, in the creation of the heavens and earth, and the alternation of night and day, there are signs for men of understanding, who remember*

> *Allah standing, sitting and while lying on their sides, and ponder over the creation of the heavens and earth (and say) our Lord, You have not created (all) this in vain. Glory be to You.*
>
> *Al-Quran*

Reason, the Test of Faith

Before the advent of Islam, learning was confined to the chosen few. The masses had to blindly accept whatever was placed before them as their religion and they were not permitted to use their intellect or judgment. In fact, before the promulgation of Islam, religion was synonymous with dogmas and doctrines, rites and rituals; and bigotry had placed an embargo on freedom of thought and enquiry. Whenever anyone conceived any new idea or propounded a new theory, he was condemned by his co-religionists as a heretic. Some of the most inhuman atrocities ever committed on men in search of truth were thus perpetrated in the name of religion. It was Islam that for the first time discountenanced all dogmatic teachings and made reason the test of faith. "The first thing created" says the Prophet of Islam, "was reason. God has not created anything better than reason." On another occasion the Prophet said, "Truly, a man may have performed prayers, fasts, charity and pilgrimages and all other good deeds, but he will not be rewarded save in proportion to the sense he employs." According to the Quran, "There is no piety in turning your face towards the East or the West." *Iman* (faith) means knowledge of a truth or principle with such conviction as to its truth as will incite one to live up to it. It does not signify belief that cannot be translated into action. All this unmistakably demonstrates that Islam does not regard rituals and ceremonies as essentials of religion. In fact, mere dogmatic doctrines have no significance for a true Muslim, who has to observe his religion in every deed and action, in every thought and conception. He may indulge in free thought and free inquiry concerning everything that man's intelligence is capable of apprehending. To him, science, the aim of which is truth, is the greatest ally of true religion. "Islam stands almost alone," says Guizot in his *History of European Civilisation* "among the religions in discountenancing the reliance on tradition without argument. It demands that its votaries should undertake the investigation of the great work of their faith." Miracle has no place in Islam to which nature itself is a revelation of God, and its laws His eternal miracles, demonstrating His Majesty, His omnipotence and His benevolence. In fact, man knew nothing of God except through His work in Nature. Islam thus gave to scientific research a religious aspect unknown and unthought of before.

By thus putting an end to all conflicts between religion and science, and by making the first principle of scientific progress—the subservience of nature to man—an article of faith, Islam revolutionised the human mind, imparted immense energy and initiative to it and strongly impelled it to investigate the marvels of creation. Moreover, it immeasurably enlarged the scope of religion, which had till then been regarded only as a means of man's future salvation, but now, for the first time, came to be looked upon also as an effective factor in his material advancement. Every branch of learning conducive to human wealth and progress thus came within the purview of Islam, which harmonised the esoteric and exoteric sides of man's life. Thus modern progress had its origin in the spirit of free thought and investigation engendered by Islam.

Education made Compulsory

I have already stated what Islam did for two of the most important factors of modern culture and civilization. Let us now see what it did for another important factor, viz., the dissemination of knowledge. It is a historical fact that no messenger of God, from Noah to Jesus, had done anything worth mentioning for the dissemination of knowledge, which was selfishly monopolised by a few priests and theologians, anxious to retain all power in their own hands. But the Prophet of Islam, though he himself did not know how to read and write, laid the greatest stress on the acquisition of knowledge and made it essentially incumbent upon all his followers, irrespective of sex, rank, colour and country. *Talabul-Ilm Farizatun Ala Kulli Muslimin Wa Muslimatin:* "Seeking of knowledge is imperative for all Muslims, male and female." "He who has been gifted with knowledge", says the Quran, "has been gifted with an abounding blessing." Convinced that an ignorant person cannot adequately realise the greatness and goodness of God, the Prophet of Islam made acquisition of knowledge an essential of faith and did not approve of his followers being entirely absorbed in meditation upon God, "an hour's contemplation and study of His creation being better than a year's adoration." Muslims were particularly enjoined to be in constant search of knowledge "from the cradle to the grave," and they were told that "the ink of the scholar was holier than the blood of the martyr."

Thus in that dark age, when the world was enveloped in ignorance and illiteracy, Islam created an insatiable thirst for knowledge and caused a tremendous upheaval of science in realms hitherto altogether unexplored. Such an extraordinary outburst of intellectual activity was unparalleled in human history. Some undreamt of discoveries and inventions were made and these contributed immensely to the progress of civilisation and the welfare of mankind. There was hardly any science of which the Muslims did not make themselves masters. They created modern Chemistry, made most important discoveries in Astronomy, added much to the knowledge of Mathematics and Medicine and conducted very valuable research in Botany, Geology, Zoology and other branches of Natural Philosophy. The foundation of what is termed Physical Science was thus laid, and the gates of investigation into the marvels of creation were flung wide open.

The Muslims, by unravelling the mysteries of Nature and widening the scope of knowledge, introduced such blessings of comfort and happiness as were unknown in the world. It was the intellectual liberty and the spirit of scientific research inaugurated by them that brought about the European Renaissance and introduced into the modern world the arts and sciences which ennobled the heart, elevated the mind, thus making a major contribution to human happiness.

The height of scientific progress forecast by the Quran has not yet been fully attained. The world is full of materials that await man's exertion and ingenuity for their development and utilisation. There are millions of things in the realm of the seas and in the bowels of the earth and the ocean that have been created for man's use. All these have to be harnessed in order to meet the increased requirements of human society. The Quran repeatedly speaks of the subservience of the physical world and phenomena to man, whose duty it is to explore them for use.

Before the advent of Islam, the West, which nowadays claims all the credit for progress in science and civilisation, was steeped in ignorance and darkness. It was the intellectual liberty and scientific research inaugurated by the Muslims which brought about the Renaissance to which Europe owed its regeneration. Medieval Europe was a hot-bed of religious fanaticism and social conservatism; and the intellectual stagnation which prevailed there is altogether beyond conception in modern times.

Persecution of Scientists in the West

In medieval Europe religion and science were thought to be quite irreconcilable to each other, and whoever ventured to express any opinion contrary to the prevailing sacerdotal belief was not merely branded as a heretic, but was relentlessly persecuted, inhumanly tortured and even mercilessly put to death. For his belief in the theory of evolution, Vanini's tongue was torn out of his mouth and he was burnt alive. Hypatia, the renowned commentator on Plato, had to pay the penalty for her intellectual audacity with her life. Copernicus tried to demonstrate that the earth revolves and not the heavens. Thereupon even Martin Luther denounced him as "an upstart astrologer," and Calvin most severely condemned him. He had, therefore, to end his life in disgrace. Bruno, who dared to advance the Copernican theory, was seized, imprisoned and at last put to death by a "fire made slow to increase the torture." Galileo, who supported the Copernican theory, was thrown into a dungeon, horribly tortured and forced to recant as follows: "I, Galileo, being in my seventieth year, being a prisoner on my knees before your Eminences, having before my eyes the Holy Gospel, abjure, curse and detest the error and the heresy of the movements of the Earth." Not content with mere recantation, the Holy Inquisition sent him into exile for the rest of his life. Thus many a devoted votary of science fell a victim to Christian fanaticism prevalent in the Middle Ages, and some famous libraries, containing the accumulated treasure of ages, were consigned to the flames.

All this conclusively proves that the credit given to Christianity, as a religion, for promoting the cause of science is nothing but a travesty of truth.

Western Civilization: Direct Offspring of Arab Civilization

It is an uncontroverted truth that modern progress in the West was not the outcome of Man's faith in Church dogmas. In fact, the West made no progress worth the name as it was in the iron grip of Christianity. This is borne out by the fact that centuries of domination of Spain, from them the utter darkness in which they were groping and the appalling ignorance in which they were immersed. The extraordinary progress made by the Christian countries during the last five hundred years is directly due to the teachings of Islam, which were promulgated six hundred years after Christianity. It was not till freedom of thought was advocated and the torch of learning was lighted by the Muslims in Spain that any progress in science and civilisation could be made in Europe, or any possibility could arise for the Renaissance and the Reformation to make their appearance in the Christian world. It was from Muslim Spain that a new life dawned upon the whole of Europe, giving birth to a new culture, which greatly stimulated the intellectual activity of its people. All that Christian Europe learnt of Greek and Hindu Philosophy and Science up to the Renaissance period emanated from the Saracenic culture of Spain.

After the conquest of Spain the Muslims established there several Universities which opened their doors to all students without distinction of creed, caste, colour or country; and also boarded and lodged them at public expense. Spain thus became the centre of European culture, and scholars from all parts of Christian Europe looked to her seats of learning. Rogers, Bacon and other pioneers of the Rationalist movements in Europe, all received their education in the Muslim University of Cordova. Even the great Emperor Charlemagne had to send his son to Spain to be educated by the Muslim teachers, for nowhere else in Europe was there any seat of learning worthy of the name.

Every branch of science was seriously investigated in Muslim Spain. Medicine achieved greater development through the discoveries of her doctors and surgeons than it had gained during all the centuries that had elapsed since the days of Galen. Astronomy, Chemistry, Geography, Natural History, all were studied at Cordova with great ardour; as for the graces of literature, there never was such a time when poetry became almost the common speech of everybody. "The taste for science and literature," writes Renan, "had by the 10th century established, in this privileged corner of the world, a toleration of which modern times hardly offer us an example. Christians, Jews and Muslims spoke the same tongue, sang the same songs, and participated in the same literary and scientific studies." All the barriers which separated the various peoples were effaced: all strove with one accord in the work of a common civilisation. The mosques of Cordova, where the students could be counted by the thousands, became the active centres of philosophical and scientific studies. "It must be owned" observes John Davenport, "that all the knowledge, whether of physics, astronomy, philosophy or mathematics, which flourished in Europe from the 10th century, was originally derived from the Arabian schools, and the Spanish Saracen may be looked upon as the father of European philosophy."

Some idea of the architectural beauty and grandeur introduced into Europe by the Muslims may be had from the Alhambra Court in the Crystal Palace in London. Stanley Lane-Pool in "The Moors in Spain" has aptly described all this; he says, "Beautiful as were the palaces and gardens of Cordova, her claims to admiration in higher matters were no less strong. The mind was as lovely as the body."

As rightly acknowledged by Gustav Diercks in his 'Europe's Debt to Islam,' there can be no denying that Europe is deeply in debt to Islam for all its scientific discoveries. In fact, it was Islam that produced scientists who anticipated Bacon, Newton, Kepler and other great scientists of Europe. But for the introduction into Europe by the Muslims of paper, gun-powder, the mariner's compass and such other instruments of progress, who knows that the condition of Europe in respect of science and civilisation would not still have been today what it was fourteen hundred years ago.

The industries developed by the Muslims during their rule in

Spain were many and of farreaching consequence. Shipbuilding, horticulture, tanyards, glassware, silver mines, cotton manufactures, silks, woollen carpets, iron and copper utensils and inlaid metal work were some of these. The Muslims gave Europe the mulberry tree, the maize, the sugar-cane, the windmill and many such other items of industry. During the reign of the Spanish king, Al-Hakam, the irrigation systems were developed in Granada, Valencia and Arragon. In short, the art of war, industry, commerce and seamanship made unprecedented progress in Muslim Spain. It is a historical fact that 477 years before Columbus, the Arabs and the moors of Spain traded with the American continent.

Though the average westerner is under the impression that Europe's salvation was caused by the defeat of the Muslims at Tours (Poitiers), the real fact is that the world's progress was retarded for ages by this check on the advance of the Muslims in the West. Perhaps the darkest pages in the annals of history, dealing with the inquisition and such other disgraceful matters, would never have been written at all and Renaissance, which ushered in an era of civilisation in Europe, would have been accelerated by 700 years if the Muslims had won that battle and Islamised the whole of Europe. Anatole France who was above racial and religious prejudice, truly said in his *La Vie En Flour*. "The most tragic event in history is that of the Battle of Poitiers, when the science, the art and the civilisation of Arabia fell before the barbarism of the Franks."

It is indeed a most happy sign of the times that not only fair-minded individuals, whose illuminating observations have been quoted, but even a whole nation has at last realised that Europe's extraordinary progress in science and civilisation, which has given her a dominating position all the world over, is to be ascribed to the civilising force of Islam. As a mark of belated justice the Spanish Republic is arranging to establish an Arabic University at Madrid in order to commemorate what Islam achieved for science and civilisation during the Muslim occupation of Spain. It is hoped this will enlighten the world about the fact that the Muslims were the most zealous promoters and protectors of knowledge and culture for full one thousand years, during which other peoples were enshrouded in ignorance, bigotry and barbarism.

Intellectual Achievements of Early Muslims

It is now an undisputed fact that the early Muslims made incomparable contributions to the culture and civilizations of the world. Far from proscribing free thought and enquiry, or placing any ban upon the cultivation of science, as early and medieval Christianity had done, Islam gave it a tremendous impetus by making it a part of religion itself. A Muslim was enjoined to look upon the universe as an expression of God's attributes, and he had to explore it and utilise its objects for the service of mankind as an item of worship of their Creator. It was this religious stimulus to scientific research that particularly impelled the early Muslims to exert themselves so zealously for the advancement of science. A detailed account of their numerous scientific achievements would fill many volumes. The more the world advances in civilization, the more will their inestimable services to humanity be adequately realised and appreciated.

History bears witness to the fact that it was Islam that raised some of the most backward nations to the highest pinnacle of moral and material progress. Wherever the Muslims conquered a country, instead of slaughtering the vanquished, as was done by the Israelites of old, they gave them new life, inspired them with lofty ideals and raised them to a high level of civilization. Thus, indeed, were many savage tribes transformed into civilized people. To whatever land the Arabs migrated, they made it their home; they absorbed the culture of the conquered people and they did their best for the intellectual, moral and material improvement of the land of their adoption. The people to whom the later intellectual development of the Muslims was due were, for the most part, not Arabs but descendants of those who had adopted the faith of the conquerors. Wherever the banner of Islam was carried, remarkable centres of learning sprangup in no time and produced illustrious men in the fields of literature, arts, science and industry. Thus Damascus, Cordova, Granada, Baghdad and Cairo became, in turn, reputed centres of Muslim culture and held aloft the torch of light and learning, art and science in Asia, Europe and Africa, at a time when the West was sunk in ignorance and superstition.

Europe's indebtedness to Islam for her scientific progress is much greater than she cares to admit. She remained barren of all progress as long as she was under the heel of the Church. Even the intellectual development that had taken place among the Greeks and Romans disappeared under the persecutions of the Church. During the centuries of moral and intellectual stagnation in Europe, it was the Muslim who led the vanguard of intellectual progress in the world. There was a time when learning in Europe could be obtained only through the medium of the Arabic tongue. The very Renaissance, that awakened her from her long lethargy, was brought about by the impact of Islamic culture and learning. But for the conquest of Spain by the Muslims, who knows how long she would have remained in that savage condition. All her later achievements in the domain of science, art and learning owe their inspiration wholly and solely to the influences that emanated from Muslim Spain and penetrated the rest of the continent. All knowledge, whether of Astronomy, Mathematics, Physics or Philosophy, of which the Europeans later made themselves masters, was originally derived from the Saracenic schools. Besides, there has been hardly any reform—religious, social or political— from the time of Martin Luther to that of Lenin, which does not bear the stamp of Islamic influence. Draper has very truly said, "In whatever direction we look, we meet in various pursuits of peace and war, of letters and science, Saracenic vestiges."

Dr Campbell, a reputed British scientist, in his book *Arabian Medicine* writes, "When Europe was lying torpid in the depth of intellectual obscurity and gloom in the dark ages, culture and civilization were spread in the Islamic States under the high patronage of the Caliphs of Baghdad and Cordova, and at a time, when the Barons and Ladies of Medieval Europe could not even sign their names, almost every adolescent boy and girl in Islam could read and write freely and with ease."

In his famous *History of Human Society*, Professor Frank Blackmore of the University of Kansas writes, "In every country that was conquered, the first duty of Islam was to build a mosque in which Allah would be worshipped and his Prophet honoured. Attached to this mosque was a school where people were taught to read and study the Qur'an. From this initial point they enlarged the study of science, literature and art, and, through the appreciation of these sublime things, they collected the treasures of art and learning wherever these could be found. From imitation they passed on to the great field of creation, and great advances were made to the sum of human knowledge. Schools were founded, great universities established, and libraries were built which laid the permanent foundations of knowledge."

The Muslims made phenomenal progress in Science in a wonderfully short time. They visualised, thirteen centuries ago, many things which are being discovered today. They explored and exploited the potentialities of objects which had remained unknown and unthought of since the creation of the world. In fact, there was hardly any conceivable subject to which they did not give serious thought. They made most important discoveries in Chemistry, in Astronomy, in Mathematics, in Medicine. They specialised in History and Geography. They unearthed Alchemy and Algebra. They initiated and developed the study of Political Economy and Sociology, which till then had been unknown sciences. They carried out valuable research in Zoology, Geology and Botany. Muslim students, accompanied by artists, travelled far and wide to study various vegetations, which were minutely described by pen and brush. Alherin, a renowned botanist, travelled to and fro in India for forty years collecting materials for his studies. Besides, Muslims investigated and wrote on various other subjects such as navigation, agriculture, irrigation, gardening, statistics, chronology and topography. Even aviation, the latest achievement of Europe and an early wonder of the twentieth century, was not left untried. The first two martyrs among the conquerors of the air were Muslims. In the reign of Khalifa Al-Mamun, a scientist named Abul Qasim invented an aeroplane, but crashed when flying and was killed.

In the eighth century, the Abbaside Khalifas established the famous academy of Baghdad, where the works of the renowned mathematicians Euclid, Archimedes and Appollonius, of the astronomer Ptolemy, and of the naturalists, Hippocrates and Diomedes were translated. In this and other Muslim centres of learning, Greek culture was kept alive at a time when, outside Byzantium, it had no abiding place in the non-Muslim world. Many were the libraries, observatories and laboratories that were established by Muslim kings. In the library attached to Baitul-ul-Hikmat, the abode of learning, a remarkable university founded by Khalifa Harun-al-Rashid, there were many hundred thousand Sanskrit, Greek, Coptic, Chaldean, and Persian books besides those in Arabic. Khalifa Al-Hakim's library was so very extensive that its catalogue had to be prepared in forty large volumes.

Chemistry: Modern Chemistry, as Humboldt rightly says, was "admittedly the invention of the Muslims" whose achievements in this sphere were of unique interest. They conclusively proved the worthlessness of ancient chemistry. They found out the chemical affinities of mercury, lead, copper, silver and gold and knew the chemical processes of oxidation and calcination. A number of words such as alembic, alkali, etc., were derived from Arabic. Jabir bin Hayyan, known as Geber in the western world, wrote some five hundred treatises on chemistry. He discovered, for the first time, nitric acid, sulphuric acid, aqua regia, silver nitrate and several compounds. The Muslims were the first to teach the world distillation, filtration, crystallisation, etc. They knew how to change a liquid into vapour. It was in Muslim Spain that chemistry was first established in Europe, and would have reached its zenith there, had the Muslims not suffered the disastrous defeat at Poitiers. Jildaki was the last great Muslim chemist. He died in 1361 A.D.

Astronomy: The Muslims may be said to have written their names on heaven itself. They identified and classified a large number of stars in their observatories. They made wonderful discoveries concerning the movements of the Solar system and other astral bodies. They ascertained the size of the earth, the variation of the lunar latitudes and the precession of the equinoxes. Averroes (Ibn-i Rushd) discovered the sun-spot: Al-Hazan (Abul Hasan) discovered atmospheric reflection; Al-Maimun determined the obliquity of ecliptic; Ibn-i-Junus, Nasiruddin Tusi and Albani constructed astronomical tables of great value. Albani's tables were translated into Latin and formed the basis of astronomical study in Europe, where that science was introduced by the translation of the works of Muhammad Farghani. Abu Junus and Al-Batan were two of the greatest Muslim astronomers. It was the Muslims who first built observatories in Europe and invented the telescope, and compass, the pendulum and many other useful astronomical instruments. The most famous of the many observatories in the Muslim Empire was that at Marghana near Taurus, built in 1259 A.D.

Mathematics: Almost every branch of higher mathematics bears the impress of Muslim genius. Many were the improvements effected by the Muslims in this important subject. The Arabic numerals, the decimal system and the art of figures, which Europe got from the Muslims, gave a great impetus to learning. By means of these the Muslims led the world in Astronomy, Mechanics and Mathematics. Algebra, Statics, Conic Sections and other branches of applied Mathematics are amongst Muslim discoveries. In Geometry the Muslims were the first of all nations to translate Euclid and use his ideas. His work was not properly translated into any European language till the sixteenth century. The Muslims for the first time applied Algebra to Geometry. They discovered equations of the second degree, and developed the theory of quadratic equations and the binomial theorem. They invented spherical Trigonometry and, by introducing the use of Sine and Cosine, they made great contributions to the science of surveying and astronomy. The Muslims were the first to use instruments of precision for the measurement of time by the use of the pendulum and the measurement of heavenly bodies by the use of the astrolabe.

Medicine: The father of the present-day European medical science was Avicenna (Ibn-i-Sina), whose *Materia Medica* is still in vogue. Aven Zoor (Ibn-i-Zoar) was a great authority on pharmacy, which was an institution of Muslim invention. He and others carefully studied the effect on the body of drugs obtained from various parts of the world, and discovered many remedies. The Muslim doctors were the first to use anaesthetics. Al-Bucasis of Cordova was an expert surgeon of world-wide reputation. There were renowned surgeons, opticians, dentists and specialists in female diseases. The science of optics owes much to Muslim research. Al-Hazan, who understood the weight of air, corrected the misconceptions of the Greeks as to the nature of vision and demonstrated, for the first time in history, that the rays of light come from the external object to the eye, and not from the eye itself, impinging on external things. He showed that the retina is the seat of vision, and proved that impressions made upon it were conveyed along the nerves to the brain. He discovered that the refraction of light varied with the density of the atmosphere and *vice* *versa.* In Baghdad, there were no less than 860 doctors of different classes, each class of whom made one particular branch of medicine their special study. Doctors as well as chemists had to pass an examination in order to obtain a license to practise. There were hospitals throughout the wide Muslim empire. All classes of people, irrespective of their creed, caste, colour and country, were freely admitted to these hospitals.

Geography and History: There are in Arabic many immortal works on Geography. The spherical shape of the globe was demonstrated by the Muslims at a time when the scientists of priest-ridden Europe emphatically asserted that it was flat. The great historical achievements of the Muslims are too well-known to require detailed mention. They produced several thousand books on history, ranging in magnitude from one to eighty volumes.

To sum up, for about one thousand years the Muslims made history; they held aloft the torch of light and learning and spread knowledge and culture throughout the world. But for-the vast intellectual heritage bequeathed by them to the people of the West, it would not have been possible for them to make the immense progress they have now made. The Muslims were in the vanguard of the world's advancement as long as they were true to Islam and faithfully followed the lofty injunctions of the Holy Quran. Their downfall began as they left the path of true Islam. Interestingly, there were orthodox Christians; in the iron grip of Christianity that they could make any appreciable advance in science and civilization. In one case the influence of a peaceful and progressive religion and in the other the effect of the disappearance of religious fervour and the presence of materialistic greed are clearly observable in the history of their respective notable achievements.

The pre-Islamic religions confined their operation to the moral aspect of human nature, and almost altogether ignored its worldly aspect. But Islam, in addition to morality, laid much stress on the practical aspect of man's everyday life. Under the inspiration of Islam, the chief mission of which is the service of humanity, the Muslims attended to such useful subjects as were calculated to contribute to the material welfare of mankind. Realising that man's material progress depends upon his mastery over nature, they devoted themselves to the development of useful sciences such as chemistry, astronomy, medicine, agriculture, irrigation, navigation, etc. Had the idea of man's capabilities to harness the forces of Nature to the service of humanity dawned on the human mind before the Holy Prophet of Islam taught it, the immense potentialites of Nature would have been utilised for the welfare of mankind long before the promulgation of Islam.

Most of the outstanding achievements of the people over whom religion has little influence and who are guided more by the fear of man than by the fear of God, have been in the domain of arms, ammunition, explosives, poisons—of death and destruction rather than of peace and construction. Had their religion had sufficient influence over them, the followers of Christ, who enjoin the turning of one cheek if the other is smitten, would have never been so very eager for the invention of all sorts of death-dealing instruments.

After the enjoyment of power, wealth and supremacy for about a thousand years, the Muslims became enervated and luxury-loving, and a sort of blight overtook them. Spiritual stagnation and intellectual sterility soon followed as a natural consequence. This has more or less been the case with all other religious communities. The Muslims themselves, and not Islam, are entirely to blame for this regrettable check on their progress. A glance at the condition of the world before and after the promulgation of Islam would convince one of what it is capable of accomplishing. The decadence of the Muslims must not, therefore, be thought to stem from their religion. It would be a great injustice to Islam to judge it by the life led by its present-day followers. True Islam, which is life and light, is very different from what goes by its name today—a bundle of dead rites and meaningless rituals.

It is, however, gratifying to note that Muslims are at last realising that they have strayed from the essentials of their noble religion and are now engaged in controversies over mere trifles. I believe true Islam will again assert itself. Signs of Islamic renaissance are already visible all over the Muslim world. Movements pregnant with great potentialities are afoot in Turkey, Persia, Arabia, Egypt, and Afghanistan. It is hoped that, before long, Muslims will shake off the languor and lethargy that have come upon them, and will be able to take their rightful place in the progressive movements of the world.

Islam, which means peace and submission to the will of God, is not a new religion promulgated by the Prophet Muhammad, but the oldest religion based on the unity of God, proclaimed by Abraham, Moses, Jesus and all other Messengers whom the Lord was pleased to send at different times and in different climes for the reclamation of degraded and debased humanity. Islam simply claims to have purged that religion of adulteration and impurities which had crept into it in the course of time. It would, therefore, be a misnomer to call it Muhammedanism. A Muslim has to believe in all the Scriptures that were revealed from time to time, and he has to respect and revere all the Prophets who preceded his own. Universalism is thus the most distinctive feature of Islam, which is intended, not like other religions for a particular time or a particular country or a particular nation, but for all time, for all countries and for all peoples.

Some of the master minds of Europe and America, like the great poet Goethe, the great historian Gibbon, the great philosopher Carlyle, the great orator Ingersoll, the great socialist George Bernard Shaw, who is perhaps the greatest intellect of the present age, among others, were most profoundly impressed by the message of Islam, and all of them lauded the greatness of its Prophet. Although an atheist himself, and hardly any dogma of any religion has passed unscathed by his trenchant pen, Bernard Shaw thinks Islam is the only religion that can satisfy all intelligent people who want a religion to guide them spiritually, morally and socially. The strongest argument advanced by him to prove the universal acceptability of Islam is that it has the great power of absorbing every form of progress made by philosophy and science.

That Bernard Shaw is not beside the mark in his forecast regarding Islam's future may be judged by what Islam, which is now in its fifteenth century, has done. Its comparison with other religions in their fifteenth century may give an idea of what it is likely to be in its twenty first century. It is, in the opinion of unbiased judges, the only power that can effectively withstand the atheism, scepticism and materialism that are gradually getting a hold over the entire civilized world.

TWO

What is Science?

Referring to *New Webster's Dictionary* the meaning of science may be (1) "knowledge" especially of facts or principles, gained by systematic study, (2) a particular branch of knowledge especially one dealing with a body of facts or truths systematically arranged and showing the operation of general laws; (3) systematized knowledge, especially of the laws and facts of the physical or material world, (4) skill resulting from training.

According to different scientists: Science is the systematic knowledge of natural phenomena and the mutual relations among them, it is the investigation or endeavour to find the inherent cause of any event and the knowledge obtained from such endeavour.

Thus we see that the subject matter of science are: to study or investigate the physical world or the nature created by Almighty and to understand as to how things have been created and as to what laws they are obeying. Knowledge thus acquired is applied or techniques evolved from such knowledge are used, for the benefit of mankind.

Thus, if we study different stars in the sky, we observe them to follow some laws; each of them rise in the east at a certain time and set in the west at a certain time. There are also different types of stars, some are near to us, some are located at infinite distance away, some are bright and some are not. Their arrangements in the sky are also different, they are being arranged in different ways as well. A group of infinite number of stars arranged in different forms make a galaxy. There are infinite number of galaxies located at infinite distances away from each other. Our sun, one of the stars of the galaxy, the Milky way, has its own characteristics. Some (at present nine) planets are revolving around the sun. The planets have no light of their own. They are seen shining bright because of sun's ray reflected from their surfaces. Our earth is a planet and the moon revolving around it is its satellite. The earth while revolving around the sun spins (rotates) around its own axis. The mystery of the heavenly bodies in the sky is studied in science. One of the branches of science, which deals with planets, stars, galaxies, cosmogony, etc., is the astrophysics.

There are other branches of science as well. Thus, studies of earth surface and its interior is the subject matter of geology. In this branch, different objects of the earth such as mountains, rivers, seas, different layers of the earth's crust, etc., are studied. There is also a subject called geography to survey and study earths surface.

Scientists' attempt to use the resources, discovered through such studies for the mankind. Crude oils, coal, different minerals, etc., discovered as a result of study are being used by the present mankind.

Study of nature includes also the atmosphere that envelopes the earth's surface. Characteristics of the atmosphere, its formation, changes, uses, etc., are studied in a branch of science called "Meteorology."

Most of the earth's surface is covered by ocean and bounties or gifts of Almighty for mankind are plenty in the ocean and beneath the ocean. Oceanography is a subject of science to study the oceans and the oceanic resources. There are ocean-related technologies studied in Marine Engineering for using ocean resources by man.

Branches of Science

Some of the various branches of science are: Botany for studying plant life, Zoology for animal life. Medical science to study human beings, Chemistry for studying elements, compounds and reactions among them.

There has been widespread involvement of different types of energy in the creation of the Universe, in otherwords, energy is inherent in the creation processes. There has been continuous changes of energy from one type to another. The different manifestations of energy are heat, light, electric, magnetic, gravitational, nuclear or atomic, etc. Matter, different types of energy, different natural objects and the physical laws are studied in Physics. There are several branches of physics as well.

Thus, it is observed that the main aims and objectives of scientists are to study or investigate and analyse different things of the universe and to gather or acquire knowledge from such studies and to realize the complexity of the creation of Almighty and to get benefited from the acquired knowledge.

Nowadays with the help of the acquired knowledge from scientific studies of nature, scientists could make various devices, machines, conveyances for use. It has become possible to improve medical treatment, advent new medicines, etc. These practical or applied branches of science is the technology. Presence of scientific knowledge has given birth to technology. Of the different technical departments, different engineering branches, electronics, computer science, communication, biotechnology are some. Because of the advancement of technology, innumerable industries and factories have been established throughout the world.

What is Directed in Al-Quran?

For common persons though surprising, it is true that Almighty has instructed or suggested or advised mankind to study His created world or in other words nature, to reflect and do research on different things and phenomena so that man may realize from the study complexity of creation, laws guiding them and find means for using natural bounties of Almighty. In fact, Al-Quran is an open invitation to mankind for studying the natural world and to get benifitted from it. This invitation or suggestion has been put forward in about 750 verses of total 6666 verses of the Holy Quran (about one eighth of the whole Quran). These verses have put stress on Al-tafaqqur (research on natural things and natural laws) and Al-taskheer (make effort to get benifit from the natural bounties through technology). Study of nature has its inner significance also. In fact, a true observer or researcher of nature can realize Almighty, the Creator of all things. In this regard Almighty has said:

> "And how many signs in the heavens and the earth Do they pass by? Yet they turn (their faces) away from them" — (12:105)

> "On the earth are Signs for those of assumed faith, as also in your own selves. will yet not then see?" — (51:20,21).

Ethical Values

It is seen in the present discussion that people are instructed or advised by Almighty to study natural things on this earth and on the sky. Man has been given this freedom and for this he has been bestowed with intellect and capacity to think. In the course of searching knowledge in scientific ways, it is to be always kept in mind that knowledge gathered thus is useful for mankind, and helpful to understand Tawheed i.e. Oneness of Almighty and is not misused in various ways such as waging wars and other such activities. Al-Quran has been revealed with the aim of making or guiding man. so that he may reach the goal of perfectness and he may maintain a balanced state in all earthly activities. It has not only explained basic philosophy of life. It also wants man to maintain a balance between philosophy and action in real life. Man must maintain congenial atmosphere with his fellow men and others i.e with the environment. That is why along with private or personal activities such as faith (*Iman*), *salat* (daily prayers), fasting, etc., man has been advised to observe or study and think (research) on natural things i.e., his environment. There is no doubt that from the study of nature i.e science man is benefited in this world, but the most basic aims of encouraging or advising people for studies of different subjects of science (which are nothing but studies of nature) are to let people know by themselves that:

(i) There is a Creator, only one Creator of the Universe. He is the Almighty, Scientist of scientists, Omnipotent, Omnipresent and He is Allah, (e.g. verse, 2:255)

(ii) The Universe has been created in a well organised and balanced way with different components. and all objects obey natural laws as framed by Almighty (e.g. verses , 41:11, 67:3)

(iii) Man is created as a servant of Almighty. He is also a viceroy of Almighty on this earth. He has been created by Almighty with many qualities and intellect so that he may learn lessons or realise examples of Almighty on observations and studies of natural things and praise Almighty. All natural things obey Almighty's order or command (natural laws). Man also should lead his life as per commands of Almighty, (e.g. verses: 2:30-31, 51:56, 55:5-6)

(iv) A time will definitely come, when this Universe will be destroyed and every man will be given as per his performance in this world, reward or punishment in the Hereafter by Allah, (e.g. verses: 14: 48-51, 40: 16-17)

Thus, the main aim of encouraging studies of nature (science) by Almighty is not just to get benefit in this world but also in the Hereafter. The Messenger of Almighty (PBUH) has cautioned the people against using knowledge for worldly purposes only. In this regard Abu Huraira reported Allah's Messenger (PBUH) as saying.

> "He who acquires knowledge, the sole purpose of which is seeking the pleasure of Allah but he does not acquire it except for gaining worldly ends, he would not smell the odour of Paradise on the Day of Resurrection."
>
> —Ahmad, Abu Dawud, Ibn Majah

Quran for Studying Science

(A) Do not ye see, look, reflect ?

Almighty has invited man in the Holy Book to study science in different ways. Almighty in many verses of the Holy Quran has asked people to observe and study or think carefully different natural objects, like, stars, rivers, plants, animals, birds etc. and learn or gather knowledge from them: Thus, Almighty says:

> ".... See how Allah did originate Creation"
>
> —(29:20)
>
> "... See they not how Allah originates creation..?"
>
> —(29:19)
>
> "... Seest thou not ..... ?"
>
> —(24:43, 31:29, 39; 35:27, 39:21)
>
> "...See ye?..."—(25:9; 56:63, 68:5,71; 71:15-16)
>
> "... Do they not look ?.."
>
> —(16:48, 79; 32:27, 36:71; 50:6; 67:19; 88:17)
>
> "...think..." —(86:5) "... Do they not reflect ?..."
>
> —(30:8)

"... Do not the unbelievers see?..." —(21:30)

"... Read in the name of Thy Lord ..." — (96:1)

In this way in many other verses also Almighty has asked man to observe His created things (natural things) and reflect or apply intellect. For this Almighty, of course, has adorned man with necessary organs such as ears, eyes, brains, etc.

"He gave you hearing and sight and intelligence
and affections that you may give thanks to Allah"
—(16:78)

It is known to everyone of us that all living creatures having ears are able to hear sound and having eyes can see objects. But simple hearing is not sufficient. On hearing it is necessary to understand as to what is being heard, it is necessary to study or reflect on the source of sound and act accordingly. Similarly simple observation of any thing visually is not an observation in the real sense. On seeing or observing a thing, it is necessary to study and do research on the thing to learn or get knowledge from it, and that will be the observation in the true sense. Almighty has asked people to observe natural things in the real sense.

(B) There are many Signs, things to learn

Almighty is supreme. He is the source of all knowledge and the Scientist of scientists.

In the creation of the Universe the slightest (*koon*) scientific talent and techniques, etc, of Almighty has been manifested. From the scientific studies of different natural things i.e. created things of Almighty one can get some idea of their Creator, techniques involved and glimpses of His infinite knowledge. The student of science may feel His existence in their studies. He gets amazed by the fact that beautiful scientific laws are involved in different natural phenomena. Tawheed or idea of Oneness of the Creator, Almighty becomes obvious from the studies of science as a set of laws are operating universally, one is not contradicting another. That's why Almighty has said repeatedly in the holy Quran that there are signs or things to learn or sources of knowledge in the observation and research of His innumerable objects in nature.

In this connection the Arabic word '*aiatoon*' has been used , whose meaning may be examples, advise, signs or sentence. Analysis of the sentences using this word gives the meaning as Signs of Almighty, His scientific talent and technique, His proof of existence, etc. One can go through the following verses of the holy Quran in this connection.

> "... Verily in these things there are Signs for those who reflect ...." —(13:3; 30:21; 45:13)

> "...... Verily in these things there are Signs for those who are wise"
> —(2:164; 13:4; 16:12, 67; 30:24; 45:5)

> "... There are indeed Signs for men of understanding" —(3:190)

> "... Signs for them ..." —(36:33, 37, 41)

> ".... Verily in this are Signs for all who constantly persevere ....." —(31:31)

> "... Do they not travel through the land, so that their hearts (and minds) may thus learn wisdom and their ears may then learn to hear?....."
> —(22:46)

> "... Verily in this is a Sign for those who listen ..."
> —(16:65)

> ".... Signs for those who fear Him ...." —(10:6)

> ".... And among His signs ...." —(30:20-25)

> ".... Signs for those who believe ...."
> —(6:99, 45:3)

> "... Signs for those of assumed faith ...."
> —(45:4)

In the verses mentioned above and in many other verses of the Holy Quran, Almighty has invited or instructed man to observe and study various things (nature) created by Him. And from the studies one can observe His signs and realise existence and oneness of Almighty. Methods of study of nature or finding the truth may be different for different observers. One may take the help of argument, logic or intellect to explain natural phenomena. These are theoretical explanations. For verifying such theories one may take the help of experiments i.e, real observation of the phenomena and see if the theories i.e theoritical explanations of the phenomena are true.

Scientists take the help of both approaches (theory and experiment) for studying natural objects and phenomena. Theoretical explanation is also based on certain observations and assumptions and takes the help of mathematics and other allied branches. Experimental observations and verification or explanation are based on real observations and takes the help of sophisticated instrumentations. Theories and experiments make a complete Science.

(C) What else is said about Science in the holy book?

Al-Quran was revealed as a guide to lead a life in the right path so that man may get benefited from this, in this world as well as in the Hereafter.

Allah has asked man repeatedly for His Ibadah as many as 82 times in the Holy Quran. This refers to daily prayers, good deeds etc. Allah has also invited or instructed man to study His creations (in natural things) and get benefited from the innumerable bounties of nature.

Study of nature has its importance in the performance of Ibadah, since it helps to understand or realize innumerable signs of Allah, His infinite scientific talent in the creation, oneness (Tawheed) of Allah, it thus brings a believer nearer to Allah. The invitation to study science (nature) has been repeated in as many as the 750 verses (about one eighth) of the whole Quran. Thus for example Allah said:

> "Do ye not see that Allah has subjected to your
> (use) all things in the heavens and on earth, and
> has made His bounties flow to you in exceeding
> measure, (both) seen and unseen?" — (31:20)

In fact Islam is not a blind faith. The Almighty has given man some faculties to use to understand things in his llfe.

> "It is He Who has created you, and made for you the faculties of hearing, seeing, and understanding: Little Thanks it is ye give."
>
> —(67:23)

In all ways, He has asked men to study nature: Look at the following verse:

> "Behold ! In the creation of the heavens skies, and the earth; In the alternation of the night and the day;
> In the sailing of the ships through the ocean for the profit of the mankind;
> In the rain which Allah sends down from the skies, and the life which He gives therewith to an earth that is dead;
> In the beasts of all kinds that He scatters through the earth;
> In the change of the winds, and the clouds which they trail their slaves between the sky and the earth; "(Here) indeed are signs for people that are wise. —(2:164)

This way the Almighty has advised man in about 750 verses to study natural things, to do research on natural phenomena and from the knowledge so gathered people may be able to use nature or harness nature for their own benefit. Studies also will enable people to realise His Signs of His might. He says:

> "And He has subjected to you, as from Him, all that is in the heavens and on earth: behold, in that are Signs indeed for those who reflect."
>
> —(45:13)

Branches of Science Mentioned in Quran

Attentive reading and analysis of the verses related to suggestions for science education reveal that in fact all branches of modern science such as Astrophysics, Space Physics, Environmental Science, Oceanography, Meteorology, Hydrology, Geology, Zoology, Botany, Medical Science, Physics, Technical Science or Engineering, etc., have been mentioned in the Holy Quran. Some are cited below:

(i) Suggestion for Studies of Geological Science

The Almighty has asked man to study geologized science in a number of verses, for example:

> "A Sign for them is the earth that is dead: We do give it life, and produce grain therefrom, of which ye do eat." — (36:33)
>
> "Do they not look on the earth, for many noble things of all kinds We have produced therein?" —(26:7)
>
> "It is He Who has made the earth manageable for you, So traverse ye through its tracts and enjoy of the sustenance, which He furnishes:" —(67:15)
>
> "(Do they not look) and at the mountains how they are placed firm and at the earth How it is spread out ?" —(88:192; 20)
>
> "It is He Who hath created for you all things that are on earth" —(2:29)

Studies of earth's surface, rocks, etc., have enabled scientists to know the time of formation of the earth (age of the earth), its different stages of formation, different materials or compositions of the surface, etc. As a result, man has become successful to discover and use different minerals found on the surface and below the surface of the earth. But it is surprising and unfortunate that in spite of Quranic instructions Muslims have not been successful in geological science. Even Islamic countries having rich oil deposits could not make progress in the fields of petroleum exploration, production, refining and other related industries. Scientific and technical aid is being taken from other countries by these countries for the purpose. It is possible to make progress in the fields of agriculture, mining, etc., if advancement is made in Geological science as well. The Almighty has created this earth with all the necessary things for the use of mankind. Geological studies, research and technical knowhow will help to harness and use such bounties available on the surface and beneath the surface of the earth.

(ii) Studies of Water Resources: (Hydrology and Hydrography)

It has been established by scientists of biological science that water is the essential life supporting ingredient for life and life began in water as well. In this regard Almighty the Creator of all things says:

> "We made from water every living thing"
> —(21:30)

Water is essential for every form of life whether it is plant or animal. The connection of water with life is intimate. The basis of all living matter in the physical world; protoplasm is water, the vital power of protoplasm seems to depend on the constant presence of water. Almighty says,

> "And Allah has created every animal from water"
> —(24:45)

> "It is He Who has created man from water"
> —(25:54)

For the sustenance of various lives on earth Almighty has arranged distribution of water throughout the world, so that all may receive its support according to needs.

> "......And We send down pure water from the sky, that with it We may give life to a dead land and slake the thirst of things. We have created, cattle and men in great numbers and We have distributed (the water) amongst them."
> — (25:48-50)

About 75 per cent of the earth's surface is covered by water. This means that water is predominant on our globe. Without water no living thing can survive. Such an important thing deserves studies, so that this unparallel bounty of Almighty could be realised and also could further be used by man for diverse purposes.

Regarding water, Almighty says:

> "See ye the water which ye drink? —(56:68)

The meaning of the above verse is simple. It asks man to study or do research on water and glorify Almighty for giving its diverse qualities. In this regard, there are points of reflection in the following verse:

> "Seest thou not that Allah sends down rain from the sky, and leads it through springs in the earth? Then He causes to grow, therewith, produce of various colours: then it withers; thou wilt see it grow yellow; then He makes it dry up and crumble away. Truly, in this, is a message of remembrance to men of understanding." —(39:21)

There are a few other verses in the holy Quran about water. Nowadays, knowledge about water has been substantially increased because of scientific studies and truth has been established regarding its universal essentiality in life formation, sustaining and surviving processes. There have been extensive studies on diverse qualities of water, chemical characteristics, etc, and techniques have been evolved for drinking pure water, supplying water for agricultural purposes, for generating electricity and for using it in many other ways. Studies on water is so extensive that a separate subject viz "Hydrology" has been created for studying different sources of surface and ground waters and for using them.

Now the question is that despite repeated instructions given in the Quran for study; research on water, do Muslims have developed or given any stress to develop Hydrology as a subject for acquiring knowledge and get benefited from it? We observe that Muslims are not at all concerned about this type of scientific studies.

(iii) Studies of Oceanic Resources

Three fourth of the surface of the earth has been covered by sea water. In addition to this vast water resource, there are innumerable things on the sea bed. Below the sea bed there are different minerals, petrols, etc. For using these oceanic resources and also for harnessing ocean in proper ways, man must study to know qualities of ocean water, ocean bed and its geographical or geological structures, different minerals available, their distribution, etc, and man must find out or make devices or ways and means for using these resources. Gratefulness to Almighty will also be associated along with the use of Almighty's bounties available in the oceans. In this regard Almighty says:

> "It is he Who has made the sea subject, that ye may eat thereof flesh that is fresh, and tender, and that ye may extract therefrom ornaments to wear, and thou seest the ships therein that plough the waves, that ye may seek (thus) of the bounty of Allah and that ye may be grateful."—(16:14)

Again in another verse He says:

> "It is Allah Who has subjected the sea to you, that ships may sail through it by His command, that ye may seek of His bounty, and that ye may be grateful." —(45:12)

In this way after getting indication or information of bounties of Almighty in the sea and instruction to harness them, no believer (Mumin) can stay away from study of sea and get benefit from it. In this modern age of science, a subject viz "Oceanography" has thus been opened in many Universities. For the profession of sailing on the sea i.e. for joining the navy and also to learn techniques of harnessing oceanic resources "Marine Engineering" is taught in many institutions. Muslims of the world can be compared with other communities as to how far they have made progress in this field.

(iv) Studies of Winds or Aerodynamics

In this modern age "Aerodyanamics" has been a major subject of science for study. Detail knowledge of the atmosphere, air motion, its pressure, temperature, density and their variations, etc., is necessary for design and manufacture of modern means of communication such as aeroplanes, means of defence and offence such as aircraft, missiles, rockets, etc. Knowledge of atmosphere is also necessary to fly all these and monitor their motions through atmosphere.

In other fields of our daily activities air or atmosphere is also used extensively. Thus, from olden days air is being used for sailing purposes. Air driven machines are also being used nowadays for generating electricity. But what is most important about air is that it is most essential for life due to the presence of oxygen in it. All these and more can be known and air can be used in proper ways if studies and researches are carried out on atmosphere. Almighty has said regarding air in the Holy Book this way:

> "Among His Signs is this that He sends the winds, as heralds of glad tidings, giving you a taste of his Mercy, that the ships may sail by His command and that ye may seek of His bounty in order that ye may be grateful."
>
> —(30:46)

In a single line of the above verse many qualities, bounties, etc., of winds have been indicated. All the benefits obtained from wind are nothing but mercy of Almighty. The winds are not only essential for surviving life, they are also means of purification and bring blessing of Almighty in terms of rain which make the soil fertile and fill the rivers and ponds with fresh water. Air helps international business and mixing up through sea-ways (sailing) and now by air-ways (floating in air). Those who know, i.e. study and do research for utilising wind, with prosper and rejoice, while those who ignore or fail to understand Sign of Almighty will perish.

(v) Meteorology

This is another branch of science which includes studies of climatic condition such as pressure, temperature of atmosphere and rainfall. All these and other informations of the atmosphere help people in various ways such as in agriculture and in communication.

Meteorological informations can be had from the studies of

atmosphere. The following verse describes different phenomena occuring in the atmosphere and ask people to observe these phenomena so that people may get benefit from such observation:

> "Seest thou not that Allah makes the clouds move gently, then joins them together, then makes them into a heap?" Then wilt thou see rain issue forth from their midst. And He sends down from the sky mountain masses (of clouds) wherein is hail: He strikes therewith whom He pleases and He turns it away from whom He pleases. The vivid flash of its lightning well-nigh binds the sight."
> —(24:43)

Not that winds, clouds in the atmosphere, together with the process of formation of rain drops, hails and lightning, all these topics of meteorology are mentioned in the above verse. By the words "seest thou not" and "then wilt thou see", Almighty has asked man to study all these phenomena.

(vi) Agriculture and Climate

There is intimate relation between climate of a place and its agriculture. Wind and the atmospheric condition control the formation of clouds alongwith their movement and cause rain. Proper rainfall converts a dead land into a living, fertile and beautiful land bearing a rich harvest. Allah said in this regard

> "It is He Who sendeth the winds like herald of glad tidings, going before His Mercy: when they have carried the heavy-laden clouds. We drive them to a land that is dead, make rain to descend thereon; and produce every kind of harvest therewith." —(7:57)

For a good harvest, only rain is not sufficient, quality of land must be good i.e. land must be fertile. Almighty has indicated this in the following verse which is the continuation of the above mentioned verse:

> "From the land that is clean and good, by the Will of its Cherisher, springs up produce, (rich)

after its kind: but from the land that is bad,
springs up nothing but that which is scanty, thus
do we explain the Signs by various (symbols) to
those who are grateful" —(7:58)

Thus, there is necessity to study and to research on climate and on quantity of land for good agricultural products. Detail knowledge of climatic conditions enable a cultivator to know pressure, temperature, wind condition and probable rainfall in the season of the place. Detail knowledge of quality of cultivating enables cultivators to know its fertility, moisture conditions, ground water, mineral contents, of the soil. Knowledge of climate and quality of land will thus help the cultivators to select suitable land, help to prepare the land and help to choose proper timing for cultivation for a good harvest.

(vii) Studies of Plant Life: Botany

Almighty has advised, suggested or directed mankind through about 750 verses of the Holy Quran to study and do research on nature i.e. science. In some verses, He mentioned His creation, in some verses He mentioned natural phenomena, in some cases. He has asked man to ponder about the creation. In short, nature includes all natural things and natural laws. Modern science also includes studies of all branches of nature. Studies of plant life is a separate subject in science called Botany. Studies of plant life include all types of plants, flowers, fruits, crops, etc. Animals including birds and man depend for their survival on plants and their products. There is necessity to study these things for getting more benefit from them. Also innumerable signs of Almighty can be realised in all the phenomena of plant life. Almighty describes about His wonderful creation of plants this way:

"It is He Who sendeth down Rain from the skies:
With it We produce vegitation of all kinds:
From some We produce green (crops), out of
which We produce, close-compounded grain out
of the date-palm and its sheaths (or spathes)
come clusters of dates hanging low and near:
and (then there are) gardens of grapes, and olives

> and pomegranates, each similar (in kind) yet
> different (in variety):
> When they begin to bear fruit; Feast your eyes
> with the fruit and the ripeness thereof:
> Behold! in these things there are Signs for people
> who believe. —(6:99)

There are many other verses of this type about plants and their products in the Holy book. It is worth noticing that instructions for study, research and reflection have been given in above verse by the sentence:

> "When they begin to bear fruit Feast your eyes
> with the fruit and ripeness thereof." —(6:99)

In the above mentioned verse, Almighty has invited man to study carefully the processes involved in plant growth, how flowers bloom and then come fruits from flowers and the changes taking them in the fruits. On study and reflection one can realise if not understand the complexity and sophistication of the processes involved and the inherent divine power which would make foundation of his faith in Almighty more deep rooted. Studies of Botany is also necessary in order to explain and understand various verses related to plant life. Further, there is some indication about the causes of their growth. We know in the cases of man and animals that a pair of male and female is necessary for the spread of their offsprings. Similar is the case in vegetable life and in other living organisms of which we do not know. Almighty said in this regard:

> "Glory to Allah, Who created in pairs all things
> that the earth produces, as well as their own
> (human) kind and (other) things of which they
> have no knowledge. —(36:36)

Almighty has asked man to observe or study the processes of germination and growth of plant from seeds and contemplate to find out the causes of their growth.

> "See ye the seed that ye sow in the ground? Is it
> ye that cause it to grow or are We the cause?
> —(:56: 63, 64)

Deep study and contemplation will reveal that only Almighty, the all powerful is behind all the phenomena.

> "It is Allah Who causeth the seed grain and the date-stone to split and sprout" —(6:95)

In the above verse the seed-grain and the date-stone are cited as examples of vegetable world. Scientists (Botanists) will notice that the seed grain includes the cereals (such as wheat, barley, rice, millet, maize, etc.) which are monocotyledons, as well as pulses (such as beans, peas, grams etc.) and other seeds which are dicotyledons. The word "split and sprout" in the above verse represents a double process: (1) the seed divides and (2) one part (plumule) shoots up seeking the light, and forming leaves and the visible parts of the future tree, and the other part (radicle) digs down into the dark, forming the roots and seeking sustenance from the soil. Thus, seed is mentioned in the above verse as one small instance of the vegetable kingdom. Studies and researches show the diversity, complexity, and supreme scientific talent involved in the processes of many other cases. In spite of such vivid and specific instructions in the Holy Quran, Muslims though followers of the Book have not shown enthusiasm to study vegetable kingdom i.e. Botany and as such their knowledge in this field is also very insignificant. Other communities or nations already have concentrated in the study of botanical science and have made progress in applying their knowledge for various purposes such as making medicines, cultivation in scientific ways and also in biotechnology.

(viii) Studies of Animals, Birds, etc: Zoology and Veterinary Science

Let us see whether Almighty has given any instruction for studies of animal life i.e. zoological science or not. Almighty mentioned varieties of animals existing in nature and asked man to contemplate on their birth, different activities and the benefit obtained by mankind. He Says:

> "Allah has created every animal from water: of them there are some that creep on their bellies, some that walk on two legs: and some that walk on four" —(24:45)

The creeping things include worms and lowly forms of animal life as well as reptiles, centipedes, spiders, and insects. Where these have legs they are small and the description of creeping or crawling is more applicable to them; fishes and sea-animals swim, their swimming is like "creeping on their bellies". Two legged animals include birds and man. Most of the mammals walk on four legs. All these include the whole animal world. This world is open for study for man. Almighty has mentioned specifically domestic animals and their use by man for carrying loads, getting milk, medicine like honey, etc. He has thus given sanction to study animal science or veterinary science.

> "And verily in cattle will ye find an instructive
> Sign. From what is within their bodies, between
> excretion and blood, we produce for your drink,
> milk, pure and agreeable to those who drink"
> —(16:66)

Again:

> "Do they not look at the camels, How they are
> made?" —(88:17)

Cattle and camels are mentioned in these verses as instances of domestic animals. Camel *is* specially common for Arabs, but cattle throughout the world. In the above two verses, indication for study is given by the words "ye find an instructive sign." and "Do they not look". It is indeed a matter of contemplation as to how milk is being produced in the body of the female. It is not wonderful that the same food, eaten by male and females, produces in the latter, the wholesome and complete food, known as milk? Also when cattle are tamed and specially bred for milk, the supply of milk is greater than is necessary for their young and it is wholesome and good diet for man. In all these there are points of contemplation. These verses encourage man to study Veterinary Science, in particular and Zoological Science, in general.

Regarding bee He says:

> "And thy Lord taught the bee to build its cells in
> hills, on trees and in (men's) habitations; then to

eat of all produce (of the earth), and follow the ways of thy Lord made smooth: their issues from within their bodies, a drink of varying colours, wherein is healing for men.

Verily in this a Sign for those who give thought."

—(16:68,69)

Production of honey by bee and its healing power for man are subjects of study and research. Science or Chemistry is involved in the production of milk by animals and honey by bees.

(ix) Chemical Science

It includes studies of different elements, minerals, compounds, chemicals, reactions between chemicals, etc., and synthesis of new chemicals or compounds, gases, etc. An example of chemical activities is the production of fire. Almighty says:

"See ye the fire which ye kindle?" — (56:71)

Again:

"(He) Who produces for you fire out of the green tree, when behold ? Ye kindle therewith (your own fire)! —(36:80)

Fire or flame or in other words burning of gases, petrols, kerosenes, woods, etc, involve lot of Chemistry. There is intimate relation of fire with trees. Nearly for all the fire, the fuel is derived from the wood of trees. Even coal is nothing but the wood of prehistoric forests petrified under the earth through ages. Studies of all these will include chemistry of the phenomena.

(x) Studies of Medical Science

Medical Science is a subject for studying different processes involved in birth and growth of man and diseases causing ailments and death of man. Ways and means such as medicines, operations, etc., for treatment of man, when attacked by diseases, are also taught in this subject. In this field also Muslims are not in the forefront. For their backwardness in learning Medical Science, Muslims may have some other reasons, but there is no religious prohibition. Rather, Almighty has given instruction or invited mankind to study the life processes and to contemplate on it. Almighty says:

> "Let man but think from what he is created."
>
> —(86:5)

With a question mark Almighty has described in the holy Quran:

> "Was he not a drop of sperm emitted (in lowly form)? Then did he become a leach-like clot; then did (Allah) make and fashion (him) in due proportion. And of him He made two sexes, male and female." —(75:37-39)

Again:

> "Has there not been over man a long period of time, when he was nothing (not even) mentioned ?" —(76:1)

In the above two verses, question mark is to be specially noted. Unless one studies or knows basic phenomena involved in the processes mentioned in the two, how one can agree to or understand the answer given in the same verses. The way of expression in the verses is clearly an invitation to study various aspects of birth, growth and other related things of the human being. In these modern days, medical science has made tremendous progress in all fronts. Fertilization (conception) in the mother's womb, gradual growth and development of different organs (embryology), birth, growth after birth, different diseases and their treatment with the help of most modern techniques are all studied in Medical Science. Now it has even become possible, because of Medical Science, to transplant or replace some organs of human body, operate upon heart and produce test tube babies. Researches are going on in full swing in different laboratories of the world to discover new medicines for various diseases and for treatment of dreaded diseases. Also scientists are busy, at the same time, to know the mystery of human life itself.

(xi) Studies of Physical Laws etc.: Physics

Almighty has created innumerable things on this earth vis-a-vis- this Universe. They are subjected to certain physical laws i.e. they are obeying certain laws which are commands of Almighty. Thus, for example, every particle of matter in the Universe attracts every other particle due to gravitation. The force of mutual attraction that acts between any two particles are directly proportional to the product of their masses and inversely proportional to the square of the distance between them. Planetary motion about sun is governed by such laws. Every object even movement of air, a leaf of a tree, flow of river water, etc., follows or obeys physical laws framed by Almighty.

Almighty says:

> "Seest thou not that to Allah prostrate all things that are in the Heavens and on earth."
>
> —(22:18)

Again:

> "Do they not look at Allah's Creation, among things, how their shadows turn round, from the right and the left, prostrating themselves to Allah, and that in the humblest manner? And to Allah doth prostrate, all that is in the heavens and on the earth, whether moving creatures or the angels: for none are arrogant....."
>
> —(16:48-49)

Prostrating means to lay flat before Almighty as a token of submission i.e. worshiping Almighty. The verses, it seems, carry mystic meaning. Inanimate things even their shadows are told as recognising Almighty and humbly worshiping Him. Even their shadows turn round according to position of light and humbly prostrate themselves on the ground to celebrate the praises of Almighty. It is known that shadows or any other things behave not on their own. They are found to obey certain laws and those laws are framed by Almighty Himself. Obeying of those laws means obeying of Almighty's commands.

By the words "Do they not look at Allah's creation," Almighty has asked man to study different laws framed by Him and obeyed by His created things including living creatures and angels. Physics include studies of these laws.

Physics, a subject of science, includes studies of different laws of natural phenomena. Further, energy is involved in the creation and maintenance of natural things. Light, heat, electricity, sound, etc., are all different manifestation of energy. Studies of these energies are also included in Physics.

(xii) Studies of Astrophysics and Space Physics

The Universe includes planets, stars, galaxies, clusters of galaxies and other bodies, all moving in controlled ways but maintaining infinite distances between any two of them. Studies of the Universe and contemplation on them enables man to realise a little of infinite scientific talent and power of Almighty, the Creator of all things of the Universe. The holy Quran declares,

> "It is Allah Who has Created the heavens and the earth and all between them;..." —(32:4)

All these objects are subject to certain laws, as framed by Almighty:

> "He has made subject to you the night and the day: the sun and the moon; and the stars are in subjection by His Command: Verily in this are Signs for men who are wise" —(16:12)

It is indeed necessary to think or study as to how night and day happen for us; sun, moon, planets and other heavenly bodies in the sky move or what laws are obeyed by them. The sky with all these objects is full of beauty and magnificence, design and order, plainness and mystery. Almighty has asked people:

> "And (Do they not look) at the sky, how it is raised high?" —(88:18)

This way Almighty has advised mankind to observe the sky, the bodies adorned with and contemplate on their origin, physical laws obeyed by them, etc., so that man can realise the power of creativity, etc., of the Almighty.

Many people worship, out of ignorance, different objects of the sky as their gods attributing to them powers of doing good or bad for the people.

He says:

> "Among His Signs are the Night and Day, and the Sun and the Moon. Prostrate to Allah, Who Created them—" —(41:37)

Studies of Astrophysics remove ignorance and prejudice from the mind and help one to identify false gods and know Almighty, the creator of all the objects.

In these modern days of science, Astrophysics and Space physics are two major subjects. Scientists are studying and doing research by observation and other theoretical methods on different objects of the sky and have succeeded in knowing many things: about their motion, evolution, etc. Because of such knowledge and because of the tremendous progress in science and technology, it has become possible for the man to venture into outer space, to land on the moon and to send space probes to collect informations of planets, galaxies and other objects. Researches are going on in full swing in this regard throughout the world.

It is a matter of concern that of the vast Muslim population a very insignificant number of them are astrophysicists.

(xiii) Space Exploration

All Praises to God, Who is the Lord of the Universe (all worlds)

One of the many aims of this book is to encourage. Muslims to come forward for science education and to remind them that Almighty has advised, instructed and also invited man to study nature or in other words science. Through studies of different branches of science, our knowledge increases and one can realise the complexity of our creation and hidden Signs of God, faith (Iman) of the faithful becomes more intense or deep rooted.

Nowadays scientists are not only engaged in study and research on terrestrial things and phenomena, but also have made progress in studying the earth's atmosphere. Knowledge gathered from such studies are being used by mankind. Now, not being satisfied with the study of atmosphere, scientists have ventured into outer space beyond the atmosphere. They are busy to explore outer space to study planets, stars, galaxies and other objects in the sky. This step is insignificant compared to the vastness of the Universe. Because of the infinite size of the Universe there is no possibility for man to explore or go beyond the boundary of the Universe. In fact there is no boundary of the Universe, He says:

> "O ye assembly of Jinns and men! If it be ye can pass beyond the zones of the heavens and the earth, pass ye! Not without authority shall ye be able to pass!" —(55:33)

This verse has given the indication of the vastness of the Universe and limited ability of man. The sun, moons, stars and other objects are created by God for the use by man, as gifts from Him. They may be studied within man's limitation and may be made useful in many ways. He has not put any condition or hindrance in studying the objects of the sky:

> "He has made subject to you the night and day; sun and the moon, and the stars are in subjection by His command: verily in this are Signs for men who are wise." —(16:12)

In the above verse, the words "subject to you" and "who are wise" are worthy of notice. Man may be more benefitted from the heavenly objects on study, reflection and applying knowledge gathered from such studies.

(xiv) Technical Education

The essence of knowledge is having it, to apply it; not having it, to confess your ignorance as put by great Confucius. Studies of nature or science has given birth to Applied Science and Technical Education. For science education many experiments are performed for observation of any phenomenon and verification of theoretical predictions or results. Experimentation needs many equipments and it is required to establish laboratories. Scientific knowledge gathered this way is used or implemented in many ways for better life style and comfort. As a result of scientific knowledge various machines, vehicles and other communication systems, ways and means for defense, etc., are being invented and being used. Industries for production of various items; whether it is medicine, food, cloth, vehicles, electronic goods, stationaries, etc., are established throughout the world. There were several messengers of Allah, the Almighty before Muhammad (PBUH) who were blessed with technical knowledge. Thus, Prophet David (Dawood) was a good technologist to make various items with iron. He says:

> "And we made the iron soft for him; (commanding), "Make thou coats of mail, balancing well the rings of chain armour, and work ye right." —(34:10-11)

Manufacture of coats of mail and defensive armour are attributed to David. In this verse, with the mention of technical knowledge of David, the God had warned David and his whole people by the words "Work ye righteousness". David made the armour, but it was to be worn not only by him but all the warriors. But he and his people were to be careful to see that they did not deviate from the paths of righteousness. This warning equally applies to todays scientists, engineers and people of the world. Manufacturing anything should be aimed at for righteous causes, it should not in any case create problems or misused by Governments or individual to creat disturbances on this earth. Prophet Solomon was also a great engineer. He used brass for making various materials, dishes, temples known as "Temple of Solomon."

Al-Quran mentions it in this way:

> "And we made a Font of molten brass to flow for him (Solomon);...." —(34:12)

> "They (Jinns) worked for him as he desired, (making) arches, images, basins as large as wells, and (cooking) Couldrons fixed (in their places)." —(34:13)

The Almighty made violent and speedy winds available to the land of Solomon. He had miraculous power over winds and could tame them for his use.

> "(we made) violent wind flow for Solomon"
> —(21.81)

> "And to Solomon (we made) this wind (obedient),
> " —(34:12)

> "Then we subjected the wind to his power, to flow gently to his order, whatsoever he willed...."
> —(38:36)

Solomon used wind energy in his own way. Nowadays wind power has become one of the major sources of energy. God has granted man intelligence and faculties by which he can tame different forces of nature like winds for his use.

The story of ship building technique or engineering may be traced back to the days of Prophet Noah. It was to be a great flood during his time. So Noah was instructed by Him to remain afloat in the flood, so that the righteous could be saved in it during the flood.

> "And construct Ark under our eyes and our inspiration." —(11:37)

> "Forthwith he (started) constructing the Ark"
> —(11:38)

Thus, we see from the verses mentioned above that there was technical culture among the people of the past and several prophets were directly involved in technical or engineering activities. They possessed knowledge of metallurgy, heavy construction work, taming wind energy for useful purposes, ship building, using iron and brass. Al-Quran has characteristics to mention history of the past so that people can learn a lesson from them. The Prophet Muhammad (PBUH) himself showed examples in his lifetime. He never hesitated to take most modern techniques of his time for defense purposes. Thus for example, he constructed trench (Khandak) to save Medina from the attack by the enemies, the people of Mecca, which was a very new technique at that time in the whole Arab world. In the expedition to Khaibar, he also adopted new techniques. He (PBUH) adopted technical tricks or knowledge whenever necessary to win a war.

Muhammad (PBUH) on Education and Knowledge

Progress of any nation is judged by the number of properly educated people of the nation. One of the ways for People to become wise or educated is by study on "Nature" and reflection or research on natural things and phenomena. Educated men and women can understand or realise the vastness of the Universe, complexity of the macro as well as microworld and also realize the greatness of the creation of the God.

Muhammad (PBUH) was illiterate, but he was enlightened by the best of knowledge by Almighty Himself. He was guided and shown the best path and he could realise the creation of the Universe better than any other human body. That is why, gathering knowledge through education, and reflection were dearer to him. Because of importance and necessity he has made education compulsory for all Muslims. Muhammad (PBUH) said: as reported by Anas:

> "The seeking of knowledge is obligatory to every Muslim" —Ibn Majah; Baihaqi

Again he (PBUH) said as reported by Anas:

> "One who goes out to search for knowledge is (devoted) to the cause of Allah till he returns"
> —Tirmizi and Darimi

Again as Abu Umama Al-Bahili reported,

> "Allah's Messenger (PBUH) said: The superiority, of a scholar over the devout is like my superiority over one who is of the lowest rank amongst you"
> —Tirmizi

Al-Azdi reported:

> "He Who acquires knowledge it is an expiation for his past sin" —Tirmizi, Darimi

Studies and teachings of religious subjects are also processes of acquiring knowledge. Abu Huraira reported Almighty's Messenger (PBUH) as saying:

> "Learn obligatory acts and the Quran and teach them to the people for I am mortal" —Tirmizi

In this hadith the Messenger (PBUH) reminded us his mortality and asked people to acquire Divine Knowledge from him and teach them to others.

Abu Huraira reported God's Messenger (PBUH) as saying:

> "Verily what a believer continues to receive (in the form of reward) for his action and his virtues after his death is the knowledge which he acquired and then disseminated...."
>
> —Ibn Majah, Baihaqui

He (PBUH) said as reported by Ibn Abbas:

> "Acquiring of knowledge in company for an hour in the night is better than spending the whole night in prayer." —Darimi

There are also other Hadiths (Traditions) on the importance of *ilm* (knowledge) or on acquiring it.

In many of the Traditions, seeking of knowledge has been termed as a part of Ibadah (Prayer). By *ibadah*, as we know, the path towards Paradise becomes easier. Similar is the case with seeking of knowledge.

When we speak of knowledge, it is not meant theological or religious knowledge only. It covers all types of knowledge. Studies of all subjects may lead one to earn more knowledge. To earn knowledge on different subjects such as theology, history, literature, science, etc., one should study those subjects. Similarly for administration or to rule a country, or for, trade and business studies are necessary to acquire knowledge on these topics. Studies of different subjects of science are very essential to understand natural phenomena and natural things and it becomes easier to realise science of creation. A true student of science becomes a true believer of the Creator. A knowledgeable person who is also a scholar has high place in Islam. The Messenger of Almighty (PBUH) said:

> "The superiority of the scholar over a worshipper is like that of moon in the night when it is full over the rest of the stars."
>
> —Ahmad, Tirmidhi, Abu Dawud, Ibn Majah, Darimi

As to how much education and hence knowledge were dearer to the Prophet (PBUH) can be guessed from the following historical incident:

In the battle of Badr the Muslims came victorious and there were about seventy prisoners of war. The Prophet (PBUH), holding a council decided to liberate them on payment of ransom. Four thousand drahmas (unit of money) was fixed as the rate of ransom for ordinary prisoners. Even the relatives of the Prophet were not exempted. In spite of all this, the Prophet (PBUH) asked the literates among the prisoners only to teach ten Muslim boys each how to read and write and this would be their ransom.

—(Ref. Ibn Sa'd Vol II / i p p14, 17, *Ibn Hambal* Vol I, p 246, Also The Battlefields of the Prophet Muhammad (PBUH) by M. Hamidullah pp 40, 41)

From the historical fact referred to above, it can be understood that both religious and general educations are essential for gathering knowledge. At the time of Rasulullah (PBUH) knowledge of the Islam (such as methods of daily prayer knowledge of Tawheed etc.) was given directly by him (PBUH) and his companions. But in spite of that he (PBUH) realised the importance of general education and as such encouraged people to acquire knowledge through general education in addition to theological knowledge. That is why, he (PBUH) set the condition for the unbelievers (prisoners of war) to teach Muslim boys reading and writing instead of paying cash as their ransom for their freedom.

Muhammad (PBUH) on Practical Education

In this modern age, many institutions are being established for different disciplines. Thus, there are Madrassas for religious education, schools and colleges for studying science, literature, history, political science, Higher institutions for medical science and engineering or technical education have also sprung up. The guardians become indecisive or get confused in selecting the type of education or institutions for their children. It is true that religious education for obligatory duties is a must for every Muslim child. There cannot be hesitation or two opinions about the urgency of Islamic education. Children must require to learn reciting Quran, know necessary things of *halal* and *haram*, also know prayers and practices and, know basic things to lead Islamic way of life. In addition to religious knowledge children should study science and also devote their time for engineering and technical education. This will help them earn more knowledge and improve their thinking capacity and family condition. The Messenger of the Almighty (PBUH) said about proper education of children in this way:

> "The best gift that a father can bestow upon his son (children) is to arrange good education and training for him."
> —Mishkat

The importance or usefulness of knowledge can be understood from the following description cited by Ziauddin Sardar in his arguments for Islamic science:

> "Knowledge is obligatory only in so far (it) is requisite for acting rightly. God condemns those who learn useless knowledge, and the Prophet (PBUH) said "I take refuge with thee from knowledge that profiteth naught". Much may be done by means of a little knowledge and knowledge should not be separated from action. The Prophet said: "The devotee without divinity is like a donkey turning a mill" because the donkey goes round and round on its tracks and never makes any advances."
>
> —(Ref *Quest for New Science* p. 47
> eds. R Ahmad and S.N. Ahmad)

More was said about the importance of practical knowledge.

> "The worst of man in the eye of Allah on the Day of Resurrection would be the scholar who does not derive benefit from knowledge"
>
> —Darimi

In fact knowledge and its application should go together. Even religious knowledge should be put into practice in religious duties. So also the case with scientific and other knowledge. Abu Huraira reported God's Messenger (PBUH) as saying:

> "The knowledge from which no benefit is derived is like a treasure out of which nothing is spent in the cause of Allah"
>
> —Ahmad and Darimi

Supremacy of God and Limitations of Scientists

Studies of nature or creation of God i.e. science is a difficult subject. If we read the different aspects of civilization, we come to know that from the primitive way of life and primitive stage of thinking, man has reached the present day state through continuous study and search of knowledge. In this long struggle to understand nature, innumerable mistakes were committed, correct or wrong paths or views were taken. Right conclusions or truth could be achieved after many ups and downs in the scientific search. Even now wrong or incorrect paths, views or conclusions are being corrected. In the field of politics, for example, sociology, communism, capitalism, monarchy, military or dictatorship or a system based on religious principles are being tried. Many people are not yet sure as to which system would be appropriate or universal for mankind. The Quran claims that Islam is the correct system for mankind. After many changes, rejection and acceptance, correct system may be found by man. Similar is the case in the studies of science. Scientists have some methods of their own to study nature in search of true knowledge behind any phenomena. Generally, to study or to know natural phenomena or laws, scientists may proceed in two ways: (1) he theoretically explains or predicts and after that he establishes the truth i.e. he proves by adopting different experiments, or (2) he observes, natural phenomena and then he finds the laws governing the observed phenomena and thus he explains as to how the phenomena happen. If the theoretical explanation and the experimental observations of the phenomena tally, then theory is accepted as correct, if there is difference between the theoretical explanation and the natural laws or phenomena then the theory is rejected and a new theory or explanation based on certain modified assumptions are put forward by scientists. Thus, scientists sometimes adopt trial and error method to find out the truth. If we read history of science, we see commission of many mistakes and their correction. Below are cited two examples:

(1) Fundamental Particles of Matter:

We can cite the examples of committing so many errors in finding the true nature of the smallest part of matter called atom. First scientists put forward the idea that the smallest part of matter which is indivisible and fundamental or building block of matter is the atom. But afterwards as a result of more scientific studies scientists could know that atom is not the fundamental particle. It is divisible and it is made up of a number of smaller particles known as proton, neutron and electron. In their search for atomic structure, scientists initially told us that atom is having positive as well as negative electric charges and the charges are equally distributed throughout the atom. But deep studies and researches revealed that the atomic structure is more complicated. It has a centre called the nucleus containing proton particles with positive charges, and neutron particles without any charges. It was also found that more smaller particles called electrons with negative charges are revolving with high velocity around the nucleus on different orbits. The total number of electrons on the orbits are same as that of the number of protons in the nucleus. These findings are not the final. With the advancement of scientific studies it was later discovered that protons and neutrons within the atom are not again fundamental particles of matter. They are made up of even more smaller particles. Thus scientists have not been successful as yet in knowing the true nature or true building block of matter. We observe that scientists have to put forward many theories to know the true nature out of which some are rejected. A sort of trial and error method is adopted. This has happened because scientists or in other words man has limitation in their thinking. Scientists in their search for knowledge can understand partially the complete phenomena of creation but can never secure the perfect knowledge. All knowledge is attributed to the Almighty only. The Holy Quran declares this:

> "To Allah belongeth the Unseen of the heavens and the earth" —(16:77)

Through studies of nature (science) one can realize the complexity of creation only, but can not understand the process of creation. Scientist should realise his weakness and his inability as well. God says:

> "Man was created weak." — (4:28)

Scientist knows that limitation and that is why he never claims finality of his research finding.

(2) The Ideas and Knowledge of Scientists Regarding Time and Place

Initially the idea of time was that it is unchangeable and it is an absolute thing. At any time under any condition time will have the same value. This means that for an observer in motion or at rest, the length of time of any event will be the same. But after the introduction of Theory of Relativity by Einstein, the notion of time has changed. According to this theory, duration of time or age of any event depends on its state of motion or its velocity. If we move with greater velocity, it will appear to us living more time compared to one at rest. This means that if we travel in space with great speed (at the speed of light for example) for sometime by a rocket or other advanced space craft and return to earth, we would see many decades already have passed on earth! This theory of relativity is not a production of mere imagination. The truth is already established by different experiments. At Geneva in the Particle research laboratory (CERN) this experiment is done easily. Here small charged particles like muon of different speeds are produced. Muons are unstable and quickly change to other particles such as electrons or neutrons. It has been observed the life times of high speed muons are larger than the life times of slow speed muons. Though it is difficult to believe that life time or age depends on speed, but it is true. Theory of Relativity changed the whole notion of time and space and the earlier idea of absolute time and space had to be abandoned.

The Apprehensions

The Uncertainty Principle put forward by Heisenberg has revealed limitation of knowledge of scientists. This theory warned us that we have limitations of knowledge by birth in knowing the absolute nature of any thing. It will be easier to illustrate this principle by an example: Thus by an experiment if a scientist knows the absolute position (co-ordinates) of an electron, he can not know by the same experiment, its motion or its velocity if it is moving. If velocity of the electron is measured, it is not possible to know its position at the same time. Here lies the limitation of knowledge of a scientist.

Thus, how a scientist can boast of his limited knowledge? He can study nature to understand creation but he can not become equal to Almighty, he even is not able to understand a small fraction of His infinite scientific talent. Scientist can not acquire smallest of the smallest portion of infinite knowledge. Though Almighty has invited mankind to study nature to realize His creativity and scientific talent, in reality Almighty is the Supreme, all knowing visible and invisible.

> "He knoweth the Unseen and that which is open:
> He is the Great, the Most High."
>
> —(13:9)

One of the greatest scientists, Newton the inventor of the Universal laws of gravitation was reported to say that he could pick up a grain of sand standing on the bank of a sea of infinite knowledge. In such a miserable situation of a scientist, religion should not have any apprehension of losing its credibility. A true scientist can not put comment or own view or change any part of the religious systems introduced by the Creator Himself. A true believing scientist, knowing his limitation of knowledge can not put suspicion on the revelation in Al-Quran. Rather he will have more faith in the Holy Book and fear Him. The Holy Quran asserts:

> "This is the Book; in it is guidance sure, without doubt to those who fear Allah; who believe in the unseen..." —(2:2-3)

And the fear of God may be the beginning of Wisdom.

Opinions about Religion

Common people want to know the views of scientists in respect of religion particularly about the existence of God and also their personal believes. Opinions of a few great scientists are mentioned below:

Cases of Believers

(i) Einstein's View: Einstein, formulator of Theory of Relativity was born in Germany and was a Jew. He was busy in his whole life studying natural phenomena and cosmogony and ultimately at the old age he became completely a religious person in the true sense. He was fascinated and overwhelmed with the Universe, the creation of God and he wrote this way:

> "A knowledge of the existence of something we can not penetrate, our perceptions of the profoundest reason and the most radiant beauty, which only in their most primitive forms are accessible to our minds—it is this knowledge and this emotion that constitute true religiosity; in this sense and in this alone, I am deeply religious man. I can not conceive of a God Who rewards and punishes His creatures, or has a will of the kind that we experience in ourselves."

Again he wrote:

> "I am satisfied with the mystery of the eternity of life and with the awareness and a glimpse of the marvellous structure of the existing world, together with the devoted striving to comprehend a portion, be it ever so tiny, of the Reason that manifests itself in nature."
>
> —(Ref: Ideas and opinions by Einstein: Translated by Sona Bargman, based on *Mein Weltbild*, Rutra & Co., Indian Edition 1979, P. 11)

(ii) Abdus Salam's View: From Muslim Ummah first and only Nobel Prize winner Abdus Salam was one of the forefront scientists of modern times. He was born near the city of Jhung of India and now

Pakistan. From matric onwards he passed different examinations with position and earned Ph.D. degree in 1950 from Cambridge. He was deeply engaged in advanced research and had published more than 250 papers in different scientific journals. He was until recently Director of International Centre for Theoretical Physics, Trieste a research institute established by him for third world scientists. It was reported that after receiving the news of his selection for Nobel Prize, he went straight to the mosque and offered thanks giving prayer to God for the award. Abdus Salam from his childhood started studying the Holy Book Al-Quran. Afterwards as a result of studies of nature or science he became a staunt believer of the Almighty. His own words are quoted below:

> "Let me say at the outset that I am both a believer as well as a practising Muslim. I am a Muslim because I believe in the spiritual message of the Holy Quran. As a scientist, the Quran speaks to me in that it emphasises reflection on the Laws of Nature, with examples drawn from Cosmology, Physics, Biology and Medicine, as Signs for all men."
>
> —(Ref. *Ideals and Realities*, Ed. C.H. Lai, World Scientific Publishing Co. 1987, P. 179)

(iii) C.V. Raman's View: C.V. Raman was a great scientist of Indian subcontinent and a Nobel Prize winner in Physics. He was religious from his childhood. After becoming famous as a scientist he was religious equally. He did not leave his religious related dress, habit of vegetarian and daily religious activities. In a party after the noble award ceremony, he was offered to drink alcohol. But because of his strong religious faith he politely refused to do so.

Views of other Indian scientists are more or less similar. Science studies are found to influence their religious belief. It is concluded from the analysis of personal life of scientists that their belief in Creator (Almighty) increases as a result of deep study of nature i.e. science. Thus the apprehension that science education may detract people from religion, has no basis. There is no reason of becoming allergic to science for Muslims.

Cases of Unbelievers

Of course there are some examples of scientists becoming athiests or unbelievers of Almighty. Famous scientist Darwin from his studies of fossils of animals and other things put forward theory of evolution of life on this earth. He did not believe the creation of mankind as envisaged in religion. But there are exceptions not only in the case of scientists but also in common people as well. Non-believers were there in the time of Rasulullah (PBUH) also. These scientists and common people do not learn to take advise from the revelations. They do not believe in Almighty and the Hereafter.

They usually say that the Universe and the life are not created. They have come into existence spontaneously. They will die and will not be created again. That means there is no Hereafter. Almighty knows these people very well and put their way of thinking in the Holy Quran this way:

> "And they say: what is there but our life in this world? We shall die and we live, and nothing but time can destroy us". But of that they have no knowledge: they merely conjecture."
>
> —(45:24)

They do not also take lessons from the innumerable Signs existing in nature or creation of the Almighty. Their different organs such as of seeing (eyes), learning (ears), etc., do not work in the true sense and they do not apply their intellect in the proper way. For these people he says in the Holy Book:

> "Those whom Allah Willeth to guide, He Openeth their breasts to Islam; Those whom He Willeth to leave straying, He maketh their breasts close and constricted." —(6:125)

In fact, there is no basic difference between science and religious belief. One is complimentary to another. Where science can not reach religion helps. Knowledge or ideas which are not realizable in science can be realized or extracted from the Holy Book. Again revelations related to science are required to be explained or understood in the light of knowledge gathered from science studies.

Thus studies of science are necessary not only for a scientific or planned and meaningful way of life but also for understanding religious thoughts and revelations and to realize them.

Man has limited knowledge and also for him it is not possible to secure perfect knowledge. Because of this, religion puts a condition to believe the Unseen, though it can not be proved by experiments. The faithful religious persons believe the revelations that the God creates every thing from nothing:

> "When He decreath a matter, He saith to it: 'Be'
> and it is." — (2:117)

Till now, scientists have not been able to find the solution of this i.e. Unseen. Researches are going on to find the riddle of life. Only time will tell the outcome of research.

Golden Age of Islamic Science

From the foregoing discussion we come to the conclusion that there is no religious bar or prohibition in studying science by Muslims. Rather God has directed and advised man in different verses of Al-Quran to gather knowledge from the studies of Nature and to get benefit from it. The Messenger of God (PBUH) himself also gave much stress on seeking of knowledge from different sources. Muslims after his (PBUH) death have been observed to follow those instructions sincerely. Only within about two hundred years after Muhammad's (PBUH) death, Muslims had undertaken plans and programmes to study science. In this first two centuries Muslim rulers, thoughts and energies were directed towards establishing the new Islamic states and consolidating their positions. We see in history how once Islamic science and technology flourished throughout the Islamic world and outside. Islam was always the positive force of achievement in science and technology.

During the glorious period of Islamic civilization which continued about seven hundred years, from about 700 A.D. to 1500 A.D., Islamic science and technology flourished., Many great Muslim scientists who ushered a new horizon of science were born during this period. Some of them are:

Jabir Ibn Haytham, Abu-Bakr Ibn Zakaria, Ibn al-Haytham, Al-Beruni, Abu Sin (Abisina) and many others.

Many Muslims polymaths were also born at this period. Some of them are al-Jahiz (d 868), al-Kindi (d 873), al-Razi (d 925), al-Idrisi (b 1166), ibn Bajjah (d 1138), Omar Khayyam (d 517) , ibn Zuhr (d 1162), ibn Tufail (d 1185), ibn Rushd 91198), al-Suyuti (d 1505) and many others.

—(Ref: Ziauddin Sardar, in *Quest for New Science*, edited by R.Ahmad and S.N. Ahmad 1984, P. 55).

As put by Z. Sardar, "these Scholars gave "emphasis on synthesis and interdisciplinary investigations, multiplicity of methods and social function and accountability before God, which produced an institution which is largely unique in Islam and is unparalleled by any other civilization."

One of the key factors of spreading and flourishing Islamic civilization was the well planned scheme for science undertaken by Muslim rulers at that time.

Steps taken for the pursuance of science education and research were many such as: Arabicising and translations of scientific topics from different sources, establishment of academics, observatories and libraries; patronage of scientists and conduct of scientific and technological research; as well as running of state industries and technological research.

For Muslims the Islam and the Arabic language have always been the two unifying forces. Because of the language of the Quran, Arabic became the language of all the people in the Islamic world. It became the language of daily life and the language of science and literature replacing other languages. Caliphs from the early days of the Umayyads realized the importance of learning science by the vast majority of Muslims in Arabic and Muslim scientists translated many scientific works into Arabic. The works of the Greeks, of the Near-East and of India were translated into Arabic. The technological books written by the Banu Musa brothers, al-Jazari, Ridwan, Taqi-al-Din and others are some of the examples of literature translated into Arabic.

By the end of the second and beginning of third Hijri (A.H) (8th to 9th centuries A.D.) some anthoritative dictionaries and grammars were compiled for scientific and literary use by some scholars such as Abu Zayd, Abayda and Al-Asma. Al Kindi (ninth century A.D.) was one of the most original thinkers and philosophers of the Arab's who wrote on a variety of subjects including mineralogy and metallurgy, geology, physics, pharmacology and medicines.

Hunayn b. Ishaq (d. 260 A.H./A.D. 873) was a famous translator - scientist who worked in Baghdad in Abbasid times. He translated many scientific works from the Greek manuscripts and also wrote on philosophical, meteorological, zoological, linguistics and religious subjects, besides composing original works. The work of translation and original scientific writing had begun before the Abbasids assumed power and it was Baghdad of the 3rd century A.H.: (9th century) which witnessed the earliest Islamic scientific activities. Over the next seven centuries, Islamic science flourished at different parts of the Muslim World.

Muslim rulers established many scientific academics, schools, libraries, observatories and other centres of higher education in their respective states. Some of the institutions were patronized by the rulers of the states, some by ministers, princes as well as rich men.

The caliphs or the rulers always patronized scientists, research scholars and engineers. In all the academics, libraries, madrasas, hospitals and observatories. Financial means were provided to enable scientists to devote all their times for study and research. They were paid salaries and granted pensions. The Caliph al-Mamun (813 A.D.), for example, established in Baghdad a scientific institution which was known as Bayt-al-Hikma (House of wisdom). Two astronomical observatories, one in Baghdad and the other in Damascus, were attached to this academy and a staff of eminent scientists were included among the members of the academy. Thus, a nucleus was formed at Bayt al-Hikma at Baghdad. Later such centres were established at different major cities of the Islamic world such as Damascus, Cairo, Nishapur, Cardova, Gernada and other places.

Caliph Harun al-Rashid established a big library called Khizanat al-Hikma (library of wisdom). During the period of Fatimids (909-1171 A.D.) libraries were parts of palaces. In A.D. 1004 al-Hakim founded Dar al-Hikma (House of wisdom) in a palace which contained a library, reading room and which was the meeting of learned scholars including doctors, mathematicians and astronomers. Houses of libraries of science, on the model of the Bayt al-Hikma in Baghdad and the Dar-al-Hikma in Cairo became numerous. Some were established by Public funds and others by individuals.

The Mosques were always centres of learning. Libraries were attached to the mosques as well. In the early days of Islam, the mosques were the centres of teaching and learning from which madrassa type education started. Gradually such education became formal and madrassa buildings were built attached to most of the mosques. Some Universities were developed from madrassas where teaching and researches were carried out on various subjects. Some important Universities established during the glorious time of Islamic science are: al-Azhar in Cairo, the Zaytuniyya in Tunis and Qarawiyyin in Fez. For teaching of medicine, pharmacology and related subjects Medical Schools were established attached to hospitals.

Studies of astronomical science also made progress in the golden days of Islamic science. In addition to two observatories attached to Bayt al-Hikma, the observatories of Ulugh Beg in Samarqand and of Taqi al-Din in Istanbul and the Maragha observatory were at peaks in the studies of astronomy.

Muslim scientists and engineers developed their science and technology through continuous process of research, experiments and inventions. Thus, Banu Musa brothers, engaged in writing or translation in their early stage, but became researchers and inventors in later stage. Their mathematical and engineering book *Kitab al-Hiyal* (Book of Ingenious Devices) described about hundred devices out of which about seventy five were of their own designs. Similar was the case with al-Jazari in 12th century. The approach of al-Jazari was more experimental. He said in his book "Compendium of the theory and practice of the Mechanical Arts", that any industrial science is a doubtful science if that is not verified by experiments. Similar was Taqial-Din, scientist of much later time.

Muslims' Contribution

There are hundreds of thousands of Islamic manuscripts in the world's libraries, dealing with scientific works of Muslim scientists of the earlier period. Mention of a few will greatly distort or omit the general picture. Nevertheless a brief mention of a few great Muslim scientists and their scientific works may help in focussing the Muslim achievement in the past.

Field of work of Muslim scientists were generally broad enough to include most of the sciences in those days. But in their later parts of life, each of them became, specialist in one or more of the sciences. Muslim contribution in science and technology are discussed below in a nutshell:

(i) In Mathematics Muslim scientists contributed most original work. The Indian system of reckoning using the nine Arabic numerals with a point for zero and application of decimal fractions were introduced by Muslims. Al-Khuwarizmi (210 A.H./A.D. 875) laid the foundation of Algebra. The word "al-gorithm" came from the name of the great mathematician Al-Khuwarizmi whose real name was Abu Jafar Muhammad bin Musa. Poet Umar Khayyam (d 526 A.H./A.D. 1131) also made significant contribution in Algebra. Muslim mathematicians made great contributions towards geometry. They applied geometry in surveying, construction of machines, etc., and used to solve problems and make calculations. Muslims were the inventors of planc and spherical trigonometry introducing functions of sine, cosine and tangent. Al-Battani (d. 317 A.H./A.D. 929) presented a formula involving three sides and one angle of a spherical triangle which has no equivalent in Ptolemy. Abul-Wafa (d. 388 A.H./A.D. 929) was one of the greatest Muslim mathematicians who invented secont and cosecount, demonstrated the sine theorem for the general spherical triangle and proposed a new technique for the construction of sine tables.

(ii) In Astronomy Muslims showed much interest in the past. They gave much interest in the observation and instrumentation. Problems or contradictions found by Ptolemy in his geocentric theory were resolved by Ibn al-Shatir in the fourteenth century A.D. Muslim astronomers developed spherical trigonometry to solve or correct astronomical problems which were equally valid in sun-centred system. They also worked on making calendar problems of time keeping and to locate the direction of

Mecca (Qibla) from any place. Astronomer al-Khalili (eight century A.H) with the help of accurate trigonometrical and computational methods could give an accurate Qibla table.

(iii) Islamic contribution to Physics (science that deals with physical laws and energies) can only be appreciated by a thorough study of Muslim physics. Ibn al-Haytham (d. 430 A.H./A.D. 1039) was a great mathematician and without any doubt the greatest physicist. His words had profound influence on later scientists. He had significant contributions in advanced level experimental optics. The Formats Principle which is known to modern students of optics was described by al-Haytham many centuries earlier. He discovered spherical aberration of light, explained refraction of sunrays through atmosphere of the earth. The law of inertia was originally introduced by al-Haytham. This law after many centuries became known as Newton's (A.D. 1642-1727) first law of motion. Unfortunately al-Haytham's name is not found in this connection even as the originator of the idea. One of his books *Kitab al-Manazir* (book on optics) was translated into Latin which had a profound influence in the Middle Ages. Al-Beruni (A.D. 973-1048) of Afghanistan was a great scientist well versed in mathematics, astronomy, physical science and other subjects. Al-Beruni was also a great experimentalist. He always tested his conclusions by observations and experiments. He was an instrument maker and constructed astrolabes and a geared-mechanical calendar. Al-Khazim wrote a fine book *Kital Mizan al Hikma* based on his work on specific gravity and discussed in it a theory of gravity and many instruments. His book is a fine work on mechanics, hydrostatics and physics.

(iv) In Chemistry and Chemical Industries, Muslim scientists also made significant contributions. The works of Jabir b. Hayyan (eighth century/A.D.), Abu Bakr al Razi (d-925/A.D.), al-Kindi (ninth century A.D.), and others were very important. Modern chemical engineering, and chemical industries of today owe much to their works. Al-Razi contributed valuable knowledge and knowhow to the modern chemists regarding distillation, solution, calcination, evaporation, crystallization, sublimation, filtration, amalgamation, ceration, etc., and the various chemical -processes involved in them. His book *Kitab al-Asrar* gave full account of different alchemical equipments. Al-Kindi was also a great chemist. His treatise *kitab kimya' al-Itr waal Tasidat* (book of perfume, chemistry and distillation) was very useful for Islamic chemical industry. Some of the major areas in which Muslim scientists and engineers had great contributions are:

(v) Mechanical Engg: Water raising for irrigation, drinking, domestic and industrial purposes, harnessing water power and wind power, water clocks and mechanical clocks, scientific equipments etc.

(vi) Civil Engg : Building technology, roads and bridges, irrigation systems such as canals, dams, reservoirs etc.

(vii) Military Technology : arms such as swords, lance, bows, shields and mace, seige engines such as missile thrower, trabuchet, incediary weapons, gun powder and cannon, construction of forts, etc.

(viii) Ships and Navigation : Ship building, navigation and navies.

(ix) Chemical Industries : Chemical equipments, distillation, manufacture of perfumes, rose water, essential oils, petroleum refining (the oil fields of Baku were developed on a commercial basis by Muslims). Discovery and production of some inorganic acids: nitric acid; sulphuric and hydrochloric acids, some organic acids, alkalis, soap etc., glass making, ceramics, pottery, writing and painting materials, such as ink and pigments, varnishes, dyes, etc.

(x) Textile Industries : Works on wool, linen, cotton, silk, paper and leather manufactures.

(xi) Agriculture and Food Technology : New crops, new farming practices, agricultural implements such as ploughs, hurrows, rakes, milling, production of sugar, edible vegetable oils, foods and drinks, preservation of foods.

(xii) Mining and Metallurgy : Development of mining technology; mining of most essential minerals such as gold, silver, copper, tin, iron and steel, mercury, salt, alum, coal, precious stones, exploitation of underwater resources such as pearls, etc.

The above mentioned branches of science are technological or applied science. Muslim scientists were thus active in studying nature and were serious in applying their knowledge for the benefit of the people. Engineers and architects were called in those days as 'al-muhandisun' which came from the word 'handasa' meaning engineering and architecture's. However, in many cases there was not much diffrence between an engineer and a scientist. Generally any scientist involved in a subject concentrated to apply the knowledge in practising fields. Thus, Jabir was a chemist and engineer, al-Kindi a physicist as well as a metallurgist and engineer, al-Razi a chemist, engineer and physician, Banu Musa brothers mathematicians, physicists and engineers; Al-Biruni an astronomer, physicist and engineer. Some like Al-Jazari devoted themselves solely to engineering.

Spread of Islamic Science

An analysis reveals that contributions of Muslim scientists from 8th century to 15th century A.D. laid the foundation of European science to be flourished now. Muslim scientists did not leave untouched any branch of science. In medicine Ibn Sina and Al-Razi, in physical science Al-Beruni, in mathematics Al-Khuwarizmi, in astronomy Al-Zarkali and Ulugh Beg, in navigation Ibn Batuta are some of many Muslim scientists whose work were the cause of progress of European science. There were many hospitals, Universities, research laboratories in Muslim countries when there was scarcity of books in science in Europe, Baghdad, Damascus, Cairo, Cordova, Gernada, etc. being the centres of Islamic science. The Arabs studied and developed algebra, calculus, optical geometry, navigation well ahead of European scientists. It is said that Muslims discovered America before Columbus. In fact, a Muslim was a guide of Columbus (Ref. *Quest for New Science* p. 150). Students from France, England, Portugal, Italy and Germany came to Gernada, Cordova, Madrid, etc., of Spain to study astronomy, medical science, chemistry, physics and mathematics. Roger Bacon, the father of modern science had been a student in Muslim institutions. Copernicus the great astronomer borrowed many ideas from Muslim astronomers. Some of these students translated the works of Muslim scientists into their native languages of Europe. The influence of these books were so great that even Newton is said to read the book of Muhammad bin Musa on motion of celestial bodies and force of attraction. Many writers translated Arabic contents of science into European languages. Many centres for translation were there. Of these centres of Toleddo, Seville and Solerno were famous. An Arabic-Latin dictionary was compiled to facilitate Arabic translation. (Ref. I, *Quest for New Science* p. 150).

The Pre-Islamic civilization from Spain to central Asia and northern India were inherited by Islam. Under the influence of Islam science and technology of these regions were developed and improved.

There was large scale technology transfer from the Islamic world to Europe. This is reflected by the many words of Arabic derivation that have entered into vocabularies of European languages to cite a few examples:

in textiles — muslin, sarsanet, damask, taffela, tabby;
in naval matters —arrival , admiral,
in chemical technology — alembic, alcohol, akali;
in paper — ream;
in food stuffs — alfalfa, sugar, syrup, sherbat,
in dye stuffs — saffron, kermes;
in leather works — cordovan, morocco;

Muslims were quite advanced in the fields of agriculture irrigation, hydraulic engg., etc.. The Muslim ideas in these fields and others passed from Spain into Italy and northern Europe. Other installations, such as the water clocks on the bank of the Tagus at Toledo, the paper mill at Jativa near Valencia were taken over by the Christians from the Muslims. Nowadays other examples of technology transfer are given in a book *Islamic Technology* compiled by Ahmad

Y. al-Hassan and Donald R. Hill. Contributions of Muslim scientists towards Western science are more than the Greeks. The Greek philosophers mainly took the help of arguments, reasonings, etc., to arrive at conclusions or to find out the truths. For this reason Aristotle, Pythogoras, Galen and Aristocres did not possess any laboratory for observational research. On the other hand, Muslim scientists favoured to experimental verification of arguments or reasonings and as such they established their own laboratories and observations. For experimental purposes they devised and fabricated many instruments and appliances. From excavation near Baghdad ruins of such a laboratory of Jabir bin Hayyan have been discovered. Western historians of science have also borne, this testimony. Also instruments invented by Muslims preserved in museums prove the above mentioned facts.

Today modern science has the foundation on experiments and observations. Its sustenance has been derived from the experimental methods of Muslim scientists and not from the deductive and analogical method of the Greeks. Because of the introduction of experimental methods, different branches of science have made tremendous progress in Europe. The role of Muslims in bringing a revolution in Europe is acknowledged by Alessandro Bausani, the Italian Orientalist, this way:

> "..... it is also true that during our middle ages the Muslim world was considered more or less like America now i.e. the world to which one had to go perfect oneself in science and technology."
> —(Ref. quoted by H.R. Siddiqui in his paper Science from the Muslim World into Europe
> —(Quest for New Science p. 134)

The Downfall

It is cléar from the discusion made above, that after the death of the Messenger of Allah (PBUH), Muslims followed instructions of the Quran and then Hadiths strictly and concentrated not only in spreading the messages of Islam but also gave much attention in learning science and for that purpose established many institutions in different parts of the Muslim world. Many Muslim rulers patronized these institutions. In course of time for various reasons unstability started in the Muslim kingdom and there had been frequent changes of rulers in many places, as a result patronization of these institutions by Muslim rulers were gradually diminished and ultimately stopped. Between the last part of the eleventh century and first part of twefth century there was much political unstability and uncertainty and religious conflicts among the Muslims. During this period real downfall of Islamic science started. In the begining the determination of spreading Islamic teaching and idealism was the guiding force to the progress of science and achievement and this was at its peak when the Muslim states were stable and their economic conditions were sound. With the political disintegration of the Muslim states and the deterioration of economic life of Muslims, progress of Islamic science and achievement began to decline. Muslims were slowly deviating themselves from the teachings of the Quran and Hadiths and their political power was declining one after another. The Christians at this time started to realize their religious superstition and there was renaissance in Europe. During this period Sufisim, a new practice of Islam, unknown to the earlier Muslims was slowly introduced. After the hanging of Mansur al-Hillaj (922 A.D.), Sufism became widespread. Common people having no advanced knowledge of religion started to accept Sufism which is an advanced and mystic religious philosophy. As a result, instead of dynamic and progressive activities in the field of searching knowledge through science education a stagnant situation was developed. Muslim Ulemas also could not escape from this. The movement of religious fanaticism by the clerical factions against science was so strong that the last observatory in Islam established in Constantinople was demolished by Taqi al-Din in 1580 A.D. In contrast the first observatory was established at this time by Tycho Brahe in the West.

On the other hand, after long and continuous sufferance and exploitation rennaissance started in Europe. Being guided by wrong idea and wrong explanations of religion a sense of repulsion from religion was developed in the minds of these people and they could easily concentrate on materialistic aspects of life. Leaving aside the degenerated religious or theological activities, they concentrated in a full fledged way in material aspects of life and in studies and researches of science. During this period many great scientists of later period such as Copernicus, Kepler, Galileo, Pascal, Newton, and many others were born. The Europeans at this time with the advancement and discovery of science started exploring different parts of the earth and setting up of colonies.

There was industrial revolution in Europe with the advancement of science and technology. On the introduction of guns the military strength of the Europeans became far superior than the Muslims. As a result Muslims were losing their controls over their land one after another. During the nineteenth and twentieth centuries most Islamic lands came under colonial rule of the western powers. Western Europe during this time witnessed a scientific and industrial revolution that started in the nineteenth century and gathered momentum in the twentieth century, but during the same period the colonial dominated Islamic lands were deterred from making scientific and industrial progress.

The condition of the Muslims under colonial rule was very bad. The westerns continued to dominate them in various ways. Their West education system were imposed in the colonies.

In Muslim dominated countries also the conditions of science education were frustrating at this time of rising of European dominance: There were number of reasons for this frustration: (1) science institutions did not have any progressive outlook or planning, (2) these institutions were isolated from other institutions, (3) no encouragement or incentives were there for new scientific ideas or discoveries, (4) instructions in the Quran and the Hadiths on science education were wrongly interpreted by some ignorants or vested interests to keep people away from science studies, (5) influence of Sufism was increasing at this time and many responsible Muslims and Ulemas started to give more attention to Sufism rather than science education, (6) an apprehension was growing at this time that as reasoning, rationalism, deduction, experiments, proof, etc, are the basis of science, there is a chance of science students of becoming un-believers of Allah or religious deserters. But this propaganda had no basis, rather it was contradictory to the instructions laid down in the Holy Book.

There were some other reasons for Muslims to show their abhorence to science. These were some ideas or theories propagated by some scientists and social workers which were apparently against religious belief. Thus, the theory of Evolution of Darwin and the socialistic principle of Freud and Marx may be mentioned in this connection.

The theory put forward by the natural scientist Darwin to explain the appearance of life on earth ignores the role of Almighty. It apparently contradicts or opposes the ideas of creation as envisaged in the Holy book and as such many Muslims started thinking science as an ism opposed to the existence of Creator. In addition, the Ulemas became alarmed on increasing popularity of socialism of Freud and Marx. There was a wave of establishing in many European countries where science was progressing, to establish Communism based on the ideas of Marx which basically ignored religious principles of ruling the society. In some countries infact Communism was established destroying the religious fabric of the society. Observing increasing popularity of a system based on reasoning and rationalism and material aspects, denying the Creator and the way of life framed by Him to follow, many Muslims were alarmed. No Muslim can accept a system which breaks or tends to break the foundation of faith (Iman). As a result Muslims of medieval period kept themselves away from science education. The Ulemas also did not encourage people for such education. Rather they encouraged an education system devoid of any sort of science. But in this vast Universe there are exceptions in the creations of Almighty. History bears this testimony. Darwin, Freud, Marx, etc., may be such exceptions. If theory of evolution of Darwin is seriously studied and analysed, we see that existence of God or the Creator has not been denied or it is not possible to deny God if theory of evolution is to be accepted. Because, for evolution to take place raw materials, proper environment and proper places are required. Darwin has not answered as to where from and why these raw materials were existing for evolution to take place. Darwin kept mum or silent in this regard which indirectly indicates not refusal or not denial of existence of Allah. It is true that the political and social systems envisaged by Freud and Marx were based on material aspects only. These were hypothetical systems not science. But all these created an unfavourable psychology in the minds of the Muslims.

But all the apprehensions of Muslims did not have any basis. There is no conflict between science and Islam. Rather, the whole Quran contains verses based on science, justice, reasoning and truth.

It invites, encourages and suggests people to study nature or science. Because of their deviation from the instruction of the Quran and the Hadiths, Muslims are lagging behind in the field of general education, science and technical education.

In the Christian world before the Renaissance in Europe, there were strong differences or conflicts, between science and religion. The great scientist Galileo was punished for pursuing truth through scientific studies. Galileo proved that the earth was not the centre of the Universe. As this was against the teaching of the church, he was condemned in 1633 by a Roman Catholic Church inquisition court which sentenced Galileo to life imprisonment, later commuted to house arrest. Thus in Christian world for many centuries scientists could not pursue and publish the truth freely. Gradually people could realize this and there was renaissance throughout Europe. The Church also could realize their fault and started to change their approach towards science. At last more than 350 years after punishing Galileo, the Vatican honoured the 17th century astronomer with two stamps on May 31, 1994.

In the history of Islam such unfortunate incidents as what happened with Galileo never occured. Many Muslims including Ulemas have realized the wrong education policy of Muslims. But it is too late. In the meantime there has been an unprecedented progress 'in the field of science and technical knowledge and the progress has been made by non-Muslims alone.

Indian Muslims and Science

During the golden period of Islamic science in the Islamic world i.e. from 9th century to about 14th century India was ruled by Muslim rulers. Though Muslims were not in majority in India, they were the vast population. India was never ruled by the Muslim rulers as per Islamic laws based on the Shariah. There were arrangements for religious education and for military training to their armies for defence of their territories and some times for conquering and territories. For religious education Maktabs, Madaris, Khankas, etc., were established at different places and they were patronized by the Muslim rulers. Sufism was also gaining popularity and it was being practised by many under famous Sufi scholars such as Nizam uddin, Moinuddin Chisti and many others. There were no institutions under the Muslim rulers to study science and to do research in a systematic way.

(i) Of course there were some progress in certain fields: the Mughals had the knowledge and practice to make arms and ammunitions which were required for defence and wars.

(ii) Also in medicine there had been some studies and progress. The Hakimi system treatment was working at that time. But there was no laboratory in the style of European chemists to improve or discover medicines.

(iii) There was some progress in the field of engineering particularly in construction and architectural engineering during the period of Muslim rulers in India. They were mainly busy in constructing palaces, forts (e.g. Red Fort of Delhi), memoirs (e.g. Taj Mahal of Agra) etc.

The conquest of many parts of the globe by the Europeans and their influence were possible mainly because of their progress in science and technology. Their strong will for studying science and their unhesitating contribution towards research for new discoveries in science were the contributing factors for further progress. After the design and fabrication of guns, the Europeans could expand their rule over many parts of the world easily. With new war tactics and new weapons, they could easily conquer scientifically backward, otherwise advanced kingdoms. The Mughals of India, though remained unparalleled in war tactics and politics for centuries in India lost to the British only because of the backwardness in science and technology. Had the Mughals been advanced in science and technology the history would have been different.

After the establishment of British rule in India, the education systems were totally changed. The British introduced science and their western education system. The Hindus without any hesitation accepted the new education system and could do progress in science education. But the Muslims under the British rule had different view about the new education system.

In an apprehension that after losing the Khilafat (the Muslim Emperors were not infact Khalifa) the religion may be lost, the Muslims rejected the education system introduced by the British. They decided instead to continue their old system of education devoid of science and technology in the schools, established and run by Muslims only. The British occupied India from the Muslim rulers and as such they considered Muslims as their rivals, they wanted Muslims to stay backward in all aspects so that Muslims can not rise against the British rule. Therefore an education system, devoid of modern subjects of that time, framed and introduced by only some Muslim Ulemas was not opposed by the British. Rather, it was supported by the British. In the same country, the Hindus and the Muslims thus adopted two education systems. As a result, in course of time, the Muslims were slowly lagging behind in education particularly in different branches of science and other modern subjects. Also as a result of constant propaganda, against learning English, science and other subjects introduced by the British, and wrong interpretation of education and encouragement to study subjects of theology only, majority of Muslims became allergic to science education and devoted their time to learn Persian, Urdu and Arabic only in addition to Hadiths and Quran. These are some reasons of Muslims becoming backward in this part of the subcontinent.

After independence of India, the scenario started to change. The country was divided. Many educated and rich Muslims migrated to Pakistan. Majority of Muslims who preferred to stay in India were illiterate or half educated and economically backward. They decided to live as minority with the vast majority of Hindus. However, these Muslims got a sense of insecurity because of the apprehension that in course of time their culture, etc., may be diluted and merged with the Hindu culture and their future offspring may even leave the religion in a hostile (hostile to Islamic laws and principles) environment. Thus, many Muslims preferred Madrassa education where stresses are given on study of Arabic, Persian, Urdu, Islamic history, Hadiths and Quran. When there is a need to increase knowledge on all fronts including mathematics and science, majority of Muslim children spend time in learning some languages such as Arabic, Urdu, Persians and other theological subjects. These students after coming out from Madrassas are unable to proceed further for higher education in modern subjects because of shortage of knowledge in these subjects. Even basic education of modern subjects including science is not imparted in many madrassas. As a result they cannot compete with the students of other communities who are already advanced in the different subjects.

Consequences of Negligence

There are numerous direct and indirect repercussions on the Muslim society both in social life as well as in family life for ignoring science education by Muslims. A few are mentioned below.

(i) Religious Work

For proper understanding of the Holy Quran, the reader should have some basic knowledge of science. Al-Quran has described briefly at many places about the natural phenomena and physical laws and asked people to ponder over them. Knowledge of science helps to understand or at least realize the inner meaning of those verses. Knowledge is very much necessary for understanding truth of the Quranic revelations.

The Almighty says in this regards:

> "Thus do we explain the Signs in detail for those who know " —(7:32)

That the Quran is easier to understand for man of knowledge (scientists are knowledgeable persons) has been said by God himself this way:

> "And that those on whom knowledge has been bestowed may learn that the (Quran) is the truth from the Lord, and that they may believe therein, and their hearts may be made humbly (open) to it." —(22:54)

In the eyes of religion, to achieve the high position or get God's favour knowledge is also necessary: He says:

> "Allah will raise up, to (suitable) ranks (and degrees), those of you who believe and who have been granted knowledge" —(58:11)

Thus from the religious point of view, there is an urgent need of acquiring highest knowledge. Its importance can be envisaged from the fact that the Quran has given stress on studying physical laws of nature (*al-tafakkur*) and control or use of nature, and natural resources or laws by inventing technical knowhow, (*al-taskheer*). In this regard, al-Quran has repeatedly advised man in about seven hundred fifty verses (one eighth of the whole Quran) to study nature (i.e. science) think or ponder over them, do_ research using intellect. Thus, al-Quran has advised to adopt an education policy based on science and scientific approach. The Prophet (PBUH) himself has stressed on education for acquiring knowledge and declared this task as 'Fardh' or obligatory. Muslim community, in spite of such religious directions or guidance, on acquiring knowledge has not adopted a proper education policy. Guidance of al-Quran and Hadiths has not been reflected in their education policy. Studies of science subjects are essential for acquiring knowledge, but these are not included in the curriculum of education in the institutions financed community.

Many are observed to misinterpret the meaning of Islamic education which according to them is the education pertaining to learning Hadiths and Quran and other activities of Shariah only. This is not true and not supported by the Quran and the Hadiths as well. The so called Ulemas prefer a system devoid of science and they even openly speak out against science education. This may, perhaps, happen, if the Quranic injunctions on science education are not understood in their proper perspective. For persons having knowledge of all branches, it becomes easier to understand Quranic revelations based on science. Those who advocate rejection of science or do not give importance on science education perhaps have not been able to grasp the spirit or inner meaning of those verses.

(ii) To be benefitted from studying science

Nature and laws governing natural objects and phenomena are studied in different branches of science such as physics, chemistry, zoology, botany, astrophysics, medical science, geography, etc. Applied sciences are the different branches of technology and engineering. Nowadays much advances have been made in the field of study and research as a result of which much has been known of the nature and natural laws. Also the mystery of creation and its complexity has been realized.

It is a fact that in this modern age progress has been made in the field of science and technology by the people of other communities except Muslims. Knowledge obtained from the studies of nature and natural laws mostly by the people of other communities have been applied for the benefit of the people. Their endeavour could enable them to discover new medicines, communication systems and innumerable new things. In this technologically advanced age different industries are being built, where only people having science and technical degree or knowledge can work.

Muslims being ignorant of scientific education and knowledge have not been able to get jobs in such types of industries or workshops.

Even for ordinary and common jobs Muslims have been found not coping with job seekers of other communities. This is because other communities are already advanced in various subjects including different subjects of science and technology. It can be easily said that in a multicommunity system or country a community lagging in all fronts can not compete in any front with others and as such will lag further behind in the race.

Nowadays, not only in getting jobs but also in other fields such as business, cultivation, etc., there is tough competition. There have been many advancements in modern cultivation. Good seeds, advanced gadgets, etc., for cultivation have been discovered. So cultivators must also be modern and must be able to use modern machines for cultivation, use proper manure at proper season and be able to take care of the crops in a scientific manner. Any crop can be cultivated nowadays at any season of the year if scientific method is applied to cultivate it. Thus a sort of scientific education or knowledge is necessary for cultivators as well. Muslims, though most of them are cultivators in eastern India are completely ignorant of such a development or change.

Not only in cultivation, pattern of business has changed. In addition to buying and selling of cultivating products, scientific or industrial products are flourishing in the market. Because of research and development, hundreds of electronic goods, cosmetics, groceries, machineries, vehicles and their parts, etc., are being made and introduced in the market. For making a business, some knowledge or ideas of these goods are necessary. Otherwise it is not possible to start a business in this competitive market. In starting an industry also the same problem will be faced if knowledge of technical education is not there. The point is that the Muslims are not able to cope with or are lagging behind in all these modern fronts.

It is a fact that "the survival of the fittest" is the common principle for all. From the beginning of human history man has been trying to change, rather improve his lifestyle and has been making efforts to acquire knowledge for the purpose. There has been always a sense of competition among the different groups of people from the very beginning though they have originated from a single family. Many groups or tribes or community, because of their own fault, ignorance or negligence or incompetence have got defeated themselves and as per wish of Almighty and have vanished from this world. Some smaller groups or tribes are still there in small islands or in accessible places on the surface of the earth. These groups because of their ignorance or lack of knowledge have been living in an uncivilized way or in a primitive way. They have not been able to make betterment of their life or think for the hereafter. This way consequence of ignorance or not trying to put into action one's knowledge is disastrous God has bestowed man all human faculties and intellect to acquire knowledge, so that he can lead a life in this world to serve Him better and get the reward hereafter. This Universe is created for man only so that he can study it and realize Almighty's greatness and submit before Him. Further, he may use nature for his welfare. People of any community should put all efforts for the welfare and progress of the community. They should make their own plan and project for their own advancement. He says in this regards:

> "Verily never will Allah change the condition of
> people until they change what is in themselves."
>
> —(13:11)

Man is surrounded with all bounties of nature given by God. He is to put his intelligence and get benefits from His bounties in order to improve himself to change his lots. If man does not endeavour himself to improve or change his backwardness He will not change his position. A man or, a community is solely responsible for his or its downfall or progress on all occasions.

THREE

Religion and Science

Religion and Science, the two words have vast connotations. Religion is generally understood to mean the recognition of the existence of a supernatural ruling power, the creator and controller of the universe, who has given to man a spiritual nature which continues to exist after the death of the body, and of man's duty to be obedient to this power. As a concept of life, it is all-encompassing. Science, on the other hand, is the study of the perceptible world. Both are extremely broad-ranging subjects, and their respective spheres are in many aspects quite separate from each other. It is not intended here to go into the details of these two subjects, but to deal only with the clash — real, or unreal — which has taken place between science and religion on an academic level, and certain of its consequences. One of the reasons for this clash is the claim that scientific discoveries have proved religion baseless, and it is principally this point on which attention has been focused here.

The traditional conflict between science and religion made itself felt in the eighteenth and nineteenth centuries. It was during this period that, in the light of new scientific discoveries, many came to feel that there was no further call to believe in God. One of the most compelling reasons for believing in God, amongst others, was that without this belief, the universe was inexplicable. The antagonists of religion were quick to point out that we no longer required the 'God' hypothesis when there was no aspect of the universe which could not be explained quite easily by the findings of scientific research. To them, the idea of God was redundant and, therefore, baseless.

This claim was quite flimsy from the academic or logical point of view even at the time it was made, and now science itself has admitted, directly or indirectly, that it had no satisfactory ground for making such a claim.

Of what nature was this discovery of science which attempted to convince people that there was no further need for the concept of God? It was no more than the discovery that the universe is bound by certain laws. In ancient times, man had simply believed that all happenings in the world were directly attributable to God. But modern findings revealed that behind every event there was a cause which was discoverable by observation. For instance, Newton observed that all the stars and planets in the vastness of space are bound by certain immutable laws and move in strict accordance with those laws. Darwin's research showed that man had not come into existence through an act of special creation but had evolved, in-consonance with general material laws, from the lower species and had gradually developed into *homo sapiens,* i.e. man as we now know him. Similar observational studies showed that all events seemed to occur as part of a known system called the 'Law of Nature.' Significantly, this law of nature functioned with such effective regularity that it was considered entirely predictable.

These discoveries were taken to mean that the universe, which we had regarded as God's domain, was actually subservient to a set of material and physical laws. When these laws were applied, they yielded consistent results, and this further convinced members of the educated elite that they were right in embracing atheism. The German philosopher, Kant, declared: 'Give me matter and I shall demonstrate how the world is made out of matter.' Haeckel even went so far as to say that, given water, chemical elements and time, he would be able to create a man. Nietsche proclaimed with triumphant finality, 'God is dead.' Another belief had it that the creator and sustainer of this universe was not an alive, intelligent being possessing power; that the universe, from beginning to end, was material. All movements and all manifestations of the universe, whether related to life or to lifeless matter were nothing but blind material processes. The world discovered by science evinced no signs whatsoever of the hand of God — which is surely the basis of all religions. Then how could it be considered rational to believe in God?

All the heroes who had discovered the laws of nature were believers in God, but, ironically, when their research was brought before the public, it was thought that their discoveries had rendered meaningless the very existence of God. Since, in order to explain events, one had only to have recourse to the causes and laws of the material universe, there seemed to be no need to postulate the existence of a God who was extraneous to that universe. It was said, for example, that the rising and setting of the sun had not been properly understood until telescopes had been made and mathematics developed. The former ascription of these phenomena to the will and power of supernatural beings had been due merely to man's poor comprehension of these matters. And now that astronomy had proved that there was a universal system of gravitation which controlled the movements of the sun, moon and stars, there was no further need to believe in God. Gradually, all those happenings in nature, which were supposed in ancient times to have invisible superhuman forces at work behind them, were shown to be the results of the action and reaction of the forces of nature. It was as if, after the natural causes of events had been described in modern scientific terms, belief in God should automatically cease. Julian Huxley, in his book, *Man in the Modern World,* says:

> If the rainbow is generated by the refraction of the sun's rays on falling rain, it is not set in the sky as a sign by God. If the plague is inevitably generated by the Bacillus pestis and spread by rat-fleas, an outbreak of plague can no longer be looked on as sign of divine wrath. If animals and plants have slowly evolved through hundreds of millions of years, there is no room for a creator of animals and plants, except in a metaphorical sense totally different from that in which the word was originally and is normally used. If hysteria and insanity are the natural results of disordered minds, there is no place remaining in them for possession by devils.

After presenting this piece of 'reasoning' with great conviction, he says that the ascription of such events 'to supernatural beings is merely due to man's ignorance combined with his passion for some sort of explanation.' He then sums up with: 'If events are due to natural causes, they are not due to supernatural causes' (pp. 18-19).

There is a serious weakness inherent in such arguments of the anti-religionists, which can be best understood through illustrations.

Think of the railway engine speeding along the track. How do its wheels revolve? If we attempt to answer this question by studying the different parts of the engine and their movements, we shall arrive at the conclusion that the movement of the wheels is an extension of the functioning of the locomotive's mechanism. But would we be justified in believing that the reason for their movement is the engine and its various parts? Obviously, we would not. We should first have to consider the respective roles of the engineer who designed the engine and the engine driver who set it in motion. Without their instrumentality, the engine could neither exist, nor move. The engine and its parts are not then the final reality. The final reality is the mind which has brought the engine into existence, and runs it at will. A Christian scholar, Cecil Boyce Hamann, has aptly said: "Nature does not explain, she is herself in need of explanation." This is because, as he puts it, nature is a fact, not an explanation.

Let us consider, for example, how a chick comes into this world. In embryo, it develops inside the smooth, hard shell of an egg, then it emerges when the shell breaks up. How does it come about that the shell breaks up at the right moment and the fledgling, which is no more than a small lump of flesh, finds its way into the outer world? In the past, the obvious answer was: "It is the hand of God." But now, microscopic studies have shown that on the completion of twenty-one days, when the chick is ready to emerge, there appears on its beak a small, hard horn with which this 'lump of flesh' is able to break through the walls of its cell. The horn, having done its job, falls off a few days later. This observation, from the point of view of the anti-religionists, contradicts the old concept that it is God who brings the chick out of the shell, because the microscope has clearly shown that a 21-day law exists which is responsible for creating conditions which make it possible for the chick to emerge from the shell. This is a mere fallacy. What modern observation has done is to add a few more links to the chain of factors which lead up to an event. It does not tell us the real cause of the occurrence. It has just shifted the problem of the breaking up of the shell to the development of the horn. The breaking of the shell by the chick is simply an intermediate stage in the occurrence rather than its cause. Will the cause of the event be understood only when we learn what made the horn appear on the chick's beak? In other words, when we have traced the event back to its primary cause, the cause which 'knew' that the chick required some hard instrument to break through the shell and, therefore, in exactly twenty-one days, compelled a hard substance to appear on the beak in the form of a horn and to fall off after having discharged its function?

'How does the shell break?' was the question that faced man previously. Now, in the light of recent observations, instead of an answer, we have another question: 'How does the horn develop?' In the context of perceived phenomena, there is no difference in the nature of these two questions. At the most, questions of the type that lead us from one link to another in the chain of cause and effect demand an extension of the observation of facts, if they are to be answered at all. On this basis, they do not elicit any valid explanation.

The discoveries held by the atheists to be an explanation of nature and, as such, an alternative to God, can just as easily be thought of as being the way nature works. We can, quite rationally, say that God implements his will through these laws, only parts of which man, with his limited skills, has been able to discover. Let us suppose that religious-minded people, who believe that it is God who causes the ebb and flow of the tides, are confronted with the scientific explanation that the tides are actually caused by the gravitational pull of the moon and vary according to the geographical configuration of the seas and land surfaces. There would be no need for them to deny this explanation in order to uphold their belief in God's instrumentality. They could accept it without causing the slightest harm to their religious beliefs. It is true that tides do occur in consonance with geographical configuration and as a result of gravitational pull. But, after all, what are these things? They too are God's creations. It is through these phenomena that God acts. As John Wilson observed: This does not destory my belief. It is still God (working through these things') who is responsible for the tides.'

Similarly, in the field of biology, the theory of evolution implies that biological processes no longer demand the existence of metaphysical realities. In other words, in order to understand the nature of life, we do not need to believe in a conscious God, modern studies having 'proved' that life automatically patterns itself along certain material lines: reproduction, variation and selective survival. That is, through reproduction, living creatures continue to be born, certain congenital variations go on developing, then after a long and complicated process of mutation, an altogether new species comes into being. Thus, according to the antagonists of religion, the application of Darwin's principle of natural selection in biology has made it not only possible but imperative to reject outright the concept of God's hand in life's development.

The supposition that the various species of living creatures have come into being through a gradual process of evolution has yet to be established as a fact, but even were we to give credence to this theory, it could still be said with equal conviction, that this is God's chosen way of creation, rather than its being the result of a blind, automatic force. Mechanical evolution can easily be proved to be a creational evolution. This being so, those anti-religionists who refer to science for support have no genuine basis on which to reject this argument of creational evolution.

This is far from being all that there is to the matter. The truth is that twentieth century science has lost its ability to convince. Today, Newton has been replaced by Einstein, and the theories of Planck and Heisenberg have overthrown those of Laplace. Now the anti-religionists, at least on an academic level, can no longer claim that science has arrived at the ultimate truth. Indeed, the theory of relativity and the quantum theory have led scientists to the conclusion that it is impossible in science to separate the observer from the observed. This means that we can see only certain external manifestations of reality; we cannot apprehend it in its essence. The revolution that has occurred in science in the twentieth century has itself proved the importance of religion from the scientific point of view.

In his book, *The Limitations of Science,* J.N. Sullivan states the case thus:

What is called the modern "revolution" in science consists of the fact that the Newtonian outlook, which dominated the scientific world for nearly two hundred years, has been found insufficient. It is in process of being replaced by a different outlook, and, although the reconstruction is by no means complete, it is already apparent that the philosophical implications of the new outlook are very different from those of the old one. We are no longer taught that the scientific method of approach is the only valid method of acquiring knowledge about reality. Eminent men of science are insisting, with what seems a strange enthusiasm, on the fact that science gives us but a partial knowledge of reality.

This change in the scientific outlook seems to have taken place suddenly. It is not yet sixty years since Tyn-dall, in his Belfast Address, claimed that science alone was competent to deal with all man's major problems. But, in truth, so far as these remarks sprang from the conviction that the sole reality is 'matter and motion,' their foundations had already been undermined. The attempt to represent nature in terms of matter and motion was already breaking down. That attempt was at its most triumphant by the end of the eighteenth century, when Laplace was emboldened to affirm that a sufficiently great mathematician, given the distribution of the particles in the primitive nebula, could predict the whole future history of the world. The fundamental concepts isolated by Newton had proved themselves so adequate in the applications that had been made of them that they were regarded as the key to everything.

The first indication that the Newtonian concepts were not all-sufficient came when men tried to fashion a mechanical theory of light. This endeavour led to the creation of the ether, the most unsatisfactory and wasteful product of human ingenuity that science has to show. For generations this monster was elaborated. Miracles of mathematical ingenuity were performed in the attempt to account for the properties of light in terms of the Newtonian concepts. The difficulties became ever more heartbreaking until, after the publication of Maxwell's demonstration that light is an electromagnetic phenomenon, they seemed to become insuperable. For it had dawned on men of science that there was, after all, nothing sacrosanct about the Newtonian entities. After a certain amount of hesitation, and a few last desperate efforts to make electricity mechanical, electricity was added to the list of irreducible elements.

This may seem to have been a simple step to take, but it was, in reality, of profound significance. For the Newtonian concepts were all of a kind that one seemed to understand intimately. Thus the mass of a body was the quantity of matter in it. Force was a notion derived from our experience of muscular effort. Nevertheless, we supposed that we knew the nature of what we were talking about. But in the case of electricity its nature is precisely what we did not know. Attempts to represent it in familiar terms — as a condition of strain in the ether, or what not — had been given up. All that we knew about electricity was the way it affected our measuring instruments. The precise description of this behaviour gave us the mathematical specification of electricity and this, in truth, was all we knew about it. It is only now, in retrospect, that we can see how very significant a step this was. An entity had been admitted into physics of which we knew nothing but its mathematical structure.

Since then other entities have been admited on the same terms, and it is found that they play precisely the same role in the formation of scientific theories as do the old entities. It has become evident that, so far as the science of physics is concerned, we do not require to know the nature of the entities we discuss, but only their mathematical structure. And, in truth, that is all we do know. It is now realized that this is all the scientific knowledge we have even of the familiar Newtonian entities. Our persuasion that we knew them in some exceptionally intimate manner was an illusion.

With this realization it is no long step to Eddington's position that a knowledge of mathematical structure is the only knowledge that the science of physics can give us. Leaving out all aesthetic, ethical, or spiritual aspects of our environment, we are faced with qualities such as massiveness, substantiality, extension, duration, which are supposed to belong to the domain of physics. In a sense they do belong; but physics is not in a position to handle them directly. The essence of their nature is inscrutable; we may use mental pictures to aid calculations, but no image in the mind can be a replica of that which is not in the mind. And so in its actual procedure physics studies not these inscrutable qualities, but pointer-readings which we can observe. The readings, it is true, reflect the fluctuations of the world-qualities; but our exact knowledge is of the readings, not of the qualities. The former have as much resemblance to the latter as a telephone number has to a subscriber.

The fact that science is confined to a knowledge of structure is obviously of great "humanistic" importance. For it means that the problem of the nature of reality is not prejudged. We are no longer required to believe that our response to beauty, or the mystic's sense of communion with God, have no objective counterpart. It is perfectly possible that they are, what they have so often been taken to be, clues to the nature of reality. Thus, our various experiences are put on a more equal footing, as it were. Our religious aspirations, our perceptions of beauty, may not be the essentially illusory phenomena they were supposed to be. In this new scientific universe even mystics have a right to exist (pp. 138-42).

Such explanations from scientific philosophers now abound. Morton White in his book *The Age of Analysis,* points out that 'the philosophically-minded scientists of the 20th century have started a new crusade, the names of Whitehead, Eddington and James Jeans are the most prominent among them.' He then bears out this notion of a 'crusade' with highly pertinent quotations from each of them.

'Nature is alive' (p. 84). Such was the interpretation of modern information by the English mathematician and philosopher, A.N. Whitehead (1861-1947).

The stuff of the world is mind stuff (p. 134). So said the English astronomer, Sir Arthur Eddington (1882-1944), deriving this conclusion from his studies in science.

The English mathematical physicist, Sir James Jeans (1877-1946), interprets modern research thus: The universe is a universe of thought' (p. 134).

The views of the most perceptive scientists, can be summed up in J.W.N. Sullivan's words: 'The ultimate nature of the universe is mental' (p. 145).

The thoughts of these scholars clearly negate any material interpretation of the universe, their special virtue being that they have been advanced in the context of modern findings in the field of physics and mathematics. That the proponents of such ideas have had to make courageous, herculean efforts to overcome the materialistic outlook is aptly expressed by Morton White with reference to Whitehead: 'He is a heroic thinker who tries to beard the lions of Intellectualism, Materialism and Positivism in their own bristling den' (p. 84). Morton White may have said this only about Whitehead, but this applies to all the scientists mentioned above.

This philosophical question as to the final reality being mind or matter is actually concerned with the question of whether the universe has developed independently and spontaneously through some material process, or whether there is a non-material being who has created it at will. If we accepted the former proposition, it would be just like saying that, in the last analysis, a machine is simply a fortuitous compound of iron and petrol. That is to say, that the machine started off as iron and petrol, but owing to some blind, automatic process, it took on the form of a machine. All a pure accident! A machine, as we all know, is the product of an engineer's mind. That mind, quite distinct from the matter, existed before the machine. It conceived it, designed it, and brought it into being. The machine's existence was clearly consequent upon the exercise of mind and will.

In determining the nature of the mind, differences can be found among those who believe the mind to be the final reality, just as believers in God have diverse concepts of God. Even so, the conclusion arrived at by academic study that the final underlying reality of the universe is mind, testifies by its very nature to the truth of religion and amounts to a rejection of atheism. The truly significant change in modern science is not to be found in its increased powers to aid man's religion and science progress, but in the change in its metaphysical foundations.'

The best exposition of this viewpoint is to be found in *The Mysterious Universe,* by Sir James Jeans. By pure scientific argument, the writer has come to the conclusion that in the light of modern physics, 'The universe cannot admit of material representation, and the reason, I think, is that it has become a mere mental concept.'

He later goes on to say that "if the universe is a universe of thought, then its creation must have been an act of thought" (pp. 133-34).

He holds that the modern concept which interprets matter in terms of waves of electrons is quite unconceivable to human thought, because these 'waves' could be only the 'waves of probabilities' without having any material existence. Such reasons have compelled Jeans to conclude that the substance of the universe is thought, not matter. Now where is this thought situated? His answer is that it exists in the mind of a great 'mathematical thinker? Because the structure of this thought that comes to our mind is a completely mathematical structure. The 'great Architect of the Universe thus begins to appear as a pure mathematician,'

Sir James Jeans then states the entire case with great precision: It seems at least safe to say that the river of knowledge has made a sharp bend in the last few years. Thirty years ago, we thought, or assumed, that we were heading towards an ultimate reality of a mechanical kind. It seemed to consist of fortuitous jumble of atoms, which was destined to perform meaningless dances for a time under the action of blind purposeless forces, and then fall back to form a dead world. Into this wholly mechanical world, through the play of the same blind forces, life had stumbled by accident. One tiny corner at least, and possibly several tiny corners of this universe of atoms had chanced to become conscious for a time, but was destined in the end, still under the action of blind mechanical forces, to be frozen out and again leave a lifeless world.

Today there is a wide measure of agreement, which on the physical side of science approaches almost to unanimity, that the stream of knowledge is heading towards a non-mechanical reality; the universe begins to look more like a great thought than like a great machine. Mind no longer appears as an accidental intruder into the realm of matter; we are beginning to suspect that we ought rather to hail it as the creator and governor of the realm of matter — not of course our individual minds, but the mind in which the atoms out of which our individual minds have grown exist as thoughts.

The new knowledge compels us to revise our hasty first impressions that we had stumbled into a universe which either did not concern itself with life or was actively hostile to life. The old dualism of mind and matter, which was mainly responsible for the supposed hostility, seems likely to disappear, not through matter becoming in any way more shadowy or insubstantial than heretofore, or through mind becoming resolved into a function of the working of matter, but through substantial matter resolving itself into a creation and manifestation of mind. We discover that the universe shows evidence of a designing or controlling power that has something in common with our own individual minds — not, so far as we have discovered, emotion, morality, or aesthetic appreciation, but the tendency to think in the way, which, for want of a better word, we describe as mathematical.

In spite of this complete about-face in science from the academic point of view, it is a fact that, in practice, there have been no noticeable changes in the attitudes of anti-religionists. On the contrary, they are engaged in seeking new arguments to support their theory. The reason for this is not to be found within any academic framework. No, the reason is to be traced, alas! to a biased mentality. How often have we seen educated people refuse to accept the truth when ample proofs have been offered to them, simply because of deeply-rooted preconceived ideas. It was just such a prejudiced attitude, in the seventeenth century, which had prevented Italian scholars from accepting Galileo's theory as an alternative to Aristotle's, although a ball thrown from the Leaning Tower had demonstrated quite conclusively that Galileo was right. Again, it was this bias which caused scholars at the end of the nineteenth century to ridicule Berlin Professor Max Planck when he gave a physical explanation of light,— the quantum theory, — which proved the Newtonian concept wrong. Planck's theory was not accepted for many years, but today it is considered one of the most important principles in physics.

There is a common belief that it is only laymen who are guilty of prejudice and not scientists; we should do well, therefore, to mark the words of A.V. Hills, himself a scientist: 'I should be the last to claim that we, scientific men, are less liable to prejudice than other educated men.

Sir James Jeans underscores this when he says, 'Our modern minds have, I think, a bias towards mechanical interpretation.'

Now, in a world where prejudice holds sway, how can we hope that a concept will be accepted only because it has been proved academically? The often-repeated experiences of history show that man has all along been governed by his emotions rather than by his intellect, in spite of the fact that academically and logically, reason occupies the higher position. More often than not, reason has played into the hands of emotion. It has seldom happened that it has gained a positive control over the emotions. Indeed, the intellect has always coined arguments to support the emotional and thus tried to prove that emotional attitudes were rational. Man finds it a psychological necessity to cling to his emotional being, even at the cost of remaining blind to reality. We must remember, therefore, that we are not dealing with machines, which ought to respond to the mere flicking of a switch. What we have to address ourselves to is man, and man accepts something only when he himself is willing to do so. If he is not, no argument, however sound it may be, will convince him. Arguments are not, sad to say, electric switches. That man, with all his capacity for reasoning, should so seldom, himself, be amenable to reasoning, is perhaps the greatest tragedy of human history.

Where Science Failed?

Modern scholars have come to the conclusion that we may have succeeded in making great discoveries about inanimate matter, but that we cannot be certain of having been successful in discovering the facts of man's nature and existence, for there exists a strange disparity between the sciences of inanimate matter and those of life. The sciences which concern themselves with the inanimate part of our world differ from the biological sciences in that the former are subject to definite laws whereas the latter are, to quote Dr. Alexis Carrel, inextricably lost 'in the midst of a magic forest whose countless trees unceasingly change their place and shape.' Unlike material phenomena, biological phenomena cannot be defined in terms of algebraic equations. The sciences of the material world are confined to description, a lower form of science altogether, because they do not unveil the ultimate nature of things, but only convey certain qualities such as weight and spatial dimensions. They do give us the power to predict future events, and often to determine at will their occurrence; in learning the secret of the constitution and properties of matter, we have gained the mastery of almost everything which exists on the surface of the earth — excepting ourselves. The science of living beings in general, and of the human individual in particular, has not made such spectacular progress. It still remains at the descriptive stage, while the elucidation of the real nature of living beings requires much more than mere description.

The Nobel prize winner, Dr. Alexis Carrel, who achieved unique fame in biological research at the Rockfeller Institute in New York, elaborates at some length in his book, *Man, the Unknown,* on what is meant by man:

Man is an indivisible whole of extreme complexity. No simple representation of him can be obtained. There is no method capable of apprehending him simultaneously in his entirety, his parts, and his relations with the outer world. In order to analyze ourselves we are obliged to seek the help of various techniques and, therefore, to utilize several sciences. Naturally, all these sciences arrive at a different conception of their common object. They abstract only from man what is attainable by their special methods. And those abstractions, after they have been added together, are still less rich than the concrete fact. They leave behind them a residue too important to be neglected. Anatomy, chemistry, physiology, psychology, pedagogy, history, sociology, political economy do not exhaust their subject. Man, as known to the specialists, is far from being the concrete man, the real man. He is nothing but a schema, consisting of other schemata built up by the techniques of each science.

He is, at the same time, the corpse dissected by the anatomists, the consciousness observed by the psychologists and the great teachers of the spiritual life, and the personality which introspection shows to everyone as lying in the depth of himself. He is the chemical substance constituting the tissues and humours of the body. He is the amazing community of cells and nutrient fluids whose organic laws are studied by the physiologists. He is the compound of tissues and consciousness that hygienists and educators endeavour to lead to its optimum development while it extends into time. He is the homoaconomicus who must ceaselessly consume manufactured products in order that the machines, of which he is made a slave, may be kept at work. But he is also the poet, the hero, and the saint. He is not only the prodigiously complex being analyzed by our scientific techniques, but also the tendencies, the conjectures, the aspirations of humanity. Our conceptions of him are imbued with metaphysics. They are founded on so many and such imprecise data that the temptation is great to choose among them those which please us. Therefore, our idea of man varies according to our feelings and our beliefs. A materialist and a spiritualist accept the same definition of a crystal of sodium chloride; but they do not agree with one another upon that of the human being. A mechanistic physiologist and a vitalistic physiologist do not consider the organism in the same light. The living being of Jacques Loeb differs profoundly from that of Hans Driesch. Indeed, mankind has made a gigantic effort to know itself. Although we possess the treasure of the observations accumulated by the scientists, the philosophers, the poets, and the great mystics of all times, we have grasped only certain aspects of ourselves. We do not apprehend man as a whole. We know him as composed of distinct parts. And even these parts are created by our methods. Each one of us is made up of a procession of phantoms, in the midst of which strides an unknowable reality.

In fact, our ignorance is profound. Most of the questions put to themselves by those who study human beings remain without answer. Immense regions of our inner world are still unknown. How do the molecules of chemical substance associate in order to form the complex and temporary organs of the cell? How do the genes contained in the nucleus of a fertilized ovum determine the characteristics of the individual deriving from that ovum? How do cells organize themselves by their own efforts into societies, such as the tissues and the organs? Like the ants and the bees, they have advance knowledge of the part they are destined to play in the life of the community. And hidden mechanisms enable them to build up an organism both complex and simple. What is the nature of our duration, of psychological time, and of physiological time? We know that we are a compound of tissues, organs, fluids, and consciousness. But the relations between consciousness and cerebrum are still a mystery. We lack almost entirely a knowledge of the physiology of nervous cells. To what extent does will power modify the organism? How is the mind influenced by the state of the organs? In what manner can the organic and mental characteristics, which each individual inherits, be changed by the mode of life, the chemical substances contained in food, the climate, and the physiological and moral disciplines?

We are very far from knowing what relations exist between skeleton, muscles, and organs, and mental and spiritual activities. We are ignorant of the factors that bring about nervous equilibrium and resistance to fatigue and to diseases. We do not know how moral sense, judgement, and audacity could be augmented. What is the relative importance of intellectual, moral, and mystical activities? What is the significance of aesthetic and religious sense? What form of energy is responsible for telepathic communications? Without any doubt, certain physiological and mental factors determine happiness or misery, success or failure. But we do not know what they are. We cannot artificially give to any individual the aptitude for happiness. As yet we do not know what environment is the most favourable for the optimum development of civilized man. Is it possible to suppress struggle, effort, and suffering from our physiological and spiritual formation? How can we prevent the degeneration of man in modern civilization? Many other questions could be asked on subjects which are to us of the utmost interest. They would also remain unanswered. It is quite evident that the accomplishments of all the sciences having man as an object remain insufficient, and that our knowledge of ourselves is still most rudimentary.

This passage more than adequately demonstrates that we still have not formulated a true science of man. About the material part of human existence we are fairly well informed, but we are completely ignorant of who or what controls it. Life is still a mystery to us, and until it is unveiled, there can be no proper apprehension of what, in essence, it is. Alexis Carrel's book, *Man, the Unknown,* is an attempt to make scientific approach to its discovery.

Today man can split an atom; he can make icy lands habitable; he has walked on the moon and sent probes into outer space. Such instances of advanced technological progress give the impression that if man can learn so much about his material environment that he is able to exploit it at will, he should certainly be able to discover himself and, in the process, set right whatever ails him. But there are strong indications in our known world that man can never be understood in the same way that matter can.

Let us look at this entity, called man, on a purely physiological basis. He is composed of millions and millions of cells of protoplasm. And what is protoplasm? We can say with certainty that it is a viscous, translucent, homogeneous, structureless substance endowed with contractility and a chemical composition allied to that of albumen: it is the physical basis of life and, clearly, we know a great deal about it as such. Yet we have to concede that we do not know why it should have this unique property of life, or how this came to be so. Moreover, it is a fact that the methods we employ to study the material world cannot be applied to protoplasm in any way which should elicit an answer to these awesome questions. All that is visible to us is a compound of certain things.

If we had the means and the resources, we should be able not only to destroy but also to create such compounds. Indeed, science has discovered the elements of which protoplasm is composed and the particular proportion of those elements have also been learnt. But it is in vain that we join together the two distinct forms of protoplasm, the nucleus and the cytoplasm, albeit in the correct proportions, for no protoplasm is thus formed which has the property of life. While other chemical compounds can be formed by combining their elements in the correct proportions, (e.g. one molecule of water is made up of one atom of oxygen and two atoms of hydrogen) the life-giving matter which is the main constituent of a human being's body can in no way be brought into existence by human agency. Our powers of creation extend only to inanimate matter, never to living entities.

This is the area in which we are the most helpless, and we have no option but to admit it. The greatest irony is that although all our physiological studies are concerned with the living man, the results they yield bear more relevance to this cadaver. Science has discovered both the elements which constitute protoplasm and their correct proportions, yet the particular order or arrangement which is responsible for the life-property of protoplasm has still to be revealed. The moment this arrangement disintegrates, the protoplasm is rendered lifeless. It is as if a particular arrangement was responsible for the existence of soul in the protoplasm. But the difficulty that confronts us is that so long as we keep this arrangement intact, the protoplasm cannot be chemically analysed. The moment we break it, life vanishes. Whenever protoplasm is subjected to chemical analysis, the soul has already left it. And this will always be the case. Science will always remain in the dark regarding the reality of life. But this is not the end of our problem. It goes much deeper than this.

Let us suppose someone sets out to unveil reality, thus disclosing to man the law of life, and, to this end, he begins the study of human settlements. After prolonged examination of different societies, he comes to the conclusion that, since society is composed of human beings, he had best concern himself with the individual, the better to understand the group. So he reduces his focus accordingly. His first preoccupation then is with psychology. But he soon realizes that no single philosophy emerges, because there are several schools of thought on the subject, all arriving at different conclusions. One school claims that the senses are central to all human actions while others say that all man's responses are reactions to impressions received consciously or unconsciously from the external world. Yet others say that it is sexual desires which provide the stimulus for all of man's actions. A different type of study shows that an unrecognized urge to realize a certain set of ideals keeps man active. Some schools of thought take consciousness to be a reality and explain the whole of man's being in relation to this; others hold that the mind and intellect, have no existence, and that there is no central power commanding the various parts of the body. Rather the parts which receive most attention are better developed and that is what makes it possible, for example, for one man to be highly skilled in dancing, another in archery and yet another in profound reflection. These differences in thinking in the field of psychology go to such extremes that one might be led to wonder if there was any such unified science as psychology.

On seeing this jungle of ideas, our inquirer thinks of studying another aspect of human existence — biology — in order to come to more cogent conclusions. But in this discipline he finds that man is treated as an amalgam of the metabolism, the respiratory system, the blood circulation, and so on. These systems are based on certain chemical changes and, judging from their action and reaction, it would appear that the different parts of the whole bodily system are sub-functions of the metabolism.

After deep reflection, he comes to the conclusion that since the existence of the human body and its development are related to chemical actions and reactions, the principles according to which chemical changes take place should first of all be properly understood, failing which no really satisfactory information about man could ever be discovered. So he engrosses himself in the study of physics and chemistry and, indeed, devotes the major part of his life to it.

This branch of study leads him on to an investigation of the molecule and the atom, from which he proceeds to study the electrons and protons of which the atom is composed. The realization then comes to him that the whole universe is nothing but electric waves, and he becomes immersed in the study of the latest discoveries in nuclear science. He thus collects a huge mass of facts, but at the end of it all, he fails to arrive at any firm conclusions about the reality of man. He has become lost in a world which, in spite of being visible, has remained impenetrable. According to Dr. C.E.M. Joad, matter is something unreal which cannot be grasped. It is a part of the four dimensional space-time continuum, a network of electric waves, or a wave of probability which perished on being looked at; and it has even been considered an extension of the observer's consciousness instead of something solid and tangible.

This pathetic end to the quest for the secret of life in the material sciences shows that the secret of life is not discoverable by man. Now just as a sick man cannot treat his disease himself and is forced to consult a doctor, so a man who is in need of spiritual sustenance cannot provide this for himself without turning to God. The fact that he cannot discover the secret either of life or of his own nature is a sure indicator that he is in need of the God who created him in the form in which he exists. Just as God has created man in such a way that he needs oxygen and then has given him oxygen in abundance, He has made him yearn to know the secret of life and then has sent His messengers to him so that all veils should fall from reality.

FOUR

Quran and Science

Really, the relationship between the Quran and science is *a priori* a surprise, especially when it turns out to be one of harmony and not of discord. A confrontation between a religious book and the secular ideas proclaimed by science is perhaps, in the eyes of many people today, something of a paradox. The majority of today's scientists, with a small number of exceptions of course, are indeed bound up in materialist theories, and have only indifference or contempt for religious questions which they often consider to be founded on legend. In the West moreover, when science and religion are discussed, people are quite willing to mention Judaism and Christianity among the religions referred to, but they hardly ever think of Islam. So many false judgements based on inaccurate ideas have indeed been made about it, that today it is very difficult to form an exact notion of the reality of Islam.

As a prelude to any confrontation between the Islamic Revelation and science, it would seem essential that an outline be given of a religion that is so little known in the West.

The totally erroneous statements made about Islam in the West are sometimes the result of ignorance, and sometimes of systematic denigration. The most serious of all the untruths told about it are however those dealing with facts; for while mistaken opinions are excusable, the presentation of facts running contrary to the reality is not. It is disturbing to read blatant untruths in eminently respectable works written by authors who *a priori* are highly qualified. The following is an example taken from the *Universalis Encyclopedia* (Encyclopedia Universalis) Vol.6. Under the heading Gospels (Evangiles) the author alludes to the differences between the latter and the Quran: "The evangelists (. . .) do not (. . .), as in the Quran, claim to transmit an autobiography that God miraculously dictated to the Prophet . . .". In fact, the Quran has nothing to do with an autobiography: it is a preaching; a consultation of even the worst translation should have made that clear to the author. The statement we have quoted is as far from reality as if one were to define a Gospel as an account of an evangelist's life. The person responsible for this untruth about the Quran is a professor at the Jesuit Faculty of Theology, Lyon! The fact that people utter such untruths helps to give a false impression of the Quran and Islam.

There is hope today however because religions are no longer as inward-looking as they were and many of them are seeking for mutual understanding. One must indeed be impressed by a knowledge of the fact that an attempt is being made on the highest level of the hierarchy by Roman Catholics to establish contact with Muslims; they are trying to fight incomprehension and are doing their utmost to change the inaccurate views on Islam that are so widely held.

In the previous chapter of this work, the great change that has taken place in the last few years was mentioned and a document produced by the Office for Non-Christian Affairs at the Vatican under the title *Orientations for a Dialogue between Christians and Muslims* (Orientations pour un dialogue entre chretiens et musulmans) was quoted. It is a very important document in that it shows the new position adopted towards Islam. As we read in the third edition of this study (1970), this new position calls for 'a revision of our attitude towards it and a critical examination of our prejudices' . . . 'We should first set about progressively changing the way our Christian brothers see it. This is the most important of all.' . . . We must clear away the 'out-dated image inherited from the past, or distorted by prejudice and slander' . . . , and 'recognize the past injustice towards the Muslims for which the West, with its Christian education, is to blame.' The Vatican document is nearly 150 pages long. It therefore expands on the refutation of classic views held by Christians on Islam and sets out the reality.

Under the title Emancipating ourselves from our worst prejudices (*Nous liberer de nos prejuges les plus notables*) the authors address the following suggestions to Christians: "Here also, we must surrender to a deep purification of our attitude. In particular, what is meant by this are certain 'set judgements' that are all too often and too lightly made about Islam. It is essential not to cultivate in the secret of our hearts views such as these, too easily or arbitrarily arrived at, and which the sincere Muslim finds confusing."

One extremely important view of this kind is the attitude which leads people to repeatedly use the term 'Allah' to mean the God of the Muslims, as if the Muslims believed in a God who was different from the God of the Christians. *Al Idh* means 'the Divinity' in Arabic: it is a single God, implying that a correct transcription can only render the exact meaning of the word with the help of the expression 'God'. For the Muslim, *al Iah* is none other than the God of Moses and Jesus.

The document produced by the Office for Non-Christian Affairs at the Vatican stresses this fundamental point in the following terms:

"It would seem pointless to maintain that Allah is not really God, as do certain people in the West! The conciliar documents have put the above assertion in its proper place. There is no better way of illustrating Islamic faith in God than by quoting the following extracts from *Lumen Gentium:* 'The Muslims profess the faith of Abraham and worship with us the sole merciful God, who is the future judge of men on the Day of Reckoning . . . '"

One can therefore understand the Muslims' protest at the all too frequent custom in European languages of saying *'Allah'* instead of 'God'... Cultivated Muslims have praised D. Masson's French translation of the Quran for having 'at last' written 'Dieu' instead of 'Allah'.

The Vatican document points out the following: "Allah is the only word that Arabic-speaking Christians have for God."

Muslims and Christians worship a single God.

The Vatican document then undertakes a critical examination of the other false judgements made on Islam.

'Islamic fatalism' is a widely-spread prejudice; the document examines this and quoting the Quran for support, it puts in opposition to this the notion of the responsibility man has, who is to be judged by his actions. It shows that the concept of an Islamic legalism is false; on the contrary, it opposes the sincerity of faith to this by quoting two phrases in the Quran that are highly misunderstood in the West:

> "There is no compulsion in religion"
> —(2:256)

> "(God) has not laid upon you in religion any hardship"
> —(22:78)

The document opposes the widely-spread notion of 'Islam, religion of fear' to 'Islam, religion of love'—love of one's neighbor based on faith in God. It refutes the falsely spread notion that Muslim morality hardly exists and the other notion, shared by so many Jews and Christians, of Islamic fanaticism. It makes the following comment on this: "In fact, Islam was hardly any more fanatical during its history than the sacred bastions of Christianity whenever the Christian faith took on, as it were, a political value." At this point, the authors quote expressions from the Quran that show how, in the West, the expression 'Holy War' has been mis-translated; "in Arabic it is *Al jihad fi sabil Allah,* the effort on God's road", "the effort to spread Islam and defend it against its aggressors." The Vatican document continues as follows: "The *jihad* is not at all the Biblical *kherem;* it does not lead to extermination, but to the spreading of God's and man's rights to new lands."—"The past violence of the *jihad* generally followed the rules of war; at the time of the Crusades moreover, it was not always the Muslims that perpetrated the worst slaughters."

Finally, the document deals with the prejudice according to which "Islam is a hide-bound religion which keeps its followers in a kind of superannuated Middle Ages, making them unfit to adapt to the technical conquests of the modern age." It compares analogous situations observed in Christian countries and states the following: "we find, (...) in the traditional expansion of Muslim thought, a principle of possible evolution in civilian society."

It is certain that this defense of Islam by the Vatican will surprise many believers today, be the Muslims, Jews or Christians. It is a demonstration of sincerity and open-mindedness that is singularly in contrast with the attitudes inherited from the past. The number of people in the West who are aware of the new attitudes adopted by the highest authorities in the Catholic Church is however very small.

Once one is aware of this fact, it comes as less of a surprise to learn of the actions that sealed this reconciliation : firstly, there was the official visit made by the President of the Office for Non-Christian Affairs at the Vatican to King Faisal of Saudi Arabia; then the official reception given by Pope Paul VI to the Grand Ulema of Saudi Arabia in the course of 1974. Henceforth, one understands more clearly the spiritual significance of the fact that His Grace Bishop Elchinger received the Grand Ulema at his cathedral in Strasbourg and invited them during their visit to pray in the choir. This they did before the altar, turned towards Makka.

Thus the representatives of the Muslim and Christian worlds at their highest level, who share a faith in the same God and a mutual respect for their differences of opinion, have agreed to open a dialogue. This being so, it is surely quite natural for other aspects of each respective revelation to be confronted. The subject of this confrontation is the examination of the scriptures in the light of scientific data and knowledge concerning the authenticity of the texts. This examination is to be undertaken for the Quran as it was for the Judeo-Christian Revelation.

The relationship between religions and science has not always been the same in any one place or time. It is a fact that there is no writing belonging to a monotheistic religion that condemns science. In practise however, it must be admitted that scientists have had great difficulties with the religious authorities of certain creeds. For many centuries, in the Christian world, scientific development was opposed by the authorities in question, on their own initiative and without reference to the authentic scriptures. We already know the measures taken against those who sought to enlarge science, measures which often made scientists go into exile to avoid being burnt at the stake, unless they recanted, changed their attitude and begged for pardon. The case of Galileo is always cited in this context: he was tried for having accepted the discoveries made by Copernicus on the rotation of the earth. Galileo was condemned as the result of a mistaken interpretation of the Bible, since not a single scripture could reasonably be brought against him.

In the case of Islam, the attitude towards science was, generally speaking, quite different. Nothing could be clearer than the famous Hadith of the Prophet: "Seek for science, even in China", or the other

Hadith which says that the search for knowledge is a strict duty for every Muslim man and woman. As we shall see further on in this section, another crucial fact is that the Quran, while inviting us to cultivate science, itself contains many observations on natural phenomena and includes explanatory details which are seen to be in total agreement with modern scientific data. There is no equal to this in the Judeo-Christian Revelation.

It would nevertheless be wrong to imagine that, in the history of Islam, certain believers had never harboured a different attitude towards science. It is a fact that, at certain periods, the obligation to educate oneself and others was rather neglected. It is equally true that in the Muslim world, as elsewhere, an attempt was sometimes made to stop scientific development. All the same, it will be remembered that at the height of Islam, between the Eighth and Twelfth centuries A.D., i.e. at a time when restrictions on scientific development were in force in the Christian world, a very large number of studies and discoveries were being made at Islamic universities. It was there that the remarkable cultural resources of the time were to be found. The Califs library at Cordoba contained 400,000 volumes. Averroes was teaching there, and Greek, Indian and Persian sciences were taught. This is why scholars from all over Europe went to study at Cordoba, just as today people go to the United States to perfect their studies. A very great number of ancient manuscripts have come down to us thanks to cultivated Arabs who acted as the vehicle for the culture of conquered countries. We are also greatly indebted to Arabic culture for mathematics (algebra was an Arabic invention), astronomy, physics (optics), geology, botany, medicine (Avicenna), etc. For the very first time, science took on an international character in the Islamic universities of the Middle Ages. At this time, men were more steeped in the religious spirit than they are today; but in the Islamic world, this did not prevent them from being both believers and scientists. Science was the twin of religion and it should never have ceased to be so.

The Medieval period was, for the Christian world, a time of stagnation and absolute conformity. It must be stressed that scientific research was not slowed down by the Judeo-Christian Revelation itself, but rather by those people who claimed to be its servants.

Following the Renaissance, the scientists' natural reaction was to take vengeance on their former enemies; this vengeance still continues today, to such an extent indeed that in the West, anyone who talks of God in scientific circles really does stand out. This attitude affects the thinking of all young people who receive a university education, Muslims included.

Their thinking could hardly be different from what it is, considering the extreme positions adopted by the most eminent scientists. A Nobel prize winner for medicine has tried in the last few years to persuade people, in a book intended for mass publication, that living matter was able to create itself by chance from several basic components. Starting, he says, with this primitive living matter, and under the influence of various external circumstances, organized living beings were formed, resulting in the formidable complex being that constitutes man.

Surely these marvels of contemporary scientific knowledge in the field of life should lead a thinking person to the opposite conclusion. The organization presiding over the birth and maintenance of life surely appears more and more complicated as one studies it; the more details one knows, the more admiration it commands. A knowledge of this organization must surely lead one to consider as less and less probable the part chance has to play in the phenomenon of life. The further one advances along the road to knowledge, especially of the infinitely small, the more eloquent are the arguments in favour of the existence of a Creator. Instead of being filled with humility in the face of such facts, man is filled with arrogance. He sneers at any idea of God, in the same way he runs down anything that detracts from his pleasure and enjoyment. This is the- image of the materialist society that is flourishing at present in the West.

What spiritual forces can be used to oppose this pollution of thought practised by many contemporary scientists?

Judaism and Christianity make no secret of their inability to cope with the tide of materialism and invasion of the West by atheism. Both of them are completely taken off guard, and from one decade to the next one can surely see how seriously diminished their resistance is to this tide that threatens to sweep everything away. The materialist atheist sees in classic Christianity nothing more than a system constructed by men over the last two thousand years designed to ensure the authority of a minority over their fellow men. He is unable to find in Judeo-Christian writings any language that is even vaguely similar to his own; they contain so many improbabilities, contradictions and incompatibilities with modern scientific data, that he refuses to take texts into consideration that the vast majority of theologians would like to see accepted as an inseparable whole.

When one mentions Islam to the materialist atheist, he smiles with a complacency that is only equal to his ignorance of the subject. In common with the majority of western intellectuals, of whatever religious persuasion, he has an impressive collection of false notions about Islam.

One must, on this point, allow him one or two excuses: Firstly, apart from the newly-adopted attitudes prevailing among the highest Catholic authorities, Islam has always been subject in the West to a so-called 'secular slander'. Anyone in the West who has acquired a deep knowledge of Islam knows just to what extent its history, dogma, and aims have been distorted. One must also take into account the fact that documents published in European languages on this subject (leaving aside highly specialized studies) do not make the work of a person willing to learn any easier.

A knowledge of the Islamic Revelation is indeed fundamental from this point of view. Unfortunately, passages from the Quran, especially those relating to scientific data, are badly translated and interpreted, so that a scientist has every right to make criticisms—with apparent justification—that the Book does not actually deserve at all. This detail is worth noting henceforth: inaccuracies in translation or erroneous commentaries (the one is often associated with the other), which would not have surprised anybody one or two centuries ago, offend today's scientists. When faced with a badly translated phrase containing a scientifically unacceptable statement, the scientist is prevented from taking the phrase into serious consideration. In the chapter on human reproduction, a very typical example will be given of this kind of error.

Why do such errors in translation exist? They may be explained by the fact that modern translators often take up, rather uncritically, the interpretations given by older commentators. In their day, the latter had an excuse for having given an inappropriate definition to an Arabic word containing several possible meanings; they could not possibly have understood the real sense of the word or phrase which has only become clear in the present day thanks to scientific knowledge. In other words, the problem is raised of the necessary revision of translations and commentaries. It was not possible to do this at a certain period in the past, but nowadays we have knowledge that enables us to render their -true sense. These problems of translation are not present for the texts of the Judeo-Christian Revelation: the case described here is absolutely unique to the Quran.

These scientific considerations, which are very specific to the Quran, were surprising. Till then it was not thought possible for one to find so many statements in a text compiled more than fourteen centuries ago referring to extremely diverse subjects and all of them totally in keeping with modern scientific knowledge. In the beginning, there was no faith whatsoever in Islam. These tests were examined with a completely open mind and a total objectivity. If there was any influence acting, it was gained from what had been taught during earlier times when people did not speak of Muslims, but of 'Mohammadens', to make it quite clear that what was meant was a religion founded by a man and which could not therefore have any kind of value in terms of God. Like many in the West, one could have retained the same false notions about Islam; they are so widely-spread today, that it is am indeed surprising when one comes across anyone, other than a specialist, who can talk in an enlightened manner on this subject. Admittedly until one was given a view of Islam different from the one received in the West, one was extremely ignorant.

I owe the fact that I was able to realize the false nature of the judgements generally made in the West about Islam to exceptional circumstances. It was in Saudi Arabia itself that an inkling was given to me of the extent to which opinions held in the West on this subject are liable to error.

The debt of gratitude I owe to the late King Faisal, whose memory I salute with deepest respect, is indeed very great: the fact that I was given the signal honour of hearing him speak on Islam and was able to raise with him certain problems concerning the interpretation of the

Quran in relation to modern science is a very cherished memory. It was an extremely great privilege for me to have gathered so much precious information from him personally and those around him.

Since it had been seen the wide gap separating the reality of Islam from the image we have of it in the West, I experienced a great need to learn Arabic (which I did not speak) to be sufficiently well-equipped to progress in the study of such a misunderstood religion. My first goal was to read the Quran and to make a sentence-by-sentence analysis of it with the help of various commentaries essential to a critical study. My approach was to pay special attention to the description of numerous natural phenomena given in the Qur'an; the highly accurate nature of certain details referring to them in the Book, which was only apparent in the original, struck me by the fact that they were in keeping with present-day ideas, although a man living at the time of Muhammad could not have suspected this at all. I subsequently read several works written by Muslim authors on the scientific aspects of the Quranic text: they were extremely helpful in my appreciation of it, but I have not so far discovered a general study of this subject made in the West.

What initially strikes the reader confronted for the first time with a text of this kind is the sheer abundance of subjects discussed: the Creation, astronomy, the explanation of certain matters concerning the earth, and the animal and vegetable kingdoms, human reproduction. Whereas monumental errors are to be found in the Bible, I could not find a single error in the Quran. I had to stop and ask myself: if a man was the author of the Quran, how could he have written facts in the Seventh century A.D. that today are shown to be in keeping with modern scientific knowledge? There was absolutely no doubt about it: the text of the Quran we have today is most definitely a text of the period, if I may be allowed to put it in these terms (in the next chapter of the present section of the book I shall be dealing with this problem). What human explanation can there be for this observation? In my opinion there is no explanation; there is no special reason why an inhabitant of the Arabian Peninsula should, at a time when King Dagobert was reigning in France (629-639 A.D.), have had scientific knowledge on certain subjects that was ten centuries ahead of our own.

It is an established fact that at the time of the Quranic Revelation, i.e. within a period of roughly twenty years straddling Hegira (622 A.D.), scientific knowledge had not progressed for centuries and the period of activity in Islamic civilization, with its accompanying scientific upsurge, came after the close of the Quranic Revelation. Only ignorance of such religious and secular data can lead to the following bizarre suggestion I have heard several times: if surprising statements of a scientific nature exist in the Quran, they may be accounted for by the fact that Arab scientists were so far ahead of their time and Mohammed was influenced by their work. Anyone who knows anything about Islamic history is aware that the period of the Middle Ages which saw the cultural and scientific upsurge in the Arab world came after Mohammed, and would not therefore indulge in such whims. Suggestions of this kind are particularly off the mark because the majority of scientific facts which are either suggested or very clearly recorded in the Quran have only been confirmed in modern times.

It is easy to see therefore how for centuries commentators on the Quran (including those writing at the height of Islamic culture) have inevitably made crrors of interpretation in the case of certain verses whose exact meaning could not possibly have been grasped. It was not until much later, at a period not far from our own, that it was possible to translate and interpret them correctly. This implies that a thorough linguistic knowledge is not in itself sufficient to understand these verses from the Quran. What is needed along with this is a highly diversified knowledge of science. A study such as the present one embraces many disciplines and is in that sense encyclopedic. As the questions raised are discussed, the variety of scientific knowledge essential to the understanding of certain verses of the Quran will become clear.

The Quran does not aim at explaining certain laws governing the Universe, however; it has an absolutely basic religious objective. The descriptions of Divine Omnipotence are what principally incite man to reflect on the works of Creation. They are accompanied by references to facts accessible to human observation or to laws defined by God who presides over the organization of the universe both in the sciences of nature and as regards man. One part of these assertions is easily understood, but the meaning of the other can only be grasped if one has the essential scientific knowledge it requires. This means that in former times, man could only distinguish an apparent meaning which led him to draw the wrong conclusions on account of the inadequacy of his knowledge at the time in question.

It is possible that the choice of verses from the Quran which are to be studied for their scientific content may perhaps seem too small for certain Muslim writers who have already drawn attention to them before I have. In general, I believe I have retained a slightly smaller number of verses than they have. On the other hand, I have singled out several verses which until now have not, in my opinion, been granted the importance they deserve from a scientific point of view. Wherever I may have mistakenly failed to take verses into consideration for this study that were selected by these writers, I hope that they will not hold it against me. I have also found, on occasion, that certain books contain scientific interpretations which do not appear to me to be correct; it is with an open mind and a clear conscience that I have provided personal interpretations of such verses.

By the same token, I have tried to find references in the Quran to phenomena accessible to human comprehension but which have not been confirmed by modern science. In this context, I think I may have found references in the Quran to the presence of planets in the Universe that are similar to the Earth: It must be added that many scientists think this is a perfectly feasible fact, although modern data cannot provide any hint of certainty. I thought I owed it to myself to mention this, whilst retaining all the attendant reservations that might be applied.

Had this study been made thirty years ago, it would have been necessary to add another fact predicted by the Quran to what would have been cited concerning astronomy; this fact is the conquest of space. At that time, subsequent to the first trials of ballistic missiles, people imagined a day when man would perhaps have the material possibility of leaving his earthly habitat and exploring space. It was then known that a verse existed in the Quran predicting how one day man would make this conquest. This statement has now been verified.

The present confrontation between Holy Scriptures and science brings ideas into play, both for the Bible and the Quran, which concern scientific truth. For this confrontation to be valid, the scientific arguments to be relied upon must be quite soundly established and must leave no room for doubt. Those who balk at the idea of accepting the intervention of science in an appreciation of the Scriptures deny that it is possible for science to constitute a valid term of comparison (whether it be the Bible, which does not escape the comparison unscathed—and we have seen why—or the Quran, which has nothing to fear from science). Science, they say, is changing with the times and a fact accepted today may be rejected later.

This last comment calls for the following observation: a distinction must be drawn between scientific theory and duly controlled observed fact. Theory is intended to explain a phenomenon or a series of phenomena not readily understandable. In many instances theory changes: it is liable to be modified or replaced by another theory when scientific progress makes it easier to analyse facts and envisage a more viable explanation. On the other hand, an observed fact checked by experimentation is not liable to modification: it becomes easier to define its characteristics, but it remains the same. It has been established that the Earth revolves around the Sun and the Moon around the Earth, and this fact will not be subject to revision; all that may be done in the future is to define the orbits more clearly.

A regard for the changing nature of theory is, for example, what made me reject a verse from the Quran thought by a Muslim physicist to predict the concept of anti-matter, a theory which is at present the subject of much debate. One can, on the other hand, quite legitimately devote great attention to a verse from the Quran describing the aquatic origins of life, a phenomenon we shall never be able to verify, but which has many arguments that speak in its favour. As for observed facts such as the evolution of the human embryo, it is quite possible to confront different stages described in the Quran with the data of modern embryology and find complete concordance between modern science and the verses of the Quran referring to this subject.

This confrontation between the Quran and science has been completed by two other comparisons: one is the confrontation of modern knowledge with Biblical data on the same subjects; and the other is the comparison from the same scientific point of view between the data in the Quran, the Book of Revelation transmitted by God to the Prophet, and the data in the Hadiths, books narrating the deeds and sayings of Muhammad that lie outside the written Revelation.

At the end of this, the third section of the present work, the detailed results of the comparison between the Biblical and Quranic description of a single event are given, along with an account of how the passage fared when subjected to the scientific criticism of each description. An examination has, for example, been made in the case of the Creation and of the Flood. In each instance, the incompatibilities with science in the Biblical description have been made clear. Also to be seen is the complete agreement between science and the descriptions in the Quran referring to them. We shall note precisely those differences that make one description scientifically acceptable in the present day and the other unacceptable.

This observation is of prime importance, since in the West, Jews, Christians and Atheists are unanimous in stating (without a scrap of evidence however) that Muhammad wrote the Quran or had it written as an imitation of the Bible. It is claimed that stories of religious history in the Quran resume Biblical stories. This attitude is as thoughtless as saying that Jesus Himself duped His contemporaries by drawing inspiration from the Old Testament during His preachings: the whole of Matthew's Gospel is based on this continuation of the Old Testament, as we have indeed seen already. What expert in exegesis would dream of depriving Jesus of his status as God's envoy for this reason? This is nevertheless the way that Muhammad is judged more often than not in the West: "all he did was to copy the Bible". It is a summary judgement that does not take account of the fact that the Quran and the Bible provide different versions of a single event. People prefer not to talk about the difference in the descriptions. They are pronounced to be the same and thus scientific knowledge need not be brought in. We shall enlarge on these problems when dealing with the description of the Creation and the Flood.

The collection of Hadiths are to Muhammad what the Gospels are to Jesus: descriptions of the actions and sayings of the Prophet. Their authors were not eyewitnesses. (This applies at least to the compilers of the collections of Hadiths which are said to be the most authentic and were collected much later than the time when Muhammad was alive). They do not in any way constitute books containing the written Revelation. They are not the words of God, but the sayings of the Prophet. In these books, which are very widely read, statements are to be found containing errors from a scientific point of view, especially medical remedies. We naturally discount anything relating to problems of a religious kind, since they are not discussed here in the context of the Hadiths. Many Hadiths are of doubtful authenticity; they are discussed by Muslim scientists themselves. When the scientific nature of one of the Hadiths is touched upon in the present work, it is essentially to put into relief all that distinguishes them from the Quran itself when seen from this point of view, since the latter does not contain a single scientific statement that is unacceptable. The difference, as we shall see, is quite startling.

The above observation makes the hypothesis advanced by those who sec Muhammad as the author of the Quran quite untenable. How could a man, from being illiterate, become the most important author, in terms of literary merit, in the whole of Arabic literature? How could he then pronounce truths of a scientific nature that no other human being could possibly have developed at the time, and all this without once making the slightest error in his pronouncements on the subject?

The ideas in this study are developed from a purely scientific point of view. They lead to the conclusion that it is inconceivable for a human being living in the Seventh century A.D. to have made statements in the Quran on a great variety of subjects that do not belong to his period and for them to be in keeping with what was to be known only centuries later. For me, there can be no human explanation to the Quran.

Authenticity of the Quran. How It Came to be Written

Thanks to its undisputed authenticity, the text of the Quran holds a unique place among the books of Revelation, shared neither by the Old nor the New Testament. In the first two sections of this work, a review was made of the alterations undergone by the Old Testament and the Gospels before they were handed down to us in the form we know today. The same is not true for the Quran for the simple reason that it was written down at the time of the Prophet; we shall see how it came to be written, i.e. the process involved.

In this context, the differences separating the Quran from the Bible are in no way due to questions essentially concerned with date. Such questions are constantly put forward by certain people without regard to the circumstances prevailing at the time when the Judeo-Christian and the Quranic Revelations were written; they have an equal disregard for the circumstances surrounding the transmission of the Quran to the Prophet. It is suggested that a Seventh century text had more likelihood of coming down to us unaltered than other texts that are as many as fifteen centuries older. This comment, although correct, does not constitute sufficient reason; it is made more to excuse the alterations made in the Judeo-Christian texts in the course of centuries than to underline the notion that the text of the Quran, which was more recent, had less to fear from being modified by man.

In the case of the Old Testament, the sheer number of authors who tell the same story, plus all the revisions carried out on the text of certain books from the pre-Christian era, constitute as many reasons for inaccuracy and contradiction. As for the Gospels, nobody can claim that they invariably contain faithful accounts of Jesus's words or a description of his actions strictly in keeping with reality. We have seen how successive versions of the texts showed a lack of definite authenticity and moreover that their authors were not eyewitnesses.

Also to be underlined is the distinction to be made between the Quran, a book of written Revelation, and the Hadiths, collections of statements concerning the actions and sayings of Muhammad. Some of the Prophet's companions started to write them down from the moment of his death. As an element of human error could have slipped in, the collection had to be resumed later and subjected to rigorous criticism so that the greatest credit is in practise given to documents that came along after Muhammad. Their authenticity varies, like that of the Gospels. Not a single Gospel was written down at the time of Jesus (they were all written long after his earthly mission had come to an end), and not a single collection of Hadiths was compiled during the time of the Prophet.

The situation is very different for the Quran. As the Revelation progressed, the Prophet and the believers following him recited the text by heart and it was also written down by the scribes in his following. It therefore starts off with two elements of authenticity that the Gospels do not possess. This continued up to the Prophet's death. At a time when not everybody could write, but everyone was able to recite, recitation afforded a considerable advantage because of the double-checking possible when the definitive text was compiled.

The Quranic Revelation was made by Archangel Gabriel to Muhammad. It took place over a period of more than twenty years of the Prophet's life, beginning with the first verses of Sura 96, then resuming after a three-year break for a long period of twenty years up to the death of the Prophet in 632 A.D., i.e. ten years before Hegira and ten years after Hegira.

The following was the first Revelation —(96:1-5)

> "Read: In the name of thy Lord who created,
> Who created man from something which clings
> Read ! Thy Lord is the most Noble
> Who taught by the pen
> Who taught man what he did not know."

Professor Hamidullah notes in the Introduction to his French translation of the Quran that one of the themes of this first Revelation was the 'praise of the pen as a means of human knowledge' which would 'explain the Prophet's concern for the preservation of the Quran in writing.'

Texts formally prove that long before the Prophet left Makka for Madina (i.e. long before Hegira), the Quranic text so far revealed had been written down. We shall see how the Quran is authentic in this. We know that Muhammad and the believers who surrounded him were accustomed to reciting the revealed text from memory. It is therefore inconceivable for the Quran to refer to facts that did not square with reality because the latter could so easily be checked with people in the Prophet's following, by asking the authors of the transcription.

Four suras dating from a period prior to Hegira refer to the writing down of the Quran before the Prophet left Makka in 622 A.D. —(80:11-16)

"By no means! Indeed it is a message of instruction
Therefore Whoever wills, should remember
On leaves held in honour
Exalted, purified
In the hands of scribes
Noble and pious."

Yusuf Ali, in the commentary to his translation, (1934), wrote that when the Revelation of this sura was made, forty-two or forty-five others had been written and were kept by Muslims in Makka (out of a total of 114).

"Nay, this is a glorious reading[1]
On a preserved tablet" —56: 21,22

"This is a glorious reading[1]
In a book well kept
Which none but the purified teach.
This is a Revelation from the Lord of the Worlds."
—25: 77-80

"They said: Tales of the ancients which he has caused to be written and they are dictated to him morning and evening." —25: 5

Here we have a reference to the accusations made by the Prophet's enemies who treated him as an imposter. They spread the rumour that stories of antiquity were being dictated to him and he was writing them down or having them transcribed (the meaning of the word is debatable, but one must remember that Muhammad was illiterate). However this may be, the verse refers to this act of making a written record which is pointed out by Muhammad's enemies themselves.

A sura that came after Hegira makes one last mention of the leaves on which these divine instructions were written:

"An (apostle) from God recites leaves
Kept pure where are decrees right and straight."
—98: 2-3

The Quran itself therefore provides indications as to the fact that it was set down in writing at the time of the Prophet. It is a known fact that there were several scribes in his following, the most famous of whom, Zaid Ibn Thabit, has left his name to posterity.

In the Preface to his French translation of the Quran (1971), Professor Hamidullah gives an excellent description of the conditions that prevailed when the text of the Quran was written, lasting up until the time of the Prophet's death:

"The sources all agree in stating that whenever a fragment of the Quran was revealed, the Prophet called one of his literate companions and dictated it to him, indicating at the same time the exact position of the new fragment in the fabric of what had already been received.. . Descriptions note that Muhammad asked the scribe to reread to him what had been dictated so that he could correct any deficiencies. . . Another famous story tells how every year in the month of Ramadan, the Prophet would recite the whole of the Quran (so far revealed) to Gabriel . . ., that in the Ramadan preceding Muhammad's death, Gabriel had made him recite it twice ... It is known how since the Prophet's time, Muslims acquired the habit of keeping vigil during Ramadan, and of reciting the whole of the Quran in addition to the usual prayers expected of them. Several sources add that Muhammad's scribe Zaid was present at this final bringing-together of the texts. Elsewhere, numerous other personalities are mentioned as well."

Extremely diverse materials were used for this first record: parchment, leather, wooden tablets, camels' scapula, soft stone for inscriptions, etc.

At the same time however, Muhammad recommended that the faithful learn the Quran by heart. They did this for a part if not all of the text recited during prayers. Thus there were *Hafizun* who knew the whole of the Quran by heart and spread it abroad. The method of doubly preserving the text both in writing and by memorization proved to be extremely precious.

Not long after the Prophet's death (632), his successor Abu Bakr, the first Caliph of Islam, asked Muhammad's former head scribe, Zaid Ibn Thabit, to make a copy; this he did. On Omar's initiative (the future second Caliph), Zaid consulted all the information he could assemble at Madina: the witness of the *Hafizun,* copies of the Book written on various materials belonging to private individuals, all with the object of avoiding possible errors in transcription. Thus an extremely faithful copy of the Book was obtained.

The sources tell us that Caliph Omar, Abu Bakr's successor in 634, subsequently made a single volume *(mushaf)* that he preserved and gave on his death to his daughter Hafsa, the Prophet's widow.

The third Caliph of Islam, Uthman, who held the caliphate from 644 to 655, entrusted a commission of experts with the preparation of the great recension that bears his name. It checked the authenticity of the document produced under Abu Bakr which had remained in Hafsa's possession until that time. The commission consulted Muslims who knew the text by heart. The critical analysis of the authenticity of the text was carried out very rigorously. The agreement of the witnesses was deemed necessary before the slightest verse containing debatable material was retained. It is indeed known how some verses of the Quran correct others in the case of prescriptions: this may be readily explained when one remembers that the Prophet's period of apostolic activity stretched over twenty years (in round figures). The result is a text containing an order of suras that reflects the order followed by the Prophet in his complete recital of the Quran during Ramadan, as mentioned above.

One might perhaps ponder the motives that led the first three Caliphs, especially Uthman, to commission collections and recensions of the text. The reasons are in fact very simple: Islam's expansion in the very first decades following Muhammed's death was very rapid indeed and it happened among peoples whose native language was not Arabic. It was absolutely necessary to ensure the spread of a text that retained its original purity: Uthman's recension had this as its objective.

Uthman sent copies of the text of the recension to the centres of the Islamic Empire and that is why, according to Professor Hamidullah, copies attributed to Uthman exist in Tashkent and Istanbul. Apart from one or two possible mistakes in copying, the oldest documents known to the present day, that are to be found throughout the Islamic world, are identical; the same is true for documents preserved in Europe (there are fragments in the Bib-liotheque Nationale in Paris which, according to the experts, date from the Eighth and Ninth centuries A.D., i.e. the Second and Third Hegirian centuries). The numerous ancient texts that are known to be in existence all agree except for very minor variations which do not change the general meaning of the text at all. If the context sometimes allows more than one interpretation, it may well have to do with the fact that ancient writing was simpler than that of the present day.

The 114 suras were arranged in decreasing order of length; there were nevertheless exceptions. The chronological sequence of the Revelation was not followed. In the majority of cases however, this sequence is known. A large number of descriptions are mentioned at several points in the text, sometimes giving rise to repetitions. Very frequently a passage will add details to a description that appears elsewhere in an incomplete form. Everything connected with modern science are, like many subjects dealt with in the Qur'an, scattered throughout the book without any semblance of classification.

Creation of Heavens and Earth

In contrast to the Old Testament, the Quran does not provide a unified description of the Creation. Instead of a continuous narration, there are passages scattered all over the Book which deal with certain aspects of the Creation and provide information on the successive events marking its development with varying degrees of detail. To gain a clear idea of how these events are presented, the fragments scattered throughout a large number of suras have to be brought together.

This dispersal throughout the Book of references to the same subject is not unique to the theme of the Creation. Many important subjects are treated in the same manner in the Quran: earthly or celestial phenomena, or problems concerning man that are of interest to scientists. For each of these themes, the same effort has been made here to bring all the verses together.

For many European commentators, the description of the Creation in the Quran is very similar to the one in the Bible and they are quite content to present the two descriptions side by side. I believe this concept is mistaken because there are very obvious differences. On subjects that are by no means unimportant from a scientific point of view. We find statements in the Quran whose equivalents we search for in vain in the Bible. The latter contains descriptions that have no equivalent in the Quran.

The obvious resemblances between the two texts are well known;

among them is the fact that, at first glance, the number given to the successive stages of the Creation is identical: the six days in the Bible correspond to the six days in the Quran. In fact however, the problem is more complex than this and it is worth pausing to examine it.

There is absolutely no ambiguity whatsoever in the Biblical description of the Creation in six days followed by a day of rest, the sabbath, analogous with the days of the week. It has been shown how this mode of narration practiced by the priests of the Sixth century B.C. served the purpose of encouraging the people to observe the sabbath. All Jews were expected to rest on the sabbath as the Lord had done after he had laboured during the six days of the week.

The way the Bible interprets it, the word 'day' means the interval of time between two successive sunrises or sunsets for an inhabitant of the Earth. When defined in this way, the day is conditioned by the rotation of the Earth on its own axis. It is obvious that logically-speaking there can be no question of 'days' as defined just now, if the mechanism that causes them to appear—i.e. the existence of the Earth and its rotation around the Sun—has not already been fixed in the early stages of the Creation according to the Biblical description. This impossibility has already been emphasized in the first part of the present book.

When we refer to the majority of translations of the Quran, we read that—analogous with the Biblical description—the process of the Creation for the Islamic Revelation also took place over a period of six days. It is difficult to hold against the translators the fact that they have translated the Arabic word by its most common meaning. This is how it is usually expressed in translations so that in the Quran, verse 54, sura 7 reads as follows:

> "Your Lord is God Who created the heavens and the earth in six days."

There are very few translations and commentaries of the Quran that note how the word 'days' should really be taken to mean 'periods'. It has moreover been maintained that if the Quranic texts on the Creation divided its stages into 'days', it was with the deliberate intention of taking up beliefs held by all the Jews and Christians at the dawn of Islam and of avoiding a head-on confrontation with such a widely-held belief.

Without in any way wishing to reject this way of seeing it, one could perhaps examine the problem a little more closely and scrutinize in the Quran itself, and more generally in the language of the time, the possible meaning of the word that many translators themselves still continue to translate by the word 'day': *yaum,* plural *ayyam* in Arabic.

Its most common meaning is 'day' but it must be stressed that it tends more to mean the diurnal light than the length of time that lapses between one day's sunset and the next. The plural *ayyam* can mean, not just 'days', but also 'long length of time', an indefinite period of time (but always long). The meaning 'period of time' that the word contains is to be found elsewhere in the Quran. Hence the following:

> ". . . in a period of time *(yaum)* whereof the measure is a thousand years of your reckoning." —32:5

(It is to be noted that the Creation in six periods is precisely what the verse preceding verse 5 refers to).

> ". . . in a period of time *(yaum)* whereof the measure is 50,000 years." —70:4

The fact that the word *'yaum'* could mean a period of time that was quite different from the period that we mean by the word 'day' struck very early commentators who, of course, did not have the knowledge we possess today concerning the length of the stages in the formation of the Universe. In the Sixteenth century A.D. for example, Abu al Su'ud, who could not have had any idea of the day as it dawned astronomically in terms of the Earth's rotation, thought that for the Creation a division must be considered that was not into days as we usually understand the word, but into 'events' (in Arabic *nauba).*

Modern commentators have gone back to this interpretation. Yusuf Ali (1934), in his commentary on each of the verses that deals with the stages in the Creation, insists on the importance of taking the word, elsewhere interpreted as meaning 'days', to mean in reality 'very long Periods, or Ages, or Aeons'.

It is therefore possible to say that in the case of the Creation of the world, the Quran allows for long periods of time numbering six. It is obvious that modern science has not permitted man to establish the fact that the complicated stages in the process leading to the formation of the Universe numbered six, but it has clearly shown that long periods of time were involved compared to which 'days' as we conceive them would be ridiculous.

One of the longest passages of the Quran, which deals with the Creation, describes the latter by juxtaposing an account of earthly events and one of celestial events.

(God is speaking to the Prophet)

> "Say: Do you disbelieve Him Who created the earth in two periods? Do you ascribe equals to Him. He is the Lord of the Worlds.
>
> "He set in the (earth) mountains standing firm. He blessed it. He measured therein its sustenance in four periods, in due proportion, in accordance with the needs of those who ask for (sustenance? or information?).
>
> "Moreover *(tumma)* He turned to heaven when it was smoke and said to it and to the earth: come willingly or unwillingly ! They said: we come in willing obedience.
>
> "Then He ordained them seven heavens in two periods, and He assigned to each heaven its mandate by Revelation. And We adorned the lower heaven with luminaries and provided it a guard. Such is the decree of the All Mighty, the Full of Knowledge." —41:9-12

These four verses of sura 41 contain several points to which we shall return: the initially gaseous state of celestial matter and the highly symbolic definition of the number of heavens as seven. We shall see the meaning behind this figure. Also of a symbolic nature is the dialogue between God on the one hand and the primordial sky and earth on the other: here however it is only to express the submission of the Heavens and Earth, once they were formed, to divine orders.

Critics have seen in this passage a contradiction with the statement of the six periods of the Creation. By adding the two periods of the formation of the Earth to the four periods of the spreading of its sustenance to the inhabitants, plus the two periods of the formation of the Heavens, we arrive at eight periods. This would then be in contradiction with the six periods mentioned above.

In fact however, this text, which leads man to reflect on divine Omnipotence, beginning with the Earth and ending with the Heavens, provides two sections that are expressed by the Arabic word *'tumma'*, translated by 'moreover', but which also means 'furthermore' or 'then'. The sense of a 'sequence' may therefore be implied referring to a sequence of events or a series of man's reflections on the events mentioned here. It may equally be a simple reference to events juxtaposed without any intention of bringing in the notion of the one following the other. However this may be, the periods of the Creation of the Heavens may just as easily coincide with the two periods of the Earth's creation. A little later we shall examine how the basic process of the formation of the Universe is presented in the Quran and we shall see how it can be jointly applied to the Heavens and the Earth in keeping with modern ideas. We shall then realize how perfectly reasonable this way is conceiving the simultaneous nature of the events here described.

There does not appear to be any contradiction between the passage quoted here and the concept of the formation of the world in six stages that is to be found in other texts in the Quran.

In the two passages from the Quran quoted above, reference was made in one of the verses to the Creation of the Heavens and the Earth (sura 7, verse 54), and elsewhere to the Creation of the Earth and the Heavens (sura 41, verses 9 to 12). The Quran does not therefore appear to lay down a sequence for the Creation of the Heavens and the Earth.

The number of verses in which the Earth is mentioned first is quite small, e.g. sura 2, verse 29 and sura 20, verse 4, where a reference is made to "Him Who created the earth and the high heavens". The number of verses where the Heavens are mentioned before the Earth is, on the other hand, much larger: (sura 7, verse 54; sura 10, verse 3; sura 11, verse 7; sura 25, verse 59; sura 32, verse 4; sura 50, verse 38; sura 57, verse 4; sura 79, verses 27 to 33; sura 91, verses 5 to 10).

In actual fact, apart from sura 79, there is not a single passage in the Quran that lays down a definite sequence; a simple coordinating conjunction (iva) meaning 'and' links two terms, or the word *tumma* which, as has been seen in the above passage, can indicate either a simple juxtaposition or a sequence.

There appears to me to be only one passage in the Quran where a definite sequence is plainly established between different events in the Creation. It is contained in verses 27 to 33, sura 79:

"Are you the harder to create or is it the heaven that (God) built? He raised its canopy and fashioned it with harmony. He made dark the night and he brought out the forenoon. And after that *(ba' da dalika)* He spread it out. Therefrom he drew out its water and its pasture. And the mountains He has fixed firmly. Goods for you and your cattle."

This list of earthly gifts from God to man, which is expressed in a language suited to farmers or nomads on the Arabian Peninsula, is preceded by an invitation to reflect on the creation of the heavens. The reference to the stage when God spreads out the earth and renders it arable is very precisely situated in time after the alternating of night and day has been achieved. Two groups are therefore referred to here, one of celestial phenomena, and the other of earthly phenomena articulated in time. The reference made here implies that the earth must necessarily have existed before being spread out and that it consequently existed when God created the Heavens. The idea of a concomitance therefore arises from the heavenly and earthly evolutions with the interlocking of the two phenomena. Hence, one must not look for any special significance in the reference in the Quranic text to the Creation of the Earth before the Heavens or the Heavens before the Earth: the position of the words does not influence the order in which the Creation took place, unless however it is specifically stated.

Basic Process

The Quran presents in two verses a brief synthesis of the phenomena that constituted the basic process of the formation of the Universe.

> "Do not the Unbelievers see that the heavens and the earth were joined together, then We clove thorn as under and We got every living thing out of the water. Will they not then believe?" —21:30

God orders the Prophet to speak after inviting him to reflect on the subject of the earth's creation:

> "Moreover (God) turned to the Heaven when it was smoke and said to it and to the earth . . ." —41:11
> There then follow the orders to submit, referred to earlier.

We shall come back to the aquatic origins of life and examine them along with other biological problems raised by the Quran. The important things to remember at present are the following:

a) The statement of the existence of a gaseous mass with fine particles, for this is how the word 'smoke' *(dukan* in Arabic) is to be interpreted. Smoke is generally made up of a gaseous substratum, plus, in more or less stable suspension, fine particles that may belong to solid and even liquid states of matter at high or low temperature;

b) The reference to a separation process *(fatq)* of a primary single mass whose elements were initially fused together *(raff]).* It must be noted that in Arabic *'fatq'* is the action of breaking, diffusing, separating, and that *'ratq* is the,action of fusing or binding together elements to make a homogenous whole.

This concept of the separation of a whole into several parts is noted in other passages of the Book with reference to multiple worlds. The first verse of the first sura in the Quran proclaims, after the opening invocation, the following: "In the name of God. the Beneficent, the Merciful", "Praise be to God. Lord of the Worlds."

The terms 'worlds' reappears dozens of times in the Quran. The Heavens are referred to as multiple as well, not only on account of their plural form, but also because of their symbolic numerical quantity: 7.

This number is used 24 times throughout the Quran for various numerical quantities. It often carries the meaning of 'many' although we do not know exactly why this meaning of the figure was used. The Greeks and Romans also seem to have used the number 7 to mean an undefined idea of plurality. In the Quran, the number 7 refers to the Heavens themselves *(samawat).* It alone is understood to mean 'Heavens'. The 7 roads of the Heavens are mentioned once:

> "(God) is the One Who created for you all that is on the earth. Moreover He turned to the heaven and fashioned seven heavens with harmony. He is Full of Knowledge of all things." —(2:29)

> "And We have created above you seven paths: We have never been unmindful of the Creation." —(23:17)
>
> "(God) is the One Who created seven heavens one above another. Thou canst see no fault in the creation of the Beneficent. Turn the vision again! Canst thou see any rift?" —(67:3)
>
> "Did you see how God created seven heavens one above another and made the moon a light therein and made the sun a lamp?[1]" —(71:15-16)
>
> "We have built above you seven strong (heavens) and placed a blazing lamp." —(78:12)

Here the blazing lamp is the Sun.

The commentators on the Quran are in agreement on all these verses: the number 7 means no more than plurality.[2]

There are therefore many Heavens and Earths, and it comes as no small surprise to the reader of the Quran to find that earths such as our own may be found in the Universe, a fact that has not yet been verified by man in our time.

Verse 12 of sura 65 does however predict the following:

> "God is the One Who created seven heavens and of the earth *(ard)* a similar number. The Command descends among them so that you know that God has power over all things and comprehends all things in His knowledge."

Since 7 indicates an indefinite plurality (as we have seen), it is possible to conclude that the Quranic text clearly indicates the existence of more than one single Earth, our own Earth *(ard)* ; there are others like it in the Universe.

Another observation which may surprise the Twentieth century reader of the Quran is the fact that verses refer to three groups of things created, i.e.

— things in the Heavens

— things on the Earth

— things between the Heavens and the Earth Here are several of these verses:

> "To Him (God) belongs what is in the heavens, on earth, between them and beneath the soil." —(20:6)
>
> ". . . the One Who created the heavens, the earth and what is between them in six periods." —(25:59)

> "God is the One Who created the heavens, the earth and what is between them in six periods." —(32:4)
>
> "We created the heavens, the earth and what is between them in six periods, and no weariness touched Us'"

The reference in the Quran to 'what is between the Heavens and the Earth' is again to be found in the following verses: sura 21, verse 16; sura 44, verses 7 and 38; sura 78, verse 37; sura 15, verse 85; sura 46, verse 3; sura 43, verse 85.

This Creation outside the Heavens and outside the Earth, mentioned several times, is *a priori* difficult to imagine. To understand these verses, reference must be made to the most recent human observations on the existence of cosmic extra-galactic material and one must indeed go back to ideas established by contemporary science on the formation of the Universe, starting with the simplest and proceeding to the most complex. These are the subjects of the following paragraph.

Before passing on to these purely scientific matters however, it is advisable to recapitulate the main points on which the Quran gives us information about the creation. According to the preceding quotations, they are as follows:

(1) Existence of six periods for the Creation in general.

(2) Interlocking of stages in the Creation of the Heavens and the Earth.

(3) Creation of the Universe out of an initially unique mass forming a block that subsequently split up.

(4) Plurality of the Heavens and of the Earths.

(5) Existence of an intermediary creation 'between the Heavens and the Earth'.

MODERN SCIENTIFIC ORDER

The Solar System

The Earth and planets rotating around the Sun constitute an organized world of dimensions which, to our human scale, appear quite colossal. The Earth is, after all, roughly 93 million miles from the Sun. This is a very great distance for a human being, but it is very small in comparison to the distance separating the Sun from the furthermost planet from it in the solar system (Pluto) ; in round numbers it is 40 times the distance from the Earth to the Sun, i.e. approximately 3,672 million miles away. This distance, when doubled, represents the largest dimension of our solar system. The Sun's light takes nearly 6 hours to reach Pluto, and yet the journey is made at the terrifying speed of over 186,000 miles per second. The light coming from stars on the very confines of the known celestial world therefore takes billions of years to reach us.

The Galaxies

The Sun, of which we are a satellite like the other planets surrounding it, is itself an infinitesmally small element among a hundred billion stars that form a whole, called a galaxy. On a fine summer night, the whole of space seems to be filled with stars that make up what is known as the Milky Way. This group has extremely large dimensions. Whereas light could cross the solar system in units of one hour, it would require something like 90,000 years to go from one extreme to the other of the most compact group of stars that make up our galaxy.

The galaxy that we belong to however, even though it is so incredibly huge, is only a small part of the Heavens. There are giant agglomerates of stars similar to the Milky Way that lie outside our galaxy. They were discovered a little over fifty years ago, when astronomy was able to make use of an optical instrument as sophisticated as the one that made possible the construction of the Mount Wilson telescope in the United States. Thus a very large number indeed of isolated galaxies and masses of galaxies have been discovered that are so far away that it was necessary to institute a special unit of light-years, the 'parsec' (the distance light travels in 3.26 years at 186,000 miles per second).

What was there originally in the immensely large space the galaxies now occupy? Modern science can only answer this question as of a certain period in the evolution of the Universe; it cannot put into numbers the length of time that separates this period from us.

Since the earliest time it can provide us with, modern science has every reason to maintain that the Universe was formed of a gaseous mass principally composed of hydrogen and a certain amount of helium that was slowly rotating. This nebula subsequently split up into multiple fragments with very large dimensions and masses, so large indeed, that specialists in astrophysics are able to estimate their mass from 1 to 100 billion times the present mass of the Sun (the latter represents a mass that is over 300,000 times that of the Earth). These figures give an idea of the large size of the fragments of primary gaseous mass that were to give birth to the galaxies.

A new fragmentation was to form the stars. There then followed the intervention of a condensing process where gravitational forces came into play, (since these bodies were moving and rotating more and more quickly), along with pressures and the influence of magnetic fields and of radiations. The stars became shiny as they contracted and transformed the gravitational forces into thermal energy. Thermonuclear reactions came into play, and heavier atoms were formed by fusion at the expense of others that were lighter; this is how the transition was made from hydrogen to helium, then to carbon and oxygen, ending with metals and metalloids. Thus the stars have a life of their own and modern astronomy classifies them according to their present stage of evolution. The stars also have a death; in the final stage of their evolution, the violent implosion of certain stars has been observed so that they become veritable 'corpses'.

The planets, and in particular the Earth, originated in a separation process starting from an initial constituent that in the beginning was the primary nebula. A fact that has no longer been contested for over twenty-five years is that the Sun condensed inside the single nebula and that the planets did the same inside the surrounding nebular disc. One must stress—and this is of prime importance for the subject in hand—that there was no sequence in the formation of the celestial elements such as the Sun nor in the formation of an earthly element. There is an evolutionary parallelism with the identity of origin.

Here, science can give us information on the period during which the events just mentioned took place. Having estimated the age of our galaxy at roughly ten billion years, according to this hypothesis, the formation of the solar system took place a little over billion years later. The study of natural radio activity makes it possible to place the age of the Earth and the time the Sun was formed at 4.5 billion years ago, to within a present-day accuracy of 100 million years, according to some scientists' calculations. This accuracy is to be admired, since 100 million years may represent a long time to us but the ratio 'maximum error/total time-to-be-measured' is 0.1/4.5, i.e. 2.2%.

Specialists in astrophysics have therefore attained a high degree of knowledge concerning the general process involved in the formation of the solar system. It may be summarized as follows: condensation and contraction of a rotating gaseous mass, splitting up into fragments that leave the Sun and planets in their places, among them the Earth. The knowledge that science has gained on the primary nebula and the way it split up into an incommensurable quantity of stars grouped into galaxies leaves absolutely no doubt as to the legitimacy of a concept of the plurality of worlds. It does not however provide any kind of certainty concerning the existence in the Universe of anything that might, either closely or vaguely, resemble the Earth.

Plurality of the Worlds

In spite of the above, modern specialists in astrophysics consider it highly likely that planets similar to Earth are present in the Universe. As far as the solar system is concerned, nobody seriously entertains the possibility of finding general conditions similar to those on Earth on another planet in this system. We must therefore seek for them outside the solar system. The likelihood of their existing outside it is considered quite probable for the following reasons:

It is thought that in our galaxy half of the 100 billion stars must, like the Sun, have a planetary system. The fifty billion stars do indeed, like the Sun, rotate very slowly; a characteristic which suggests that they are surrounded by planets that are their satellites. These stars are so far away that the possible planets are unobservable, but their existence is thought to be highly probable on account of certain trajectory characteristics; a slight undulation of the star's trajectory indicates the presence of a companion planetary satellite. Thus the Barnard Star probably has at least one planetary companion with a mass greater than that of Jupiter and may even have two satellites. As P. Guerin writes: "All the evidence point to the fact that planetary systems are scattered in profusion all over the universe. The solar system and the Earth are not unique." And as a corollary: "Life, like the planets that harbour it, is scattered throughout the universe, in those places where the physico-chemical conditions necessary for its flowering and development are to be found."

The basic process in the formation of the Universe therefore lay in the condensation of material in the primary nebula followed by its division into fragments that originally constituted galactic masses. The latter in their turn split up into stars that provided the sub-product of the process, i.e. the planets. These successive separations left among the groups of principle elements what one might perhaps call 'remains'. Their more scientific name is 'interstellar galactic material'. It has been described in various ways; there are bright nebulae that reflect the light received from other stars and are perhaps composed of 'dusts' or 'smokes', to use the terminology of experts in astrophysics, and then there are the dark nebulae that are less dense, consisting of interstellar material that is even more modest, known for its tendency to interfere with photometric measurements in astronomy. There can be no doubt about the existence of 'bridges' of material between the galaxies themselves. Although these gases may be very rarefied, the fact that they occupy such a colossal space, in view of the great distance separating the galaxies, could make them correspond to a mass possibly greater than the total mass of the galaxies in spite of the low density of the former. A. Boichot considers the presence of these intergalactic masses to be of prime importance which could "considerably alter ideas on the evolution of the Universe."

We must now go back to the basic ideas on the Creation of the Universe that were taken from the Quran and look at them in the light of modern scientific data.

Confronting Points

We shall examine the five main points on which the Quran gives information about the Creation.

(1) The six periods of the Creation of the Heavens and the Earth covered, according to the Quran, the formation of the celestial bodies and the Earth, and the development of the latter until (with its 'sustenance') it became inhabitable by man. In the case of the Earth, the events described in the Quran happened over four periods. One could perhaps see in them the four geological periods described by

modern science, with man's appearance, as we already know, taking place in the quaternary era. This is purely a hypothesis since nobody has an answer to this question.

It must be noted however, that the formation of the heavenly bodies and the Earth, as explained in verses 9 to 12, sura 41 required two phases. If we take the Sun and its sub-product the earth as an example (the only one accessible to us), science informs us that their formation occurred by a process of condensation of the primary nebula and then their separation. This is exactly what the Quran expresses very clearly when it refers to the processes that produced a fusion and subsequent separation starting from a celestial 'smoke'. Hence there is complete correspondence between the facts of the Quran and the facts of science.

(2) Science showed the interlocking of the two stages in the formation of a star (like the Sun) and its satellite (like the Earth). This interconnection is surely very evident in the text of the Quran examined.

(3) The existence at an early stage of the Universe of the 'smoke' referred to in the Quran, meaning the predominently gaseous state of the material that composes it, obviously corresponds to the concept of the primary nebula put forward by modern science.

(4) The plurality of the heavens, expressed in the Quran by the number 7, whose meaning we have discussed, is confirmed by modern science due to the observations experts in astrophysics have made on galactic systems and their very large number. On the other hand the plurality of earths that are similar to ours (from certain points of view at least) is an idea that arises in the text of the Quran but has not yet been demonstrated to be true by science; all the same, specialists consider this to be quite feasible.

(5) The existence of an intermediate creation between 'the Heavens' and 'the Earth' expressed in the Quran may be compared to the discovery of those bridges of material present outside organized astronomic systems.

Although not all the questions raised by the descriptions in the Quran have been completely confirmed by scientific data, there is in any case absolutely no opposition between the data in the Quran on the Creation and modern knowledge on the formation of the Universe.

This fact is worth stressing for the Quranic Revelation, whereas it is very obvious indeed that the present-day text of the Old Testament provides data on the same events that are unacceptable from a scientific point of view. It is hardly surprising, since the description of the Creation in the Sacerdotal version of the Bible was written by priests at the time of the deportation to Babylon who had the legalist intentions already described and therefore compiled a description that fitted their theological views. The existence of such an enormous difference between the Biblical description and the data in the Quran concerning the creation is worth underlining once again on account of the totally gratuitous accusations leveled against Muhammad since the beginnings of Islam to the effect that he copied the Biblical descriptions. As far as the Creation is concerned, this accusation is totally unfounded. How could a man living fourteen hundred years ago have made corrections to the existing description to such an extent that he eliminated scientifically inaccurate material and, on his own initiative, made statements that science has been able to verify only in the present day? This hypothesis is completely untenable. The description of the Creation given in the Quran is quite different from the one in the Bible.

Answers to Objections

Indisputably, resemblances do exist between narrations dealing with other subjects, particularly religious history, in the Bible and in the Quran. It is moreover interesting to note from this point of view how nobody holds against Jesus the fact that he takes up the same sort of facts and Biblical teachings. This does not, of course, stop people in the West from accusing Muhammad (PBUH) of referring to such facts in his teaching with the suggestion that he is an imposter because he presents them as a Revelation. As for the proof that Muhammad (PBUH) reproduced in the Quran what he had been told or dictated by the rabbis, it has no more substance than the statement that a Christian monk gave him a sound religious education. One would do well to re-read what R. Blachere in his book, *The Problem of Muhammad* (Le Prob-leme de Mahomet), has to say about this 'fable'.

A hint of a resemblance is also advanced between other

statements in the Quran and beliefs that go back a very long way, probably much further in time than the Bible.

More generally speaking, the traces of certain cosmogenic myths have been sought in the Holy Scriptures; for example the belief held by the Polynesians in the existence of primeval waters that were covered in darkness until they separated when light appeared; thus Heaven and Earth were formed. This myth is compared to the description of the Creation in the Bible, where, there is undoubtedly a resemblance. It would however be superficial to then accuse the Bible of having copied this from the cosmogenic myth.

It is just as superficial to see the Quranic concept of the division of the primeval material constituting the Universe at its initial stage — a concept held by modern science — as one that comes from various cosmogenic myths in one form or another that express something resembling it.

It is worth analysing these mythical beliefs and descriptions more closely. Often an initial idea appears among them which is reasonable in itself, and is in some cases borne out by what we today know (or think we know) to be true, except that fantastic descriptions are attached to it in the myth. This is the case of the fairly widespread concept of the Heavens and the Earth originally being united then subsequently separated. When, as in Japan, the image of the egg plus an expression of chaos is attached to the above with the idea of a seed inside the egg (as for all eggs), the imaginative addition makes the concept lose all semblance of seriousness. In other countries, the idea of a plant is associated with it; the plant grows and in so doing raises up the sky and separates the Heavens from the Earth. Here again, the imaginative quality of the added detail lends the myth its very distinctive character. Nevertheless a common characteristic remains, i.e. the notion of a single mass at the beginning of the evolutionary process leading to the formation of the Universe which then divided to form the various 'worlds' that we know today.

The reason these cosmogenic myths are mentioned here is to underline the way they have been embroidered by man's imagination and to show the basic difference between them and the statements in the Quran on the same subject. The latter are free from any of the whimsical details accompanying such beliefs; on the contrary, they are distinguished by the sober quality of the words in which they are made and their agreement with scientific data.

Such statements in the Quran concerning the Creation, which appeared nearly fourteen centuries ago, obviously do not lend themselves to a human explanation.

Quran on Astronomy

The Quran is full of reflections on the Heavens. In the preceding chapter on the Creation, we saw how the plurality of the Heavens and Earths was referred to, as well as what the Quran calls an intermediary creation 'between the Heavens and the Earth': modern science has verified the latter. The verses referring to the creation already contain a broad idea of what is to be found in the heavens, i.e. of everything outside the earth.

Apart from the verses that specifically describe the Creation, there are roughly another forty verses in the Quran which provide information on astronomy complementing what has already been given. Some of them are not much more than reflections on the glory of the Creator, the Organizer of all the stellar and planetary systems. These we know to be arranged according to balancing positions whose stability Newton explained in his law of the mutual attraction of bodies.

The first verses to be quoted here hardly furnish much material for scientific analysis: the aim is simply to draw attention to God's omnipotence. They must be mentioned however to give a realistic idea of the way the Quranic text described the organization of the Universe fourteen centuries ago.

These references constitute a new fact of divine Revelation. The organization of the world is treated in neither the Gospels nor the Old Testament (except for a few notions whose general inaccuracy we have already seen in the Biblical description of the Creation). The Quran however deals with this subject in depth. What it describes is important, but so is what it does not contain. It does not in fact provide an account of the theories prevalent at the time of the Revelation that deal with the organization of the celestial world, theories that science was later to show were inaccurate. An example of this will be given later. This negative consideration must however be pointed out.

The subject is man in general.

> "Do they not look at the sky above them, how We have built it and adorned it, and there are no rifts in it."
> —(50:16)
>
> "(God) created the heavens without any pillars that you can see..." —(31:10)
>
> "God is the One Who raised the heavens without any pillars that you can see, then He firmly established Himself on the throne and He subjected the sun and moon. . ."
> —(13:2)

These two verses refute the belief that the vault of the heavens was held up by pillars, the only things preventing the former from crushing the earth.

> "the sky (God) raised it . . ." —(55:7)
>
> "(God) holds back the sky from falling on the earth unless by His leave . . ." —(22:65)

It is known how the remoteness of celestial masses at great distance and in proportion to the magnitude of their mass itself constitutes the foundation of their equilibrium. The more remote the masses are, the weaker the force that attracts one to the other is. The nearer they are, the stronger the attraction is that one has to the other: this is true for the Moon, which is near to the Earth (astronomically speaking) and exercises an influence by laws of attraction on the position occupied by the waters of the sea, hence the phenomenon of the tides. If two celestial bodies come too close to one another, collision is inevitable. The fact that they are subjected to an order is the *sine qua non* for the absence of disturbances.

The subjection of the Heavens to divine order is often referred to as well:

God is speaking to the Prophet.

> "Say: Who is Lord of the seven heavens and Lord of the tremendous throne?" —(23:86)

We have already seen how by 'seven heavens' what is meant is not 7, but an indefinite number of heavens.

> "For you (God) subjected all that is in the heavens and on the earth, all from Him. Behold! In that are signs for people who reflect." —(45:13)

> "The sun and moon (are subjected) to calculations" —(55:5)
>
> " (God) appointed the night for rest and the sun and the moon for reckoning."
>
> "For you (God) subjected the sun and the moon, both diligently pursuing their courses. And for you He subjected the night and the day." —(14:33)

Here one verse completes another: the calculations referred to result in the regularity of the course described by the heavenly bodies in question, this is expressed by the word *da'ib,* the present participle of a verb whose original meaning was 'to work eagerly and assiduously at something'. Here it is given the meaning of 'to apply oneself to something with care in a perseverant, invariable manner, in accordance with set habits'.

God is speaking:

> "And for the moon We have appointed mansions till she returns like an old shriveled palm branch." —(36:39)

This is a reference to the curled form of the palm branch which, as it shrivels up, takes on the moon's crescent. This commentary will be completed later.

> "For you (God) subjected the night and the day, the sun and the moon; the stars are in subjection to His Command. Verily in this are signs for people who are wise." —(16:12)

The practical angle from which this perfect celestial order is seen is underlined on account of its value as an aid to man's travel on earth and by sea, and to his calculation of time. This comment becomes clear when one bears in mind the fact that the Quran was originally a preaching addressed to men who only understood the simple language of their everyday lives. This explains the presence of the following reflections:

> "(God) is the One Who has set out for you the stars, that you may guide yourselves by them through the darkness of the land and of the sea. We have detailed the Signs for people who know." —(16:97)
>
> "(God sets on the earth) landmarks and by the stars (men) guide themselves." —(16:16)

> "God is the One Who made the sun a shining glory and the moon a light and for her ordained mansions, so that you might know the number of years and the reckoning (of the time). God created this in truth. He explains the Signs in detail for people who know."

This calls for some comment. Whereas the Bible calls the Sun and Moon 'lights', and merely adds to one the adjective 'greater' and to the other 'lesser', the Quran ascribes differences other than that of dimension to each respectively. Agreed, this is nothing more than a verbal distinction, but how was one to communicate to men at this time without confusing them, while at the same time expressing the notion that the Sun and Moon were not absolutely identical 'lights'?

Sun and Moon

The Sun is a shining glory *(diya')* and the Moon a light *(nur).* This translation would appear to be more correct than those given by others, where the two terms are inverted. In fact there is little difference in meaning since *diya'* belongs to a root *(dw')* which, according to Kazimirski's authoritative Arabic/French dictionary, means 'to be bright, to shine' (e.g. like a fire). The same author attributes to the substantive in question the meaning of 'light'.

The difference between Sun and Moon will be made clearer by further quotes from the Quran.

> "Blessed is the One Who placed the constellations in heaven and placed therein a lamp and a moon giving light." —(25:61)
>
> "Did you see how God created seven heavens one above another and made the moon a light therein and made the sun a lamp?" —(71:15-16)
>
> "We have built above you seven strong (heavens) and placed a blazing lamp." —(78:12-13)

The blazing lamp is quite obviously the Sun.

Here the moon is defined as a body that gives light *(munir)* from the same root as *nur* (the light applied to the Moon). The Sun however is compared to a torch *(siraj)* or a blazing *(wahhaj)* lamp.

A man of Muhammad's time could easily distinguish between the Sun, a blazing heavenly body well known to the inhabitants of the desert, and the Moon, the body of the cool of the night. The comparisons found in the Quran on this subject are therefore quite normal. What is interesting to note here is the sober quality of the comparisons, and the absence in the text of the Quran of any elements of comparison that might have prevailed at the time and which in our day would appear as phantasmagoria!.

It is known that the Sun is a star that generates intense heat and light by its internal combustions, and that the Moon, which does not give off light itself, and is an inert body (on its external layers at least) merely reflects the light received from the sun.

There is nothing in the text of the Quran that contradicts what we know today about these two celestial bodies.

Stars

As we know, the stars are heavenly bodies like the Sun. They are the scene of various physical phenomena of which the easiest to observe is their generation of light. They are heavenly bodies that produce their own light.

The word 'star' appears thirteen times in the Quran (*najm,* plural *nujum*) it comes from a root meaning to appear, to come into sight. The word designates a visible heavenly body without saying of what kind, i.e. either generator of light or mere reflector of light received. To make it clear that the object so designated is a star, a qualifying phrase is added as in the following sura:

> "By the sky- and the Night-Visitor, who will tell thee what the Night-Visitor is, the Star of piercing brightness."
>
> —(86:1-3)

The evening star is qualified in the Quran by the word *takib* meaning 'that which pierces through something' (here the night shadows). The same word is moreover used to designate shooting stars (sura 37, verse 10) : the latter are the result of combustion.

The Planets

It is difficult to say whether these are referred to in the Quran with the same exact meaning that is given to the heavenly bodies in the present day.

The planets do not have their own light. They revolve around the Sun, Earth being one of them. While one may presume that others exist elsewhere, the only ones known are those in the solar system.

Five planets other than Earth were known to the ancients: Mercury, Venus, Mars, Jupiter and Saturn. Three have been discovered in recent times: Uranus, Neptune and Pluto.

The Quran would seem to designate these by the word *kaukab* (plural *kawakib*) without stating their number. Joseph's dream (sura 12) refers to eleven of them, but the description is, by definition, an imaginary one.

A good definition of the meaning of the word *kaukab* in the Quran seems to have been given in a very famous verse. The eminently spiritual nature of its deeper meaning stands forth, and is moreover the subject of much debate among experts in exegesis. It is nevertheless of great interest to offer an account of the comparison it contains on the subject of the word that would seem to designate a 'planet'.

Here is the text in question:

> "God is the light of the heavens and the earth. The similitude of His light is as if there were a niche and within it a luminary. The luminary is in a glass. The glass is as if it were a planet glittering like a pearl."—(24:35)

Here the subject is the projection of light onto a body that reflects it (glass) and gives it the glitter of a pearl, like a planet that is lit by the sun. This is the only explanatory detail referring to this word to be found in the Quran.

The word is quoted in other verses. In some of them it is difficult to distinguish which heavenly bodies are meant (sura 6, verse 76; sura 82, verses 1-2).

In one verse however, when seen in the light of modern science, it would seem very much that these can only be the heavenly bodies that we know to be planets. In sura 37, verse 6, we see the following:

> "We have indeed adorned the lowest heaven with an ornament, the planets."

Is it possible that the expression in the Quran 'lowest heaven' means the 'solar system'? It is known that among the celestial elements nearest to us, there are no other permanent elements apart from the planets: the Sun is the only star in the system that bears its name. It is difficult to see what other heavenly bodies could be meant if not the planets. The translation given would therefore seem to be correct and the Quran to refer to the existence of the planets as defined in modern times.

Lowest Heaven

The Quran mentions the lowest heaven several times along with the heavenly bodies of which it is composed. The first among these would seem to be the planets, as we have just seen. When however the Quran associates material notions intelligible to us, enlightened as we are today by modern science, with statements of a purely spiritual nature, their meaning becomes obscure.

Thus the verse quoted could easily be understood, except that the following verse (7) of the same sura 37 speaks of a 'guard against every rebellious evil spirit', 'guard' again being referred to in sura 21, verse 32 and sura 41, verse 12, so that we are confronted by statements of quite a different kind.

What meaning can one attach moreover to the 'projectiles for the stoning of demons' that according to verse 5, sura 67 are situated in the lowest heaven? Do the 'luminaries' referred to in the same verse have something to do with the shooting stars mentioned above?

All these observations seem to lie outside the subject of this study. They have been mentioned here for the sake of completeness. At the present stage however, it would seem that scientific data are unable to cast any light on a subject that goes beyond human understanding.

Celestial Organisation

The information the Quran provides on this subject mainly deals with the solar system. References are however made to phenomena that go beyond the solar system itself: they have been discovered in recent times.

There are two very important verses on the orbits of the Sun and Moon:

> "(God is) the One Who created the night, the day, the sun and the moon. Each one is travelling in an orbit with its own motion." —(21:33)

> "The sun must not catch up the moon, nor does the night outstrip the day. Each one is travelling in an orbit with its own motion." —(36:40)

Here an essential fact is clearly stated: the existence of the Sun's and Moon's orbits, plus a reference is made to the travelling of these bodies in space with their own motion.

A negative fact also emerges from a reading of these verses: it is shown that the Sun moves in an orbit, but no indication is given as to what this orbit might be in relation to the Earth. At the time of the Quranic Revelation, it was thought that the Sun moved while the Earth stood still. This was the system of geocentrism that had held sway since the time of Ptolemy, Second century B.C., and was to continue to do so until Copernicus in the Sixteenth century A.D. Although people supported this concept at the time of Muhammad, it does not appear anywhere in the Quran, either here or elsewhere.

The Arabic word *falak* has here been translated by the word 'orbit'; many French translators of the Quran attach to it the meaning of a 'sphere'. This is indeed its initial sense. Hamidullah translates it by the word 'orbit'.

The word caused concern to older translators of the Quran who were unable to imagine the circular course of the Moon and the Sun and therefore retained images of their course through space that were either more or less correct, or hopelessly wrong. Si Hamza Boubekeur in his translation of the Quran cites the diversity of interpretations given to it: "A sort of axle, like an iron rod, that a mill turns around; a celestial sphere, orbit, sign of the zodiac, speed, wave . . .", but he adds the following observation made by Tabari, the famous Tenth century commentator: "It is our duty to keep silent when we do not know." (XVII, 15). This shows just how incapable men were of understanding this concept of the Sun's and Moon's orbit. It is obvious that if the word had expressed an astronomical concept common in Muhammad's day, it would not have been so difficult to interpret these verses. A new concept therefore existed in the Quran that was not to be explained until centuries later.

Today, the concept is widely spread that the Moon is a satellite of the Earth around which it revolves in periods of twenty-nine days. A correction must however be made to the absolutely circular form of its orbit, since modern astronomy ascribes a certain eccentricity to this, so that the distance between the Earth and the.Moon (240,000 miles) is only the average distance.

We have seen above how the Quran underlined the usefulness of observing the Moon's movements in calculating time (sura 10, verse 5, quoted at the beginning of this chapter.)

This system has often been criticized for being archaic, impractical and unscientific in comparison to our system based on the Earth's rotation around the Sun, expressed today in the Julian calendar.

This criticism calls for the following two remarks:

(a) Nearly fourteen centuries ago, the Quran was directed at the inhabitants of the Arabian Peninsula who were used to the lunar calculation of time. It was advisable to address them in the only language they could understand and not to upset the habits they had of locating spatial and temporal reference-marks which were nevertheless quite efficient. It is known how well-versed men living in the desert are in the observation of the sky; they navigated according to the stars and told the time according to the phases of the Moon. Those were the simplest and most reliable means available to them.

(b) Apart from the specialists in this field, most people are unaware of the perfect correlation between the Julian and the lunar calendar: 235 lunar months correspond exactly to 19 Julian years of 86514 days. Then length of our year of 365 days is not perfect because it has to be rectified every four years (with a leap year). With the lunar calendar, the same phenomena occurs every 19 years (Julian). This is the Metonic cycle, named after the Greek astronomer Meton, who discovered this exact correlation between solar and lunar time in the Fifth century B.C.

It is more difficult to conceive of the Sun's orbit because we are so used to seeing our solar system organized around it. To understand the verse from the Quran, the position of the Sun in our galaxy must be considered, and we must therefore call on modern scientific ideas.

Our galaxy includes a very large number of stars spaced so as to form a disc that is denser at the centre than at the rim. The Sun occupies a position in it which is far removed from the centre of the disc. The galaxy revolves on its own axis which is its centre with the result that the Sun revolves around the same centre in a circular orbit. Modern astronomy has worked out the details of this. In 1917, Shapley estimated the distance between the Sun and the centre of our galaxy at 10 kiloparsecs i.e., in miles, circa the figure 2 followed by 17 zeros. To complete one revolution on its own axis, the galaxy and Sun take roughly 250 million years. The Sun travels at roughly 150 miles per second in the completion of this.

The above is the orbital movement of the Sun that was already referred to by the Quran fourteen centuries ago. The demonstration of the existence and details of this is one of the achievements of modern astronomy.

This concept does not appear in those translations of the Quran that have been made by men of letters. Since the latter know nothing about astronomy, they have translated the Arabic word that expresses this movement by one of the meanings the word has: 'to swim'. They have done this in both the French translations and the, otherwise remarkable, English translation by Yusuf Ali.

The Arabic word referring to a movement with a self-propelled motion is the verb *sabaha* (*yasbahuna* in the text of the two verses). All the senses of the verb imply a movement that is associated with a motion that comes from the body in question. If the movement takes place in water, it is 'to swim'; it is 'to move by the action of one's own legs' if it takes place on land. For a movement that occurs in space, it is difficult to see how else this meaning implied in the word could be rendered other than by employing its original sense. Thus there seems to have been no mistranslation, for the following reasons:

(a) The Moon completes its rotating motion on its own axis at the same time as it revolves around the Earth, i.e. 29 days (approx.), so that it always has the same side facing us.

(b) The Sun takes roughly 25 days to revolve on its own axis. There are certain differences in its rotation at its equator and poles, (we shall not go into them here) but as a whole, the Sun is animated by a rotating motion.

It appears therefore that a verbal nuance in the Quran refers to the Sun and Moon's own motion. These motions of the two celestial bodies are confirmed by the data of modern science, and it is inconceivable that a man living in the Seventh century A.D.—however knowledgeable he might have been in his day (and this was certainly not true in Muhammad's case)—could have imagined them.

This view is sometimes contested by examples from great thinkers of antiquity who indisputably predicted certain data that modern science has verified. They could hardly have relied on scientific deduction however; their method of procedure was more one of philosophical reasoning. Thus the case of the Pythagoreans is often advanced. In the Sixth century B.C., they defended the theory of the rotation of the Earth on its own axis and the movement of the planets around the Sun. This theory was to be confirmed by modern science. By comparing it with the case of the Pythagoreans, it is easy to put forward the hypothesis of Muhammad as being a brilliant thinker, who was supposed to have imagined all on his own what modern science was to discover centuries later. In so doing however, people quite simply forget to mention the other aspect of what these geniuses of philosophical reasoning produced, i.e. the colossal blunders that litter their work. It must be remembered for example, that the Pythagoreans also defended the theory whereby the Sun was fixed in space; they made it the centre of the world and only conceived of a celestial order that was centered on it. It is quite common in the works of the great philosophers of antiquity to find a mixture of valid and invalid ideas about the Universe. The brilliance of these human works comes from the advanced ideas they contain, but they should not make us overlook the mistaken concepts which have also been left to us. From a strictly scientific point of view, this is what distinguished them from the Quran. In the latter, many subjects are referred to that have a bearing on modern knowledge without one of them containing a statement that contradicts what has been established by present-day science.

Sequence of Day and Night

At a time when it was held that the Earth was the centre of the world and that the Sun moved in relation to it, how could any one have failed to refer to the Sun's movement when talking of the sequence of night and day ? This is not however referred to in the Quran and the subject is dealt with as follows:

"(God) covers the day with the night which is in haste to follow it . . ." —(7:54)

"And a sign for them (human beings) is the night. We strip it of the day and they are in darkness." —(36:37)

"Hast thou not seen how God merges the night into the day and merges the day into the night." —(31:29)

". . . He coils the night upon the day and He coils the day upon the night." —(39:5)

The first verse cited requires no comment. The second simply provides an image.

It is mainly the third and fourth verses quoted above that provide interesting material on the process of interpenetration and especially of winding the night upon the day and the day upon the night, (sura 39, verse 5).

'To coil' or 'to wind' seems, as in the French translation by R. Blachere, to be the best way of translating the Arabic verb *kawivara.* The original meaning of the verb is to 'coil' a turban around the head; the notion of coiling is preserved in all the other senses of the word.

What actually happens however in space? American astronauts have seen and photographed what happens from their spaceships, especially at a great distance from Earth, e.g. from the Moon. They saw how the Sun permanently lights up (except in the case of an eclipse) the half of the Earth's surface that is facing it, while the other half of the globe is in darkness. The Earth turns on its own axis and the lighting remains the same, so that an area in the form of a half-sphere makes one revolution around the Earth in twenty-four hours while the other half-sphere, that has remained in darkness, makes the same revolution in the same time. This perpetual rotation of night and day is quite clearly described in the Quran. It is easy for the human understanding to grasp this notion nowadays because we have the idea of the Sun's (relative) immobility and the Earth's rotation. This process of perpetual coiling, including the interpenetration of one sector by another is expressed in the Quran just as if the concept of the Earth's roundness had already been conceived at the time—which was obviously not the case.

Further to the above reflections on the sequence of day and night, one must also mention, with a quotation of some verses from the Quran, the idea that there is more than one Orient and one

Occident. This is of purely descriptive interest because these phenomena rely on the most commonplace observations. The idea is mentioned here with the aim of reproducing as faithfully as possible all that the Quran has to say on this subject.

The following are examples:

— In sura 70 verse 40, the expression 'Lord of Orients and Occidents'.

— In sura 55, verse 17, the expression 'Lord of the two Orients and the two Occidents'.

— In sura 43, verse 38, a reference to the 'distance between the two Orients', an image intended to express the immense size of the distance separating the two points.

Anyone who carefully watches the sunrise and sunset knows that the Sun rises at different points of the Orient and sets at different points of the Occident, according to season. Bearings taken on each of the horizons define the extreme limits that mark the two Orients and Occidents, and between these there are points marked off throughout the year. The phenomenon described here is rather commonplace, but what mainly deserves attention in this chapter are the other topics dealt with, where the description of astronomical phenomena referred to in the Quran is in keeping with modern data.

Evolution of the Heavens

Having called modern concepts on the formation of the Universe to mind, reference was made to the evolution that took place, starting with primary nebula through to the formation of galaxies, stars and (for the solar system) the appearance of planets beginning with the Sun at a certain stage of its evolution. Modern data lead us to believe that in the solar system, and more generally in the Universe itself, this evolution is still continuing.

How can anybody who is aware of these ideas fail to make a comparison with certain statements found in the Quran in which the manifestations of divine Omnipotence are referred to.

The Quran reminds us several times that: "(God) subjected the sun and the moon: each one runs its course to an appointed term."

This sentence is to be found in sura 13, verse 2; sura 31, verse 29; sura 35, verse 13 and sura 39, verse 5.

In addition to this, the idea of a settled place is associated with the concept of a destination place in sura 36, verse 38: "The Sun runs its course to a settled place. This is the decree of the All Mighty, the Full of Knowledge."

'Settled place' is the translation of the word *mustaqarr* and there can be no doubt that the idea of an exact place is attached to it.

How do these statements fare when compared with data established by modern science?

The Quran gives an end to the Sun for its evolution and a destination place. It also provides the Moon with a settled place. To understand the possible meanings of these statements, we must remember what modern knowledge has to say about the evolution of the stars in general and the Sun in particular, and (by extension) the celestial bodies that automatically followed its movement through space, among them the Moon.

The Sun is a star that is roughly 4.5 billion years old, according to experts in astrophysics. It is possible to distinguish a stage in its evolution, as one can for all the stars. At present, the Sun is at an early stage, characterized by the transformation of hydrogen atoms into helium atoms. Theoretically, this present stage should last another 5½ billion years according to calculations that allow a total of 10 billion years for the duration of the primary stage in a star of this kind. It has already been shown, in the case of these other stars, that this stage gives way to a second period characterized by the completion of the transformation of hydrogen into helium, with the resulting expansion of its external layers and the cooling of the Sun. In the final stage, its light is greatly diminished and density considerably increased; this is to be observed in the type of star known as a 'white dwarf.

The above dates are only of interest in as far as they give a rough estimate of the time factor involved, what is worth remembering and is really the main point of the above, is the notion of an evolution. Modern data allow us to predict that, in a few billion years, the conditions prevailing in the solar system will not be the same as they are today. Like other stars whose transformations have been recorded until they reached their final stage, it is possible to predict an end to the Suri.

The second verse quoted above (sura 36, verse 38) referred to the Sun running its course towards a place of its own.

Modern astronomy has been able to locate it exactly and has even given it a name, the Solar Apex: the solar system is indeed evolving in space towards a point situated in the Constellation of Hercules (alpha lyrae) whose exact location is firmly established; it is moving at a speed already ascertained at something in the region of 12 miles per second.

All these astronomical data deserve to be mentioned in relation to the two verses from the Quran, since it is possible to state that they appear to agree perfectly with modern scientific data.

Expansion of Universe

The expansion of the Universe is the most imposing discovery of modern science. Today it is a firmly established concept and the only debate centres around the way this is taking place.

It was first suggested by the general theory of relativity and is backed up by physics in the examination of the galactic spectrum; the regular movement towards the red section of their spectrum may be explained by the distancing of one galaxy from another. Thus the size of the Universe is probably constantly increasing and this increase will become bigger the further away the galaxies are from us. The speeds at which these celestial bodies are moving may, in the course of this perpetual expansion, go from fractions of the speed of light to speeds faster than this.

The following verse of the Quran (sura 51, verse 47) where God is speaking, may perhaps be compared with modern ideas:

> "The heaven, We have built it with power. Verily. We are expanding it."

'Heaven' is the translation of the word '*sama*' and this is exactly the extra-terrestrial world that is meant.

'We are expanding it' is the translation of the plural present participle *musi'una* of the verb *ausa'a* meaning 'to make wider, more spacious, to extend, to expand'.

Some translators who were unable to grasp the meaning of the latter provide translations that appear to me to be mistaken, e.g. "we give generously" (R. Blachere). Others sense the meaning, but are afraid to commit themselves: Hamidullah in his translation of the Quran talks of the widening of the heavens and space, but he includes a question mark. Finally, there are those who arm themselves with authorized scientific opinion in their commentaries and give the meaning stated here. This is true in the case of the *Muntakab*, a book of commentaries edited by the Supreme Council for Islamic Affairs, Cairo. It refers to the expansion of the Universe in totally unambiguous terms.

Conquering Space

From this point of view, three verses of the Quran should command our full attention. One expresses, without any trace of ambiguity, what man should and will achieve in this field. In the other two, God refers for the sake of the unbelievers in Makka to the surprise they would have if they were able to raise themselves up to the Heavens; He alludes to a hypothesis which will not be realized for the latter.

(1) The first of these verses is sura 55, verse 33: "O assembly of Jinns and Men, if you can penetrate regions of the heavens and the earth, then penetrate them! You will not penetrate them save with a Power."

The translation given here needs some explanatory comment:

(a) The word 'if expresses in English a condition that is dependant upon a possibility and either an achievable or an unachievable hypothesis. Arabic is a language which is able to introduce a nuance into the condition which is much more explicit. There is one word to express the possibility (i&a), another for the achievable hypothesis (in) and a third for the unachievable hypothesis expressed by the word (lau). The verse in question has it as an achievable hypothesis expressed by the word (in). The Quran therefore suggests the material possibility of a concrete realization. This subtle linguistic distinction formally rules out the purely mystic interpretation that some people have (quite wrongly) put on this verse.

(b) God is addressing the spirits (*jinn*) and human beings (*ins*), and not essentially allegorical figures.

(c) 'To penetrate' is the translation of the verb *nafada* followed by the preposition *min*. According to Kazimirski's dictionary, the phrase means 'to pass right through and come out on the other side of a body' (e.g. an arrow that comes out on the other side). It therefore suggests a deep penetration and emergence at the other end into the regions in question.

(d) The Power (sultan) these men will have to achieve this enterprise would seem to come from the All-Mighty.

There can be no doubt that this verse indicates the possibility men will one day achieve what we today call (perhaps rather improperly) 'the conquest of space'. One must note that the text of the Quran predicts not only penetration through the regions of the Heavens, but also the earth, i.e. the exploration of its depths.

(2) The other two verses are taken from sura 15, (verses 14 and 15). God is speaking of the unbelievers in Makka, as the context of this passage in the sura shows:

> "Even if We opened unto them a gate to Heaven and they were to continue ascending therein, they would say: our sight is confused as in .drunkenness. Nay, we are people bewitched."

The above expresses astonishment at a remarkable spectacle, different from anything man could imagine.

The conditional sentence is introduced here by the word *lau* which expresses a hypothesis that could never be realized as far as it concerned the people mentioned in these verses.

When talking of the conquest of space therefore, we have two passages in the text of the Quran: one of them refers to what will one day become a reality thanks to the powers of intelligence and ingenuity God will give to man, and the other describes an event that the unbelievers in Makka will never witness, hence its character of a condition never to be realized. The event will however be seen by others, as intimated in the first verse quoted above. It describes the human reactions to the unexpected spectacle that travellers in space will see: their confused sight, as in drunkenness, the feeling of being bewitched.

This is exactly how astronauts have experienced this remarkable adventure since the first human spaceflight around the world in 1961. It is known in actual fact how once one is above the Earth's atmosphere, the Heavens no longer have the azure appearance we see from Earth, which results from phenomena of absorption of the Sun's light into the layers of the atmosphere. The human observer in space above the Earth's atmosphere sees a black sky and the Earth seems to be surrounded by a halo of bluish colour due to the same phenomena of absorption of light by the Earth's atmosphere. The Moon has no atmosphere, however, and therefore appears in its true colors against the black background of the sky. It is a completely new spectacle therefore that presents itself to men in space, and the photographs of this spectacle are well known to present-day man.

Here again, it is difficult not to be impressed, when comparing the text of the Quran to the data of modern science, by statements that simply cannot be ascribed to the thought of a man who lived more than fourteen centuries ago.

The Earth

As in the case of the subjects already examined, the verses of the Quran dealing with the Earth are dispersed throughout the Book. It is difficult to classify them, and the scheme adopted here is a personal one.

To explain them more clearly, one might begin by singling out a certain number of verses that deal with more than one subject at a time. These verses are largely general in their application and constitute an invitation extended to men to reflect on divine Beneficence by pondering on the examples provided.

Other groups of verses may be singled out which deal with more specific subjects, as follows :

— the water cycle and the seas.
— the Earth's relief.
— the Earth's atmosphere.

General Statements

Although these verses provide arguments intended to lead man to meditate on the Beneficence of God towards His creatures, here and there they contain statements that are interesting from the point of view of modern science. They are perhaps especially revealing by virtue of the fact that they do not express the varied beliefs concerning natural phenomena that were current at the time of the Quranic Revelation. These beliefs were later to be shown by scientific knowledge to be mistaken.

On the one hand, these verses express simple ideas readily understood by to those people to whom, for geographical reasons, the Quran was first directed : the inhabitants of Makka and Madina, the Bedouins of the Arabian Peninsula. On the other hand, they contain reflections of a general nature from which a more cultivated public of any time and place may learn something instructive, once it starts to think about them: this is a mark of the Quran's universality.

As there is apparently no classification of such verses in the Quran, they are presented here in the numerical order of the suras:

> "(God) is the One who made the earth a couch for you and the heavens an edifice, and sent down water from the sky. He brought forth therewith fruits for your sustenance. Do not join equals with God when you know." —(2:22)
>
> "Behold! In the creation of the heavens and the earth,
> In the disparity of night and day,
> In the ship which runs upon the sea for the profit of mankind, —(2:164)
> In the water which God sent down from the sky thereby reviving the earth after its death,
> In the beasts of all kinds He scatters therein, In the change of the winds and the subjected clouds between the sky and earth,
> Here are Signs for people who are wise." —(13:3)
>
> "(God) is the One who spread out the earth and set therein mountains standing firm and rivers. For every fruit He placed two of a pair. He covers the day with the night. Verily in this there are Signs for people who reflect." —(13:3)
>
> God is speaking:
>
> "The earth, We spread it out and set thereon mountains standing firm. We caused all kind of things to grow therein in due balance. Therein We have provided you and those

> you do not supply with means of subsistence and there is not a thing but its stores are with Us. We do not send it down save in appointed measure." —(15:19-21)
>
> "(God is) the One Who has made for you the earth like a cradle and inserted roads into it for you. He sent water down from the sky and thereby We brought forth pairs of plants, each separate from the other. Eat! Pasture your cattle! Verily in this are Signs for people endued With intelligence." —(20:55-54)
>
> "He Who made the earth an abode and set rivers in its interstices and mountains standing firm. He placed a barrier between the two seas. Is there any divinity besides God? Nay, but most people do not know." —(27:61)

Here a reference is made to the general stability of the Earth's crust. It is known that at the early stages of the Earth's existence before its crust cooled down, the latter was unstable. The stability of the Earth's crust is not however strictly uniform, since there are zones where earthquakes intermittently occur. As to the barrier between the two seas, it is an image which signifies that the waters of the great rivers and the waters of the sea do not mix at the level of certain large estuaries.

> "(God is) the One Who made the earth docile to you. So walk upon its shoulders! Eat of His sustenance! Unto Him will be the Resurrection." —(67:15)
>
> "After that (God) spread the earth out. Therefrom He drew out its water and its pasture. And the mountains He has firmly fixed. Goods for you and for your cattle." —(79:30-33)

In many such verses, emphasis is laid upon the importance of water and the practical consequences of its presence in the earth's soil, i.e. the fertility of the soil. There can be no doubt that in desert countries, water is the most important element governing man's survival. The reference in the Quran however goes beyond this geographical detail. According to scientific knowledge the character the Earth has of a planet that is rich in water is unique to the solar system, and this is exactly what is highlighted in the Quran. Without water, the Earth would be a dead planet like the Moon. The Quran gives first place to water among the natural phenomena of the Earth that it refers to. The water cycle is described with remarkable accuracy in the Quran.

Water Cycle and Seas

When the verses of the Quran concerning the role of water in man's existence are read in succession today, they all appear to us to express ideas that are quite obvious. The reason for this is simple: in our day and age, we all, to a lesser or greater extent, know about the water cycle in nature.

If however, we consider the various concepts the ancients had on this subject, it becomes clear that the data in the Quran do not embody the mythical concepts current at the time of the Revelation which had been developed more according to philosophical speculation than observed phenomena. Although it was empirically possible to acquire on a modest scale, the useful practical knowledge necessary for the improvement of the irrigation, the concepts held on the water cycle in general would hardly be acceptable today.

Thus it would have been easy to imagine that underground water could have come from the infiltration of precipitations in the soil. In ancient times however, this idea, held by Vitruvius Polio Marcus in Rome, 1st century B.C., was cited as an exception. For many centuries therefore (and the Quranic Revelation is situated during this period) man held totally inaccurate views on the water cycle.

Two specialists on this subject, G. Gastany and B. Blavoux, in their entry in the *Universalis Encyclopedia* (Encyclopedia Universalis) under the heading Hydrogeology (Hydrogeologie), give an edifying history of this problem.

"In the Seventh century B.C., Thales of Miletus held the theory whereby the waters of the oceans, under the effect of winds, were thrust towards the interior of the continents; so the water fell upon the earth and penetrated into the soil. Plato shared these views and thought that the return of the waters to the oceans was via a great abyss, the Tartarus'. This theory had many supporters until the Eighteenth century, one of whom was Descartes. Aristotle imagined that the water vapour from the soil condensed in cool mountain caverns and formed underground lakes that fed springs. He was followed by Seneca (1st Century A.D.) and many others, until 1877, among them O. Volger . . . The first clear 13 formulation of the water cycle must be attributed to Bernard Palissy in 1580: he claimed that underground water came from rainwater infiltrating into the soil. This theory was confirmed by E. Mariotte and P. Perrault in the Seventeenth century.

In the following passages from the Quran, there is no trace of the mistaken ideas that were current at the time of Muhammad (PBUH):

> "We sent down from the sky blessed water whereby We caused to grow gardens, grains for harvest, tall palm-trees with their spathes, piled one above the other—sustenance for (Our) servants. Therewith We gave (new) life to a dead land. So will be the emergence (from the tombs)." —(50:9-11)

> "We sent down water from the sky in measure and lodged it in the ground. And We certainly are able to withdraw it. Therewith for you We gave rise to gardens of palm-trees and vineyards where for you are abundant fruits and of them you eat." —(23:18-19)

> "We sent forth the winds that fecundate. We cause the water to descend from the sky. We provide you with the water—you (could) not be the guardians of its reserves." —(15:22)

There are two possible interpretations of this last verse. The fecundating winds may be taken to be the fertilizers of plants because they carry pollen. This may, however, be a figurative expression referring by analogy to the role the wind plays in the process whereby a non-rain carrying cloud is turned into one that produces a shower of rain. This role is often referred to, as in the following verses:

> "God is the One Who sends forth the winds which raised up the clouds. We drive them to a dead land. Therewith We revive the ground after its death. So will be the Resurrection." —(35:9)

It should be noted how the style is descriptive in the first part of the verse, then passes without transition to a declaration from

God. Such sudden changes in the form of the narration are very frequent in the Quran.

> "God is the One Who sends forth the winds which raised up the clouds. He spreads them in the sky as He wills and breaks them into fragments. Then thou seest raindrops issuing from within them. He makes them reach such of His servants as He wills. And they are rejoicing." —(30:48)
>
> "(God) is the One Who sends forth the winds like heralds of His Mercy. When they have carried the heavy-laden clouds, We drive them to a dead land. Then We cause water to descend and thereby bring forth fruits of every kind. Thus We will bring forth the dead. Maybe you will remember." —(7:57)
>
> "(God) is the One Who sends forth the winds like heralds of His Mercy. We cause pure water to descend in order to revive a dead land with it and to supply with drink the multitude of cattle and human beings We have created." —(25:48-49)
>
> ". . . In the provision that God sends down from the sky and thereby He revives the ground after its death and in the change (of direction) of winds, there are Signs for people who are wise." —(45:5)

The provision made in this last verse is in the form of the water sent down from the sky, as the context shows. The accent is on the change of the winds that modify the rain cycle.

> "(God) sends water down from the sky so that the rivers flow according to their measure. The torrent bears away an increasing foam." —(13:17)
>
> God commands the Prophet:
>
> "Say: Do you see if your water were to be lost in the ground, who then can supply you with gushing water?" —(67:30)
>
> "Hast thou not seen that God sent water down from the sky and led it through sources into the ground ? Then He caused sown fields of different colours to grow." —(39:21)

> "Therein We placed gardens of palm-trees and vineyards and We caused water springs to gush forth." —(36:34)

The importance of springs and the way they are fed by rainwater conducted into them is stressed in the last three verses. It is worth pausing to examine this fact and call to mind the predominance in the Middle Ages of views such as those held by Aristotle, according to whom springs were fed by underground lakes. In his entry on Hydrology (Hydrologie) in the *Universalis Encyclopedia* (Encyclopedia Universalis) M.R. Remenieras, a teacher at the French National School of Agronomy (Ecole nationale du Genie rural, des Eaux et Forets), describes the main stages of hydrology and refers to the magnificent irrigation works of the ancients, particularly in the Middle East. He notes however that an empirical outlook ruled over everything, since the ideas of the time proceeded from mistaken concepts. He continues as follows:

"It was not until the Renaissance (between circa 1400 and 1600) that purely philosophical concepts gave way to research based on the objective observation of hydrologic phenomena. Leonardo da Vinci (1452-1519) rebelled against Aristotle's statements. Bernard Palissy, in his wonderful discourse on the nature of waters and fountains both natural and artificial (Discours admirable de la nature des eaux et fontaines tant naturelles qu'artificielles (Paris, 1570)) gives a correct interpretation of the water cycle and especially of the way springs are fed by rainwater."

This last statement is surely exactly what is mentioned in verse 21, sura 39 describing the way rainwater is conducted into sources in the ground.

The subject of verse 43, sura 24 is rain and hail:

> "Hast thou not seen that God makes the clouds move gently, then joins them together, then makes them a heap. And thou seest raindrops issuing from within it. He sends down from the sky mountains of hail, He strikes therewith whom He wills and He turns it away from whom He wills. The flashing of its lightning almost snatches away the sight."

The following passage requires some comment:

> "Have you observed the water you drink? Do you bring it

> down from the rainclouds? Or do We? If it were Our will, We could make it salty. Then why are you not thankful?"
> —(56:68-70)

This reference to the fact that God could have made fresh water salty is a way of expressing divine Omnipotence. Another means of reminding us of the same Omnipotence is the challenge to man to make rain fall from the clouds. In modern times however, technology has surely made it possible to create rain artificially. Can one therefore oppose the statement in the Quran to man's ability to produce precipitations?

The answer is no, because it seems clear that one must take account of man's limitations in this field. M.A. Facy, an expert at the French Meteorological Office, wrote the following in the *Universalis Encyclopedia* (Encyclopedia Universalis) under the heading Precipitations (Precipitations) : "It will never be possible to make rain fall from a cloud that does not have the suitable characteristics of a raincloud or one that has not yet reached the appropriate stage of evolution (maturity)". Man can never therefore hasten the precipitation process by technical means when the natural conditions for it are not present. If this were not the case, droughts would never occur in practice—which they obviously do. To have control over rain and fine weather still remains a dream therefore.

Man cannot wilfully break the established cycle that maintains the circulation of water in nature. This cycle may be outlined as follows, according to modern ideas on hydrology:

The calories obtained from the Sun's rays cause the sea and those parts of the Earth's surface that are covered or soaked in water to evaporate. The water vapour that is given off rises into the atmosphere and, by condensation, forms into clouds. The winds then intervene and move the clouds thus formed over varying distances. The clouds can then either disperse without producing rain, or combine their mass with others to create even greater condensation, or they can fragment and produce rain at some stages in their evolution. When rain reaches the sea (70% of the Earth's surface is covered by seas), the cycle is soon repeated. When rain falls on the land, it may be absorbed by vegetation and thus aid the latter's growth; the vegetation in its turn gives off water and thus returns some water to the atmosphere. The rest, to a lesser or greater extent, infiltrates into the soil, whence it is either conducted through channels into the sea, or comes back to the Earth's surface network through springs or resurgences.

When one compares the modern data of hydrology to what is contained in the numerous verses of the Quran quoted in this paragraph, one has to admit that there is a remarkable degree of agreement between them.

The Oceans

Whereas the above verses from the Quran have provided material for comparison between modern knowledge about the water cycle in nature, this is not the case for the seas. There is not a single statement in the Quran dealing with the seas which could be used for comparison with scientific data per se. This does not diminish the necessity of pointing out however that none of the statements in the Quran on the seas refers to the beliefs, myths or superstitions prevalent at the time of its Revelation.

A certain number of verses deal with the seas and navigation. As subjects for reflection, they provide indications of divine omnipotence that arise from the facts of common observation. The following verses are examples of this:

> "(God) has made the ship subject to you, so that it runs upon the sea at His Command." —(14:32)
>
> " (God) is the One Who subjected the sea, so that you eat fresh meat from it and you extract from it ornaments which you wear. Thou seest the ships ploughing the waves, so that you seek of His Bounty. Maybe, you will be thankful." —(16:4)
>
> "Hast thou seen that the ship runs upon the sea by the Grace of God, in order to show you His Signs. Verily in this are Signs for all who are persevering and grateful." —(31:31)
>
> "His are the ships erected upon the sea like tokens." —(55:24)
>
> "A sign for them is that We bore their offspring in the loaded Ark. We have created for them similar (vessels) on

which they ride. If We will, We drown them and there is no help and they will not be saved unless by Mercy from Us and as a gratification for a time." —(36:41-44)

The reference here is quite clearly to the vessel bearing man upon the sea, just as, long ago, Noah and the other occupants of the vessel were carried in the Ark that enabled them to reach dry land.

Another observed fact concerning the sea stands out, because of its unusual nature, from the verses of the Quran devoted to it: three verses refer to certain characteristics shared by great rivers when they flow out into the ocean.

The phenomenon is well known and often seen whereby the immediate mixing of salty seawater and fresh riverwater does not occur. The Quran refers to this in the case of what is thought to be the estuary of the Tigris and Euphrates where they unite to form what one might call a 'sea' over 100 miles long, the Shatt Al Arab. At the inner parts of the gulf, the effect of the tides is to produce the welcome phenomenon of the reflux of fresh water to the interior of the dry land, thus ensuring adequate irrigation. To understand the text correctly, one has to know that the English word 'sea' conveys the general meaning of the Arabic word *bahr* which designates a large mass of water and is equally used for both the sea and the great rivers: the Nile, Tigris and Euphrates for example.

The following are the three verses that describe this phenomenon:

> "(God) is the One Who has let free the two seas, one is agreeable and sweet, the other salty and bitter. He placed a barrier between them, a partition that it is forbidden to pass." —(25:53)
>
> "The two seas are not alike. The water of one is agreeable, sweet, pleasant to drink. The other salty and bitter. You eat fresh meat from it and you extract from it ornaments which you wear." —(35:12)
>
> "He has loosed the two seas. They meet together. Between them there is a barrier which they do not transgress. Out of them come pearls and coral." —(55:19-20, 22)

In addition to the description of the main fact, these verses refer to what may be obtained from fresh water and seawater: fish, personal adornment, i.e. coral and pearls. With regard to the phenomenon whereby the river water does not mix with seawater at the estuary, one must understand that this is not peculiar to the Tigris and Euphrates; they are not mentioned by name in the text, but it is thought to refer to them. Rivers with a very large outflow, such as the Mississippi and the Yangtze, have the same peculiarity: the mixing of their fresh water with the salty water of the sea does not often occur until very far out at sea.

More About Earth

The constitution of the Earth is highly complex. Today, it is possible to imagine it very roughly as being formed of a deep layer, at very high temperature, and especially of a central area where rocks are still in fusion, and of a surface layer, the Earth's crust which is solid and cold. The crust is very thin; its thickness is estimated in units of miles or units of ten miles at the most. The Earth's radius is however slightly over 3,750 miles, so that its crust does not represent (on average) one hundredth of the sphere's radius. It is upon this skin, as it were, that all geological phenomena have taken place. At the origin of these phenomena are folds that were to form the mountain ranges; their formation is called 'orogenesis' in geology: the process is of considerable importance because with the development of a relief that was to constitute a mountain, the Earth's crust was driven in proportionately far down: this process ensures a foundation in the layer that underlies it.

The history of the distribution of the sea and land on the surface of the globe has only recently been established and is still very incomplete, even for the most recent and best known periods. It is likely that the oceans appeared and formed the hydrosphere circa half a billion years ago. The continents were probably a single mass at the end of the primary era, then subsequently broke apart. Some continents or parts of continents have moreover emerged through the formation of mountains in maritime zones (e.g. the North Atlantic continent and part of Europe).

According to modern ideas, the dominating factor in the formation of the land that emerged was the development of mountain ranges. The evolution of the land, from the primary to the quaternary era, is classed according to 'orogenic phases' that are themselves grouped into 'cycles' of the same name since the formation of all mountain reliefs had repercussions on the balance between the sea and the continents. It made some parts of the land disappear and others emerge, and for hundreds of millions of years it has altered the surface distribution of the continents and oceans: the former at present only occupying three tenths of the surface of this planet.

In this way it is possible to give a very rough outline of the transformations that has taken place over the last hundreds of millions of years.

When referring to the Earth's relief, the Quran only describes, as it were, the formation of the mountains. Seen from the present point of view, there is indeed little one can say about the verses that only express God's Beneficence to man with regard to the Earth's formation, as in the following verses:

> "For you God made the earth a carpet so that you travel along its roads and the paths of valleys." —(71:19-20)
>
> "The earth, We have spread it out. How excellently We did that." —(51:48)

The carpet which has been spread out is the Earth's crust, a solidified shell on which we can live, since the globe's sub-strata" are very hot, fluid and hostile to any form of life.

The statements in the Quran referring to the mountains and the references to their stability subsequent to the phenomenon of the folds are very important.

The context invites unbelievers to consider certain natural phenomena, among them:

> ". . . the mountains, how they have been.pitched (like a tent). The Earth how it was made even." —(88:19-20)

The following verses give details about the way in which the mountains were anchored in the ground:

> "Have We not made the earth an expanse and the mountains stakes." —(78:6-7)

The stakes referred to are the ones used to anchor a tent in the ground (*autad*, plural of *watad*).

Modern geologists describe the folds in the Earth as giving foundations to the mountains, and their dimensions go roughly one mile to roughly 10 miles. The stability of the Earth's crust results from the phenomenon of these folds.

So it is not surprising to find reflections on the mountains in certain passages of the Quran, such as the following:

"And the mountains (God) has fixed them firmly."
—(79:32)

> "(God) has cast into the ground (mountains) standing firm, so that it does not shake with you." —(31:10)

The same phrase is repeated in sura 16, verse 15; and the same idea is expressed with hardly any change in sura 21, verse 31:

"We have placed in the ground (mountains) standing firm so that it does not shake with them."

These verses express the idea that the way the mountains are laid out ensures stability and is in complete agreement with geological data.

In addition to certain statements specifically relating to the sky, examined in the preceding chapter, the Quran contains several passages dealing with the phenomena that occur in the atmosphere. As for the comparison between them and the data of modern science, it is to be noted here, as elsewhere, that there is absolutely no contradiction between today's modern scientific knowledge and the phenomena described.

A familiar feeling of discomfort experienced at high altitude, which increases the higher one climbs, is expressed in verse 125, sura 6:

> "Those whom God wills to guide, He opens their breasts to Islam. Those whom He wills lose their way, He makes their breasts narrow and constricted, as if they were climbing in the sky."

Some commentators have claimed that the notion of discomfort at high altitude was unknown to the Arabs of Muhammad's time. It appears that this was not true at all: the existence on the Arabian Peninsula of peaks rising over two miles high makes it extremely implausible that they should not have known of the difficulty of breathing at high altitude. Others have seen in this verse a prediction of the conquest of space, an opinion that appears to require categorical denial, at least for this passage.

On Electricity

Electricity in the atmosphere and the consequences of this, i.e. lightning and hail, are referred to in the following verses:

> "(God) is the One Who shows you the lightning, with fear and covetousness. He raised up the heavy clouds. The thunder glorifies His Praise and so do the angels for awe. He sends the thunder-bolt and strikes with them who He wills while they are disputing about God. He is All Mighty in His Power." —(13:12-13)

In this verse there is the expression of an obvious correlation between the formation of heavy rainclouds or clouds containing hail and the occurrence of lightning: the former, the subject of covetousness on account of the benefit it represents and the latter, the subject of fear, because when it falls, it is at the will of the All-Mighty. The connection between the two phenomena is verified by present-day knowledge of electricity in the atmosphere.

On Shadows

The phenomenon of shadows and the fact that they move is very simply explained today. It forms the subject of the following observations:

> "Out of the things He created, God has given you shade . . ." —(16:81)
>
> "Have (the Unbelievers) not observed that for all the things God created, how their shadow shifts right and left, prostating themselves to God while they are full of humility." —(16:48)
>
> "Hast thou not seen how thy Lord has spread the shade. If He willed, He could have made it stationary. Moreover We made the sun its guide and We withdraw it towards Us easily." —(25:45-46)

Apart from the phrases dealing with the humility before God of all the things He created, including their shadow, and the fact that God can take back all manifestations of His Power, as He wills, the text of the Quran refers to the relationship between the Sun and the shadows. One must bear in mind at this point the fact that, in Muhammad's day, it was believed that the way a shadow moved was governed by the movement of the sun from east to west. This principle was applied in the case of the sun dial to measure the time between sunrise and sunset. In this instance, the Quran speaks of the phenomenon without referring to the explanation current at the time of the Revelation. It would have been readily accepted for many centuries by those who came after Muhammad. In the end however, it would have been shown to be inaccurate. The Quran only talks moreover of the function the sun has as an indicator of shadow. Evidently there is no contradiction between the way the Quran describes shadow and what we know of this phenomenon in modern times.

Animals and Vegetables

Numerous verses describing the origins of life have been assembled in this chapter, along with certain aspects of the vegetable kingdom and general or specific topics relating to the animal kingdom. The grouping of verses scattered throughout the Book afford a general view of the data the Quran contains on these subjects.

In the case of the subject of this and the following chapter, the examination of the Quranic text has sometimes been particularly delicate on account of certain difficulties inherent in the vocabulary. These have only been overcome through the fact that scientific data which have a bearing on the subject have been taken into consideration. It is particularly so in the case of living beings, i.e. animal, vegetable and human, where a confrontation with the teachings of science is shown to be indispensable in the search for the meaning of certain statements on these topics contained in the Quran.

It will become clear that numerous translations of these passages in the Quran, made by men of letters, must be deemed inaccurate by the scientist. The same holds true for commentaries made by those who do not possess the scientific knowledge necessary for an understanding of the text.

Origin of Life

This question has always preoccupied man, both for himself and for the living things around him. It will be examined here from a general point of view. The case of man, whose appearance on Earth and reproduction processes are the subject of lengthy exposes, will be dealt with in the next chapter.

When the Quran describes the origins of life on a very broad basis, it is extremely concise. It does so in a verse that also mentions the process of the formation of the Universe, already quoted and commented on:

> "Do not the Unbelievers see that the heavens and the earth were joined together, then We clove them as under and We got every living thing out of the water. Will they then not believe?" —(21:30)

The notion of 'getting something out of something' does not give rise to any doubts. The phrase can equally mean that every living thing was made of water (as its essential component) or that every living thing originated in water. The two possible meanings are strictly in accordance with scientific data. Life is in fact of aquatic origin and water is the major component of all living cells. Without water, life is not possible. When the possibility of life on another planet is discussed, the first question is always: does it contain a sufficient quantity of water to support life?

Modern data lead us to think that the oldest living being must have belonged to the vegetable kingdom: algae have been found that date from the pre-Cambrian period, i.e. the time of the oldest known lands. Organisms belonging to the animal kingdom probably appeared slightly later: they too came from the sea.

What has been translated here by 'water' is the word ma' which means both water in the sky and water in the sea, plus any kind of liquid. In the first meaning, water is the element necessary to all vegetable life:

> "(God is the One Who) sent water down from the sky and thereby We brought forth pairs of plants each separate from the other." —(20:53)

This is the first reference to the notion of a pair in the vegetable kingdom. We shall return to this later.

In the second meaning, a liquid without any further indication of what kind, the word is used in its indeterminate form to designate what is at the basis of the formation of all animal life:

> "God created every animal from water." —(24:45)

We shall see further on how this word may also be applied to seminal fluid.

Whether it deals therefore with the origins of life in general, or the element that gives birth to plants in the soil, or the seed of animals, all the statements contained in the Quran on the origin of life are strictly in accordance with modern scientific data. None of the myths on the origins of life that abounded at the time the Quran appeared are mentioned in the text.

The Vegetables: It is not possible to quote in their entirety all the numerous passages in the Quran in which divine Beneficence is referred to concerning the salutary effect of the rain which makes vegetation grow. Here are just three verses on this subject:

> "(God) is the One Who sends water down from the sky. For you this is a drink and out of it (grow) shrubs in which you let (cattle) graze freely. Therewith for you He makes sown fields, olives, palm-trees, vineyards and all kinds of fruit grow." —(16:10-11)
>
> "(God) is the One Who sent water down from the sky. There—with We brought forth plants of all kinds and from them the verdure and We brought forth from it the clustered grains, and from the palm-tree its spathes with bunches of dates (hanging) low, the gardens of grapes, olives and pomegranates similar and different. Look at their fruit, when they bear it, and their ripening. Verily, in that there are Signs for people who believe." —(6:99)
>
> "We sent down from the sky blessed water.whereby We caused to grow gardens, grains for harvest, tall palm-trees with their spathes, piled one above the other—sustenance for (Our) servants. Therewith We give (new) life to a dead land. So will be the emergence (from the tombs)." —(50:9-11)

The Quran adds to these general data, others that refer to more specialized subjects:

> "The earth . . . We caused all kinds of things to grow therein in due balance." —(15:19)

On various food materials, the Quran says:

> "On the earth are adjacent parts; vineyards, sown fields, palm-trees, similar and not similar, watered with the same water. We make some of them more excellent than others to eat and verily in this are Signs for wise people."
>
> —(13:4)

It is interesting to note the existence of these verses because they show the sober quality of the terms used, and the absence of any description that might highlight the beliefs of the times, rather than fundamental truths. What particularly attracts our attention however, are the statements in the Quran concerning reproduction in the vegetable kingdom.

One must bear in mind that there are two methods of reproduction in the vegetable kingdom: one sexual, the other asexual. It is only the first which in fact deserves the term 'reproduction', because this defines a biological process whose purpose is the appearance of a new individual identical to the one that gave it birth.

Asexual reproduction is quite simply multiplication. It is the result of the fragmentation of an organism which has separated from the main plant and developed in such a way as to resemble the plant from which it came. It is considered by Guilliermond and Mangenot to be a 'special case of growth'. A very simple example of this is the cutting: a cutting taken from a plant is placed in suitably watered soil and regenerated by the growth of new roots. Some plants have organs specially designed for this, while others give off spores that behave like seeds, as it were, (it should be remembered that seeds are the results of a process of sexual reproduction).

Sexual reproduction in the vegetable kingdom is carried out by the coupling of the male and female parts of the generic formations united on the same plant or located on separate plants. This is the only form that is mentioned in the Quran.

> "(God is the One Who) sent water down from the sky and thereby We brought forth pairs of plants each separate from the other." —(20:53)

'One of a pair' is the translation of *zauj* (plural *azwaj*) whose original meaning is: 'that which, in the company of another, forms a pair'; the word is used just as readily for a married couple as for a pair of shoes.

> "Thou seest the grounds lifeless. When We send down water thereon it shakes and grows and puts forth every magnificent pair (of plants)." —(22:5)
>
> "We caused to grow (on the earth) every noble pair (of plants)." —(31:10)
>
> "Of all fruits (God) placed (on the earth) two of a pair." —(13:3)

We know that fruit is the end-product of the reproduction process of superior plants which have the most highly developed and complex organization. The stage preceding fruit is the flower, which has male and female organs (stamens and ovules). The latter, once pollen has been carried to them, bear fruit which in turn matures and frees its seeds. All fruit therefore implies the existence of male and female organs. This is the meaning of the verse in the Quran.

It must be noted that for certain species, fruit can come from non-fertilized flowers (parthenocarpic fruit), eg., bananas, certain types of pineapple, fig, orange, and vine. They can nevertheless also come from plants that have definite sexual characteristics.

The culmination of the reproductive process comes with the germination of the seed once its outside casing is opened (sometimes it is compacted into a fruit-stone). This opening allows roots to emerge which draw from the soil all that is necessary for the plant's slowed-down life as a seed while it grows and produces a new plant.

A verse in the Quran refers to this process of germination:

> "Verily, God splits the grain and the fruit-stone." —(6:95)

The Quran often restates the existence of these components of a pair in the vegetable kingdom and brings the notion of a couple into a more general context, without set limits:

> "Glory be to Him Who created the components of couples of every kind: of what the ground caused to grow, of themselves (human beings) and of what you do not know." —(36:36)

One could form many hypotheses concerning the meaning of, the 'things men did not know' in Muhammad's day. Today we can distinguish structures or coupled functions for them, going from the infinitesimally small to the infinitely large, in the living as well as the non-living world. The point is to remember these clearly expressed ideas and note, once again, that they are in perfect agreement with modern science.

The Animals: There are several questions in the Quran concerning the animal kingdom which are the subject of comments that call for a confrontation with modern scientific knowledge. Here again, however, one would gain an incomplete view of all that the Quran contains on this subject if one were to leave out a passage such as the extract which follows. In this passage, the creation of certain elements in the animal kingdom is described with the purpose of making man reflect upon the divine Beneficence extended to him. It is quoted basically to provide an example of the way in which the Quran describes the harmonious adaptation of Creation to man's needs; it relates in particular the case of those people who live in a rural setting, since there is nothing that could be examined from a different point of view.

> "(God) created cattle for you and (you find) in them warmth, useful services and food, sense of beauty when you bring them home and when you take them to pasture. They bear your heavy loads to lands you could not reach except with great personal effort. Verily, your Lord is Compassionate and Merciful; (He created) horses, mules and donkeys for you to ride and for ornament. And He created what you do not know." —(16:5-8)

Alongside these general remarks, the Quran sets out certain data on highly diversified subjects:

— reproduction in the animal kingdom.

— references to the existence of animal communities.

— statements concerning bees, spiders and birds.

— remarks on the source of constituents of animal milk.

The reproduction in animals is very summarily dealt with in these verses:

> "(God) fashioned the two of a pair, the male and the female, from a small quantity of liquid when it is poured out." —(53:45-46)

The 'pair' is the same expression that we have already encountered in the verses which deal with reproduction in the vegetable kingdom. Here, the sexes are given. The detail which is absolutely remarkable is the precision with which it is stated that a small quantity of liquid is required for reproduction. The word itself signifying 'sperm' is used.

Mention is made of animal communities in holy Quran, in this manner:

> "There is no animal on earth, no bird which flies on wings, that (does not belong to) communities like you. We have not neglected anything in the Book (of Decrees). Then to their Lord they will be gathered." —(6:38)

There are several points in this verse which require comment. Firstly, it would seem that there is a description of what happens to animals after their death: Islam does not apparently, have any doctrine on this point. Then there is predestination in general[1] which would seem to be mentioned here. It could be conceived as absolute predestination or relative, i.e. limited to structures and a functional organization that condition modes of behaviour: the animal acts upon various exterior impulses in terms of a particular conditioning.

Blachere states that an older commentator, such as Kazi, thought that this verse only referred to instinctive actions whereby animals worship God. Sheik Si Boubakeur Hamza, in the commentary to his translation of the Quran, speaks of "the instinct which, according to Divine Wisdom, pushes all beings to group together, so that they demand that the work of each member serve the whole group."

Animal behaviour has been closely investigated in recent decades, with the result that genuine animal communities' have been shown to exist. Of course, for a long time now the results of a group or community's work have been examined and this has led to the acceptance of a community organization. It has only been recently however, that the mechanisms which preside over this kind of organization have been discovered for certain species. The most studied and best known case is undoubtedly that of bees, to whose behaviour the name von Frisch is linked. Von Frisch, Lorenz and Tinbergen received the 1973 Nobel Prize for their work in this field.

When specialists on the nervous system wish to provide striking examples of the prodigious organization directing animal behaviour, possibly the animals referred to most frequently are bees, spiders and birds (especially migratory birds). Whatever the case, there is no doubt that these three groups constitute a model of highly evolved organization.

The fact that the text of the Quran refers to this exemplary trio in the animal kingdom is in absolute keeping with the exceptionally interesting character that each of these animals has from a scientific point of view.

In the Quran, bees are the subject of the longest commentary:

> "Thy Lord inspired the bees: Choose your dwelling in the hills, in the trees and in what (man) built. Eat of all fruit and follow the ways of your Lord in humility. From within their bodies comes a liquor of different colours where is a remedy for men." —(16:68-69)

It is difficult to know what exactly is meant by the order to follow the ways of the Lord in humility, unless it is to be seen in general terms. All that may be said, with regard to the knowledge that has been gained of their behaviour, is that here—as in each of the three animal cases mentioned as cxamples in the Quran—there is a remarkable nervous organization supporting their behaviour. It is known that the pattern of a bee's dance is a means of communication to other bees; in this way, bees are able to convey to their own species the direction and distance of flowers from which nectar is to be gathered. The famous experiment performed by von Frisch has shown the meaning of this insect's movement which is intended to transmit information between worker bees.

Spiders are mentioned in the Quran to stress the flimsiness of their dwelling which is the most fragile of all. They have a refuge that is as precarious, according to the Quran, as the dwelling of those who have chosen masters other than God.

> "Those who choose masters other than God are like the spider when it takes for itself a dwelling. Verily, the flimsiest dwelling is the dwelling of the spider. If they but knew." —(29:41)

A spider's web is indeed constituted of silken threads secreted by the animal's glands and their calibre is infinitely fine. Its fragility cannot be imitated by man. Naturalists are intrigued by the extraordinary pattern of work recorded by the animal's nervous cells, which allows it to produce a geometrically perfect web.

Birds are frequently mentioned in the Quran. They appear in episodes in the life of Abraham, Joseph, David, Solomon and Jesus. These references do not however have any bearing on the subject in hand.

The verse concerning the existence of animal communities on the ground and bird communities in the sky has been noted above:

Two other verses highlight the birds' strict submission to God's Power :

> "Do they not look at the birds subjected in the atmosphere of the sky? None can hold them up (in His Power) except God." —(16:79)
>
> "Have they not looked at the birds above them spreading their wings out and folding them? None can hold them up (in His power) except the Beneficent." —(67:19)

The translation of one single word in each of these verses is a very delicate matter. The translation given here expresses the idea that God holds the birds up in His power. The Arabic verb in question is *amsaka*, whose original meaning is 'to put one's hand on, seize, hold, hold someone back.

An illuminating comparison can be made between these verses, which stress the extremely close dependence of the birds' behavior on divine order, to modern data showing the degree of perfection attained by certain species of bird with regard to the programming of their movements. It is only the existence of a migratory programme in the genetic code of birds that can account for the extremely long and complicated journeys which very young birds, without any prior experience and without any guide, are able to accomplish. This is in addition to their ability to return to their departure point on a prescribed date. Professor Hamburger in his book, *Power and Fragilitil* (La Puissance et la Fragilite), gives as an example the well-known case of the 'mutton-bird' that lives in the Pacific, with its journey of over 15,500 miles in the shape of the figure 8. It must be acknowledged that the highly complicated instructions for a journey of this kind simply have to be contained in the bird's nervous cells. They are most definitely programmed, but who is the programmer?

The source of the constituents of animal milk is defined in the Quran in strict accordance with the data of modern knowledge.

Holy Quran says:

> "Verily, in cattle there is a lesson for you. We give you to drink of what is inside their bodies, coming from a conjunction between the contents of the intestine and the blood, a milk pure and pleasant for those who drink it." —(16:66)

This interpretation is very close to the one given in the Muntakab, 1973, edited by the Supreme Council for Islamic Affairs, Cairo, which relies for its support on modern physiology.

The notion of a 'primary origin' of the constituents of milk is expressed by the word *min* (in English 'from') and the idea of a conjunction by the word *baini*. The latter not only signifies 'among' but also 'between' in the other translations quoted. It is however also used to express the idea that two things or two people are brought together.

From a scientific point of view, physiological notions must be called upon to grasp the meaning of this verse.

The substances that ensure the general nutrition of the body come from chemical transformations which occur along the length of the digestive tract. These substances come from the contents of the intestine. On arrival in the intestine at the appropriate stage of chemical transformation, they pass through its wall and towards the systemic circulation. This passage is effected in two ways: either directly, by what are called the 'lymphatic vessels', or indirectly, by the portal circulation. This conducts them first to the liver, where they undergo alterations, and from here they then emerge to join the systemic circulation. In this way everything passes through the bloodstream.

The constituents of milk are secreted by the mammary glands. These are nourished, as it were, by the product of food digestion brought to them via the bloodstream. Blood therefore plays the role of collector and conductor of what has been extracted from food, and it brings nutrition to the mammary glands, the producers of milk, as it does to any other organ.

Here the initial process which sets everything else in motion is the bringing together of the contents of the intestine and blood at the level of the intestinal wall itself. This very precise concept is the result of the discoveries made in the chemistry and physiology of the digestive system. It was totally unknown at the time of the Prophet Muhammad and has been understood only in recent times. The discovery of the circulation of the blood, was made by Harvey roughly ten centuries after the Quranic Revelation.

I consider that the existence in the Quran of the verse referring to these concepts can have no human explanation on account of the period in which they were formulated.

Reproduction in Human Beings

From the moment ancient human writings enter into detail (however slight) on the subject of reproduction, they inevitably make statements that are inaccurate. In the Middle Ages— and even in more recent time—reproduction was surrounded by all sorts of myths and superstitions. How could it have been otherwise, considering the fact that to understand its complex mechanisms, man first had to possess a knowledge of anatomy, the discovery of the microscope had to be made, and the so-called basic sciences had to be founded which were to nurture physiology, embryology, obstetrics, etc.

The situation is quite different in the Quran. The Book mentions precise mechanisms in many places and describes clearly-defined stages in reproduction, without providing a single statement marred by inaccuracy. Everything in the Quran is explained in simple terms which are easily understandable to man and in strict accordance with what was to be discovered much later on.

Human reproduction is referred to in several dozen verses of the Quran, in various contexts. It is explained through statements which deal with one or more specific points. They must be assembled to give a general idea of the verses as a whole, and here, as for the other subjects already examined, the commentary is in this way made easier.

It is imperative to recall certain basic concepts which were unknown at the time of the Quranic Revelation and the centuries that followed.

Human reproduction is effected by a series of processes which we share in common with mammals. The starting point is the fertilization of an ovule which has detached itself from the ovary. It takes place in the Fallopian tubes half-way through the menstrual cycle. The fertilizing agent is the male sperm, or more exactly, the spermatozoon, a single fertilizing cell being all that is needed. To ensure fertilization therefore, an infinitely small quantity of spermatic liquid containing a large number of spermatozoons (tens of millions at a time) is required. This liquid is produced by the testicles and temporarily stored in a system of reservoirs and canals that finally lead into the urinary tract; other glands are situated along the latter which contribute their own additional secretions to the sperm itself.

The implantation of the egg fertilized by this process takes place at a precise spot in the female reproductive system: it descends into the uterus via a Fallopian tube and lodges in the body of the uterus where it soon literally implants itself by insertion into the thickness of the mucosa and of the muscle, once the placenta has been formed and with the aid of the latter. If the implantation of the fertilized egg takes place, for example, in the Fallopian tubes instead of in the uterus, pregnancy will be interrupted.

Once the embryo begins to be observable to the naked eye, it looks like a small mass of flesh at the centre of which the appearance of a human being is at first indistinguishable. It grows there in progressive stages which are very well known today; they lead to the bone structure, the muscles, the nervous system, the circulation, and the viscerae, etc.

These notions will serve as the terms of reference against which the statements in the Quran on reproduction are to be compared.

It is not easy to gain an idea of what the Quran contains on this subject. The first difficulty arises from the fact already mentioned, i.e. that the statements dealing with this subject are scattered throughout the book. This is not however a major difficulty. What is more likely to mislead the inquiring reader is, once again, the problem of vocabulary.

In fact there are still many translations and commentaries in circulation today that can give a completely false idea of the Quranic Revelation on this subject to the scientist who reads them. The majority of translations describe, for example, man's formation from a 'blood clot' or an 'adhesion'. A statement of this kind is totally unacceptable to scientists specializing in this field. In the paragraph dealing with the implantation of the egg in the maternal uterus, we shall see the reasons why distinguished Arabists who lack a scientific background have made such blunders.

This observation implies how great the importance of an association between linguistic and scientific knowledge is when it comes to grasping the meaning of Quranic statements on reproduction.

The Quran sets out by stressing the successive transformations the embryo undergoes before reaching its destination in the maternal uterus.

> 'O Man! Who deceives you about your Lord the Noble, Who created you and fashioned you in due proportion and gave you any form He willed." —(82:6-8)
>
> "(God) fashioned you in (different) stages." —(71:14)

Along with this very general observation, the text of the Quran draws attention to several points concerning reproduction which might be listed as follows:

(1) fertilization is performed by only a very small volume of liquid.
(2) the constituents of the fertilizing liquid.
(3) the implantation of the fertilized egg.
(4) the evolution of the embryo.

The Quran repeats this concept eleven times using the following expression:

> "(God) fashioned man from a small quantity (of sperm.)."
>
> The Arabic word *nutfa* has been translated by the words 'small quantity (of sperm)' because we do not have the terms that are strictly appropriate. This word comes from a verb signifying 'to dribble, to trickle'; it is used to describe what remains at the bottom of a bucket that has been emptied out. It therefore indicates a very small quantity of liquid. Here it is sperm because the word is associated in another verse with the word sperm. —(16:4)
>
> "Was (man) not a small quantity of sperm which has been poured out?" —(75:37)

Here the Arabic word *mani* signifies sperm.

Another verse indicates that the small quantity in question is put in a 'firmly established lodging' (*qarar*) which obviously means the genital organs.

God is speaking:

> "Then We placed (man) as a small quantity (of sperm) in a safe lodging firmly established." —(23:13)

It must be added that the adjective which in this text refers to the 'firmly established lodging' *makin* is, I think, hardly translatable. It expresses the idea of a firmly established and respected place. However this may be, it refers to the spot where man grows in the maternal organism. It is important to stress the concept of a very small quantity of liquid needed in the fertilization process, which is strictly in agreement with what we know on this subject today.

The Quran describes the liquid enabling fertilization to take place in terms which it is interesting to examine:

(a) 'sperm', as has been stated precisely (sura 75, verse 37)

(b) 'a liquid poured out': "Man was fashioned from a liquid poured out" (sura 86, verse 6)

(c) 'a despised liquid' (sura 32, verse 8 and sura 77, verse 20) The adjective 'despised' (*mahin*) would, it seems, be interpreted not so much on account of the nature of the liquid itself, as more the fact that it is emitted through the outlet of the urinary tract, using the channels that are employed for passing urine.

(d) 'Mixtures' or 'mingled liquids' (*amsaj*): "Verily, we fashioned man from a small quantity of mingled liquids" (sura 76, verse 2)

Many commentators, like professor Hamidullah, consider these liquids to be the male and female agents. The same view was shared by older commentators, who could not have had any idea of the physiology of fertilization, especially its biological conditions in the case of the woman. They thought that the word simply meant the unification of the two elements.

Modern authors however, like the commentator of the *Muntakab* edited by the Supreme Council for Islamic Affairs, Cairo, have corrected this view and note here that the 'small quantity of sperm' is made up of various component parts. The commentator in the Muntakab does not go into detail, but in my opinion it is a very judicious observation.

What are the component parts of sperm?

Spermatic liquid is formed by various secretions which come from the following glands:

(a) the testicles: the secretion of the male genital gland contains spermatozoons, which are elongated cells with a long flagellum; they are bathed in a sero-fluid liquid.
(b) the seminal vesicles: these organs are reservoirs of spermatozoons and are placed near the prostate gland; they also secrete their own liquid but it does not contain any fertilizing agents.
(c) the prostate gland: this secretes a liquid which gives the sperm its creamy texture and characteristic odour.
(d) the glands annexed to the urinary tract: Cooper's or Mery's glands secrete a stringy liquid and Littre's glands give off mucous.

These are the origins of the 'mingled liquids' which the Quran would appear to refer to.

There is, however, more to be said on this subject. When the Quran talks of a fertilizing liquid composed of different components, it also informs us that man's progeny will be maintained by something which may be extracted from this liquid. This is the meaning of verse 8, sura 32:

"(God) made his progeny from the quintessence of a despised liquid."

The Arabic word, translated here by the word 'quintessence', is *sulala*. It signifies 'something which is extracted, the issue of something else, the best part of a thing'. In whatever way it is translated, it refers to a part of a whole.

Fertilization of the egg and reproduction are produced by a cell that is very elongated: its dimensions are measured in ten-thousandths of a millimetre. In normal conditions, only one single cell among several tens of millions produced by a man will actually penetrate the ovule; a large number of them are left behind and never complete the journey which leads from the vagina to the ovule, passing through the uterus and Fallopian tubes. It is therefore an infinitesimally small part of the extract from a liquid whose composition is highly complex which actually fulfills its function.

In consequence, it is difficult not to be struck by the agreement between the text of the Quraṅ and the scientific knowledge we possess today of these phenomena.

Once the egg has been fertilized in the Fallopian tube it descends to lodge inside the uterus; this is called the 'implantation of the egg'. The Quran names the lodging of the fertilized egg womb:

> "We cause whom We[2] will to rest in the womb for an appointed term." —(22:5)

The implantation of the egg in the uterus (womb) is the result of the development of villosities, veritable elongations of the egg, which, like roots in the soil, draw nourishment from the thickness of the uterus necessary to the egg's growth. These formations make the egg literally cling to the uterus. This is a discovery of modern times.

The act of clinging is described five different times in the Quran. Firstly in verses 1 and 2 of sura 96:

> "Read, in the name of thy Lord Who fashioned man from something which clings."

'Something which clings' is the translation of the word '*alaq*. It is the original meaning of the word. A meaning derived from it, 'blood clot', often figures in translation; it is a mistake against which one should guard: man has never passed through the stage of being a 'blood clot'. The same is true for another translation of this term, 'adhesion' which is equally inappropriate. The original sense of 'something which clings' corresponds exactly to today's firmly established reality.

This concept is recalled in four other verses which describe successive transformations from the small quantity of sperm through to the end:

> "We have fashioned you from . . . something which clings." —(22:5)
>
> "We have fashioned the small quantity (of sperm) into something which clings." —(23:14)
>
> "(God) fashioned you from a small quantity (of sperm), from something which clings." —(40:67)
>
> "Was (man) not a small quantity of sperm which has been poured out? After that he was something which clings; then God fashioned him in due proportion." —(75:37-38)

The organ which harbours the pregnancy is qualified in the Quran by a word which, as we have seen, is still used in Arabic to signify the uterus. In some suras, it is called a 'lodging firmly established' (sura 23, verse 13, quoted above and sura 77, verse 21).

The Quranic. description of certain stages in the development of the embryo corresponds exactly to what we today know about it, and the Quran does not contain a single statement that is open to criticism from modern science.

After 'the thing which clings' (an expression which is well-founded, as we have seen) the Quran informs us that the embryo passes through the stage of 'chewed flesh', then osseous tissue appears and is clad in flesh (defined by a different word from the preceding which signifies 'intact flesh').

> "We fashioned the thing which clings into a chewed lump of flesh and We fashioned the chewed flesh into bones and We clothed the bones with intact flesh." —(23:14)

'Chewed flesh' is the translation of the word *mudga*; 'intact flesh' is *lahm*. This distinction needs to be stressed. The embryo is initially a small mass. At a certain stage in its development, it looks to the naked eye like chewed flesh. The bone structure develops inside this mass in what is called the mesenchyma. The bones that are formed are covered in muscle; the word *lahm* applies to them.

It is known how certain parts appear to be completely out of proportion during embryonic development with what is later to become the individual, while others remain in proportion.

This is surely the meaning of the word *mukallaq* which signifies 'shaped in proportion' as used in the following verse:

> "We fashioned . .. into something which clings . . . into a lump of flesh in proportion and out of proportion."
>
> —(5:22)

The Quran also describes the appearance of the senses and the viscerae:

> "(God) appointed for you the sense of hearing, sight and the viscerae." —(32:9)

It refers to the formation of the sexual organs:

> "(God) fashioned the two of a pair, the male and the female, from a small quantity (of sperm) when it is poured out." —(53:45-46)

The formation of the sexual organs is described in two sura of the Qur'an:

> "God created you from dust, then from a sperm-drop, then He made you pairs (the male and female)."
>
> —(35:11)
>
> "And, (God) made of him a pair, the male and female."
>
> —(75:39)

As has already been noted, all statements in the Quran must be compared with today's firmly established concepts: the agreement between them is very clear. It is however very important to compare them with the general beliefs on this subject that were held at the time of the Quranic Revelation in order to realize just how far people were in those days from having views on these problems similar to those expressed here in the Quran. There can be no doubt that they would have been unable to interpret the Revelation in the way we can today because we are helped by the data modern knowledge affords us. It was, in fact, only during the Nineteenth century that people had a slightly clearer view of this question.

Throughout the Middle Ages, the most diversified doctrines originated in unfounded myths and speculations: they persisted for several centuries after this period. The most fundamental stage in the history of embryology was Harvey's statement (1651) that "all life initially comes from an egg". At this time however, when nascent science had nevertheless benefited greatly (for the subject in hand) from the invention of the microscope, people were still talking about the respective roles of the egg and the spermatozoon. Buffon, the great naturalist, was one of those in favor of the egg theory, but Bonnet supported the theory of the seeds being 'packed together': the ovaries of Eve, the mother of the human race, were supposed to have contained the seeds of all human beings, packed together one inside the other. This hypothesis came into favor in the Eighteenth century.

More than a thousand years before our time, at a period when whimsical doctrines still prevailed, men had a knowledge of the Quran. The statements it contains express in simple terms truths of primordial importance which man has taken centuries to discover.

On Sex Education

Our epoch believes that it has made manifold discoveries in all possible fields. It is thought that great innovations have been made in the field of sex education, and the knowledge of the facts of life which has been opened up to young people is regarded as an achievement of the modern world. Previous centuries were noted for their deliberate obscurity on this point and many people say that religion—without stating which religion—is the cause of it.

The information set out above is proof however that fourteen centuries ago theoretical questions (as it were) on human reproduction were brought to man's attention. This was done as far as was possible, taking into account the fact that the anatomical and physiological data needed for further explanations were lacking. One should also remember that, to be understood, it was necessary to use simple language suited to the level of comprehension of those who listened to the Preaching.

Practical considerations have not been silently ignored. There are many details in the Quran on the practical side of life in general, and the way man should behave in the many situations of his existence. His sex life is no exception.

Two verses in the Quran deal with sexual relations themselves. They are described in terms which unite the need for precision with that of decency. When translations and explanatory commentaries are consulted however, one is struck by the divergences between them. I have pondered for a long time on the translation of such verses, and am indebted to Doctor A. K. Giraud, Former Professor at the Faculty of Medicine, Beirut, for the following:

> "(Man) was fashioned from a liquid poured out. It issued (as a result) of the conjunction of the sexual area of the man and the sexual area of the woman." —(86:6-7)

The sexual area of the man is indicated in the text of the Quran by the world *sulb* (singular). The sexual areas of the woman are designated in the Quran by the word *tara'ib* (plural).

This is the translation which appears to be most satisfactory. It is different from the one that is often given by English and French translators, i.e. "(Man) has been created by a liquid poured out which issues from between the vertebral column and the bones of the breast." This would seem more to be an interpretation than a translation. It is hardly comprehensible.

The behavior of a man in his intimate relationships with his wife is stated explicitly.

There is the order concerning the menstruation period contained in following verses. God gives the following command to the Prophet:

> "They (the Believers) question thee concerning menstruation. Say: This is an evil. Keep away from women during menstruation and do not approach them until they are clean. When they have purified themselves, go to them, as God ordered it to you.
>
> "Verily, God loves the repentants and loves those who purified themselves.
>
> "Your wives are a tilth. Go to your tilth as you will. Do (some good act) for your souls beforehand."
>
> —(2:222-223)

The beginning of this passage is very clear in meaning: it formally forbids a man to have sexual contact with a woman who has her period. The second part describes the process of tilling which the sower performs before sowing the seed which is to germinate and produce a new plant. Through this image therefore, stress is indirectly laid on the importance of bearing in mind the final purpose of sexual contact, i.e. reproduction. The translation of the final phrase is by R. Blachere: it contains an order which seems to refer to the preliminaries before sexual contact.

The orders given here are of a very general kind. The problem of contraception has been raised with regard to these verses : neither here, nor anywhere else, is reference made to this subject.

Nor is provoked abortion referred to. The numerous passages quoted above on the successive transformations of the embryo make it quite clear, however, that man is considered to be constituted as of the stage described by the existence of 'something which clings. This being so, the absolute respect of the individual human being, which is referred to so often in the Quran, brings with it a total condemnation of provoked abortion. This attitude is today shared by all monotheistic religions.

Sexual relations are permitted at night during the Fast in the month of Ramadan. The verse concerning Ramadan is as follows:

> "Permitted to you, on the night of the fast, is to break chastity with your wives. They are a garment for you and you are a garment for them. So hold intercourse with them and seek what God has ordained for you."
>
> —(2:187)

In contrast to this, no exception to the rule is made for pilgrims in Makka during the celebration days of the Pilgrimage.

> "For whom undertakes (the duty of) the Pilgrimage in its time, no wooing and no license." —(2:197)

This prohibition is formal, as is the fact that other activities are forbidden, e.g. hunting, fighting, etc.

Menstruation is again mentioned in the Quran in connection with divorce. The Book contains the following verse:

> "For your wives who despair of menstruation, if you doubt about them, their period of waiting will be three months. For those who never have their monthly periods and those who are pregnant their period will be until they lay down their burden." —(65:4)

The waiting period referred to here is the time between the announcement of the divorce and the time it comes into effect. Those women of whom it is said 'they despair of menstruation have reached the menopause. A precautionary period of three months is envisaged for them. Once this period is completed, divorced women who have reached the menopause may remarry.

For those who have not yet menstruated, the pregnancy period has to be awaited. For pregnant women, divorce only comes into effect once the child is born.

All these laws are in perfect agreement with physiological data. One can, furthermore, find in the Quran the same judicious legal provision in the texts dealing with widowhood.

Thus, the theoretical statements dealing with reproduction, and the practical instructions on the sex life of couples, do not contradict and cannot be placed in opposition to the data we have from modern knowledge, nor with anything that can be logically derived from it.

FIVE

Greek Sciences Transferred to Arabs

Conquest of Syria

A map of the physical features of Western Asia and North-East Africa shows two important river valleys, one of the Tigris and Euphrates, the other of the Nile, and between them high ground, broken rather abruptly by the Red Sea. These conditions are due to geological changes with which we are not at present directly concerned: we start from a point when the two great river valleys already existed, with a good deal of barren highland between. Those two valleys were the homes of two primitive civilizations, which was the earlier is still not decided. In both cases the rivers concerned overflowed and flooded the surrounding country regularly every year, and the particular river-valley culture which grew up there was based on the artificial control of these regular inundations, draining the swamps and directing the water so as to fertilize the fields. It is commonly assumed that in primitive society land was held in common, each member of the tribe entitled to his share, but not to permanent ownership of any particular piece. Whether this is universally true is disputed, probably it does apply so long as tribes are nomadic. But in the river-valley culture of Mesopotamia and Egypt the productivity of each field depended a great deal on human labour, irrigating and draining the land, so that private ownership developed at a fairly early date and population became stationary. The people of the barren highlands between the river valleys remained nomads, not recognizing the rights of private property and in all respects at a much more primitive stage of social evolution than the settled inhabitants of the valleys. The life of those nomads was hard and bare, it generally was, and still is, on the border of starvation ; there always was a temptation for those nomads to raid the fertile and productive settlements, and when their numbers became too great to be able to make a living out of the meagre resources of the desert highlands, they tended to overflow into the valleys. Thus all through ancient history the kingdoms of Assyria, Babylonia, and Egypt found their nomadic neighbours a perpetual nuisance, and it was always necessary to provide for the protection of the frontiers, those frontiers being the precise level at which it ceased to be practicable to raise the water from the rivers to irrigate and fertilize the land. Whenever military power so far decreased as to make the guardianship of the frontiers insufficient to protect the settled country from Arab raiders, then Arabs came down to raid the country, then to settle in the rich and productive territory and reap the benefits of a cultivation at others' expense, usually subjugating and sometimes enslaving the unwarlike population already settled there.

Such a raiding and settlement took place towards the end of the seventh century A.D., when the raiding Arabs were united in a religious fraternity based on the religion taught by the Prophet Muhammad (PBUH). It does not seem that Muhammad himself had any project of foreign conquest, but such conquest followed because the people of the area invaded were exhausted by prolonged warfare, distracted by internal divisions, and disaffected by harsh government, though some of that harshness was the inevitable result of war conditions. The success of their expeditions seems to have surprised the Arabs and encouraged them to undertake the permanent occupation of the countries they had conquered. They had not the least desire to cultivate the soil or settle down to agricultural work, their idea was to establish a military occupation and live on the fruits of the toil of the native inhabitants. In this they were, no doubt, influenced by the precedent of the Arabs stationed along the Persian and Roman frontiers, On both those frontiers it had been found impossible to dislodge the Arab tribes and both countries tried the same solution, permitting the tribesmen to settle there and paying them a subsidy on condition that they guarded the frontier against any other Arabs who tried to invade the Persian or Roman territories. The Arabs already settled and paid were greatly envied by the hungry nomads of the desert, their existence seemed an ideal one, and when they conquered the eastern provinces of the Roman Empire and the kingdom of Persia they counted on living a similar kind of life, occupied in hunting and occasional warfare and supported by the tribute paid them by the conquered population. Nor were the conquered people unwilling to toil and pay tribute, as they were to be disarmed and freed from the hated military service which was the task they most disliked.

It is a debated point whether Muhammad intended his religion to be a universal one, or for the Arabs alone. Quran 34, 27, says, " We have sent thee to mankind at large, to announce and threaten." But the context shows that this refers to the Prophet warning men of the approaching end of the world and is itself one of the signs that the end is near, and is thus interpreted by tradition (Bukhari, Sahih, i, 93, 43, d. i : Muslim, Sahih, i, 53, 55). It is necessary for all Arabs to believe in Muhammad if they are to escape hell (Muslim, i, 54), but it is not stated to be necessary for non-Arabs to believe, though those who join gods to God, that is to say, arc polytheists, are doomed to hell in any case. As regards the non-Arab world, the Quran seems to contemplate conquest rather than conversion (Qur., ix, 19-23). One passage in the Quran says, " and one day We will summon up in every people a witness against them from themselves : and We will bring thee (Muhammad) up as a witness against them : for to thee We have sent down the book which makes all things clear, a guidance and a mercy, and glad tidings to those who reconcile themselves with God " (Qur., 18, 91). In another place the Quran says, " thus We have made you a central people that ye may be witnesses in regard to mankind, and that the Apostle (Muhammad) may be a witness in regard to you" (Qur., 2, 137). But these passages fall far short of a definite missionary command to go forth and preach Islam to all the nations of the earth.

In the later years of his ministry Muhammad preached his religion to all the Arabs and endeavoured to unite the tribes in one confederacy. " Fight until there is no more civil discord and no worship save that of God" (Qur., 2, 189) : " fight against those who oppose you, but do not attack first " (Qur., 2, 186), "kill and expel them" (Qur., 2, 187) : "when the sacred month is over slay the polytheists, but spare the pagan Arabs who are in league with you"

(Qur., 9, 1-4), but these commands were preparatory to the reduction and unification of Arabia. They find their best explanation in Muhammad's own conduct, for he strove hard to draw all the Arabs into his fold, though tolerating those who were " people of the book ", i.e. Christians or Jews. His attitude was endorsed by the policy of the early khalifs, men who had been his intimate companions and trained by him, men who knew his outlook as no others could, and they for some time insisted on all converts to the religion of Islam also becoming members of an Arab tribe. Much weight must be attached to the expressed reluctance of the older Muslims to spread wider into the outside world lest the multitude of strangers brought in as converts might outnumber the native Arabs, by their influence changing the character of their religion and mode of life, apprehensions which subsequent events showed were justified.

The traditional and legendary biography of Muhammad attributed to Ibn Ishaq and known to us in an edition expurgated by Ibn Hisham represents him as sending letters to foreign monarchs, the King of Persia, the Roman Emperor, and others, inviting them to become Muslims, but that biography was composed in its earliest form about a century after Muhammad and contains a great deal which cannot be regarded as historical.

There can be no question that Muhammad intended to include all the Arabs in the brotherhood of Islam. Those Arabs were the inhabitants of Arabia, not quite the artificial Arabia marked on the atlas, but all the desert highlands of Western Asia, spreading up into a tongue in Syria. In that northern area, between the two great monarchies of Parthia-Persia and Rome were the two groups of border tribes subsidized by the monarchies and to some extent settled and civilized. Muhammad was very anxious to draw these border tribes into his fraternity. The Arabs along the Persian frontier had some grievances against Persia and joined the Muslims, but threw off their allegiance as soon as Muhammad was dead. In order to gain the Arabs of the Syrian (Roman) frontier Muhammad sent an envoy to invite them to embrace Islam, but that envoy was killed at Bosra, a crime against the Arab tradition of the sacred character of an ambassador. So an army was sent under Zayd to avenge this. But the border Arabs being in Roman employ obtained the help of Roman legionaries and defeated the Arabs. For some time no further action could be taken as the Arabs were busily engaged elsewhere, but in 632 an army was assembled and preparations were made to invade Syria. But Muhammad died whilst the expedition was waiting to set out. Then Abu Bakr was appointed khalif or " successor " and ordered the army to set out. After forty days it returned laden with booty, so there was no difficulty in raising new forces. In 634 these forces invaded Syria, where they met small resistance, and that only from an ill-trained local militia. No one as yet supposed that the Arabs were venturing on more than an ordinary raid, nor do the Arabs themselves seem to have thought that they had undertaken more than that.

Certainly these Arabs were not fanatics who tried to force their religion on the conquered : they preferred them to remain toilers as before and themselves to live on the produce of their labour. Such was the system laid down in the "Constitution of Umar", an apocryphal production of later date, but indicating in general outline what was the earlier Arab policy. The picture sometimes given of a host of fanatical Arabs rushing forward with a sword in one hand, a Quran in the other, and forcing people to turn Muslims or be killed is very far from the fact. The cynical Arab is not inclined to be a fanatic. There have been plenty of fanatical Muslims, but they were not Arabs but converts of other races who were converted to Islam at a later date. The Arabs did not force the people they conquered to embrace their religion, they left the conquered population to follow their own religion, laws, customs, and use their own languages. They were to be tribute producing and the Arab ideal was to live at ease on the product of their labour.

In Syria, which was of primary importance because in 661 the khalif with his court and government settled in Damascus where they remained for more than eighty years, the Arabs found themselves rulers of an area which had been a Roman province subject to the fully developed Roman law and with a highly organised administration. This they took over as it was. Any Roman official who wished to remain under Roman rule were given every facility to remove to some part which still remained Roman. Many did so remove, but many others were content to live under Arab rule, and of these numbers rose to high office and dignity in the Muslim state. For the first twenty years or more the records continued to be kept in Greek, and the civil service was almost exclusively Christian. There already were a number of Arab tribes settled along the border, they had been subsidized by the Byzantine government as defenders of the frontier, and these were Christians. As old established settlers they had become wealthy and considered themselves socially superior to the Muslim invaders, poor hungry nomads of the desert, and had no hesitation in asserting themselves, the Muslim Arabs admitting their claims to aristocratic status. Some of the ruling dynasty married women of these Christian tribes, and that was rather resented by the Muslims. Under the khalif 'Abd al-Malik (685-705) there was a good deal of jealousy because the Christians had a monopoly of all the posts in the civil administration, and the khalif tried to employ Arabs in their place. But the change was not successful, the Arabs did not understand the details of business and the Christian officials had to be restored. This is easy to understand because the oriental practice is, not to draw up accounts so that an outside auditor can understand and check them, but to keep them in such a way that nobody but the established officials can possibly understand them : it is done deliberately so that the established officials may keep the business in their own hands and secure a permanent monopoly. The most that 'Abd al-Malik could do was to get the records kept in Arabic instead of Greek, and to use Arabic on the coinage. Bishop Arculf of Gaul made a tour of the Holy Land in about 700 A.D. and speaks with much appreciation of the hospitable way he was received by the Muslim rulers, the freedom with which he was allowed to travel about, and the generally friendly attitude of the Arabs and their rulers. Until the days of the Crusades, Syria and Egypt were practically Christian lands under the rule of the Muslim Arabs, their rule mainly confined to the collection of taxes, and that they did very thoroughly.

In the earlier period of the 'Umayyad khalifate at Damascus there was even a fashionable tendency to deride Islamic ways and customs. This is well illustrated by the poetry of Abu Malik Ghiyath ibn Salt ibn Tariqa al-Akhtal, who was born at Hira about 640 and died about 710. He belonged to the Taghlib clan of the Jusham ibn Bakr tribe and lived and died a Monophysite Christian. His poems refer to St. Sergius, the Holy'Cross, to monks, and he uses Christian oaths, though there are very few direct references to Christianity in his Diwan. He refused to change his religion (Diwan, p. 154), and derided those whom he described as becoming Muslims by pressure of hunger rather than by conviction (ibid., 315). He composed poems in honour of Yazid, the son of the khalif Mu'awiya, 'his brother 'Abdallah, and others of the royal family. He was formally recognized as poet laureate by 'Abd al-Malik, whom he celebrated as well as his relations and derided their enemies, a real courtier. In his poems there appears evidence of the survival of ancient pagan Arab usages in the days of the Umayyads, and some striking instances of the tolerant attitude of that dynasty. Many of his verses contain biting sarcasms on Islam, and such passages have prevented many Muslims from full appreciation of his poetic merits, but in his times he and his rival Jarir were the leading poets of the Arabs. He particularly expresses his contempt for all those who abandoned their ancestral religion, Christian or pagan, to conform with that of the reigning monarch. The most admired passage in his works is his panegyric of the Umayyads (Diwan, 98-112). In spite of his contemptuous attitude towards Islam this poet was patronized by the khalif 'Abd al-Malik, though not greatly favoured by his successor Walid I. He probably died before the end of Walid's reign, though Ibn 'Abd Rabbihi prolongs his life to the reign of Umar II. Probably his death should be dated about 710 A.D.

A loose tone about religion prevailed at the Umayyad court, which did not find favour with the stricter Muslims, and it was one of the causes of the hostile atmosphere and Umayyad feeling which grew in intensity until it led to the downfall of the dynasty. The old tribal rivalries of pre-Muslim days still influenced the Arabs, and there was a deep-rooted antagonism between the worldly tone of Damascus, and the cities of Mecca an,d Medina, and the more orthodox attitude of those who regarded themselves as Muslims in the first place, and Arabs only in a secondary place. The only exception to this among the Umayyad khalifs was Walid I (705-715), who was a really religious man and put the interests of Islam before political or racial considerations. At the other extreme Yazid I (680-683) is still cursed by the orthodox as an enemy of religion. It was an army sent by him which engaged in the battle of Kerbela (10th October, 680), and was responsible for the tragic death of al-Husayn, the surviving son of Ali the Prophet's son-in-law. And it was an army sent by him which besieged the holy city of Mecca and (accidentally) burned the sanctuary of the Ka'ba (November, 683).

Damascus, the official capital of Syria, was a partly Greek city, not so thoroughly Hellenized as Antioch. It was the seat of Christian Bishops who ranked next after the patriarchs of Antioch in the ecclesiastical hierarchy of Syria : it possessed a school which, though not equal to those of Alexandria and Antioch, yet had attained considerable eminence by the time of the Arab conquest, and retained its good repute after that event. Amongst its alumni were the theologian Sophronius, who became Bishop of Jerusalem (634-38), and Andrew of Crete (circ. 650-720), who studied there after the Arab conquest, became a monk in Jerusalem, and finally Bishop of Crete. The Arabic historians say that at the time of the conquest the financial agent of the Roman government in the city was Sergius (Sarjun) who was responsible for making terms with the invaders, on which account Eutychius calls him a traitor. But the citizens, deserted by the government, had no choice in the matter and it is probable that everyone supposed that the Arab attack was no more than a raid on a large scale and that after plundering the town the Arabs would go back again to the desert. The governor of such a city normally was a financial agent whose duty it was to raise the imperial taxes and commonly bore the honorary title of Patricius which had been granted to all superior officials by Constantine. He had been appointed by the Emperor Heraclius, but like many other officials continued in office after the Arab conquest under Mu'awiya, when he was governor of the province, and remained when Mu'awiya became khalif. Finally he acted as minister of finance for the whole Islamic state and paymaster-in-chief of the Arab army. Yet he remained a Christian, and long after becoming minister of finance built a Christian church. His son was treasurer under 'Abd al-Malik, and his grandson was chief minister under some of the later khalifs. The office and title of Wazir had not yet come into existence.

It is said that the second member of this family purchased a slave named Cosmas, a monk who had been captured by the Arabs during a raid on Italy, and employed him as tutor to his son John. When Cosmas had taught him all that he could he begged permission to retire to a monastery, and on obtaining leave he went to the Laura of St. Sahas, near Jerusalem. The author of this John's biography was John of Jerusalem who lived in the tenth century, a good while after the events he records, and like many hagiographers of the time used freely matter which would now be regarded as legendary, but the main lines of John's life seem to be reliable. It appears that this John was the son of Sergius, afterwards known as St. John of Damascus, son of an important official in the Arab state, was himself attached to the court and acted as " chief adviser " to the khalif, probably Hisham (724-743). After serving the khalif for some years John asked leave to resign, and followed his tutor to the Laura of St. Sabas where, after a period of rigorous discipline, he was ordained to the priesthood some time before 735. He died before 743. To him is due the earliest treatise on the controversy between Christianity and Islam, the "*Disputatio Christiani et Saraceni*" which is printed in Migne's Patrologia Graeca, xcvi, 1335-1363. This work shows that there was great freedom of religious discussion in eighth-century Damascus, and that Christians were permitted to criticize the established religion very freely. The text says, " When the Saracen says. . . . You reply. . . ." John gives proof of a good knowledge of the Quran and familiarity with Muslim ritual and doctrine. The identification of St. John of Damascus with the son of Sarjun ibn Mansur was first made by William of Tripoli.

Theodorus Abucara (d. 826) was St. John's pupil, and he also left works on the controversy with Islam. Obviously there was unrestrained intercourse between the two religions and no reluctance was felt about discussing religious differences quite freely. It may reasonably be supposed that such intercourse introduced the Muslims of Damascus to a general knowledge of Christian theology and philosophy, and within the next following generations ideas and problems suggested by Greek philosophy appear affecting Muslim thought.

A parallel infiltration of Greek thought took place in jurisprudence so that the earliest speculations of the Muslim jurists are tinctured by theories gathered from the Roman law which itself contains elements gathered from Stoic philosophy, and thus Greek philosophical teaching was passed on to the Arabs through a legal medium. Roman law at the time of the Arab conquest circulated in the eastern provinces in Greek, and slightly modified by local conditions, but it contained the Stoic principles which the lawyers of Rome had drawn from Greek sources. Prominent among these philosophical-legal theories was the doctrine that man has an innate sense of what is just and right, of what the Stoics called the Law of Nature. This was also assumed by the early Muslim jurists who appealed to "opinion" to supplement and even to supplant the written law when cases arose for which no provision had been made. Here, however, it is to be noted that the earlier indications of this Stoic doctrine appear, not in Syria where the Roman law was established, but in Iraq, and especially at Basra. That the Arabs were first brought into contact with Roman law in Syria and Egypt is certain. They had conquered those provinces and found there a complicated system of land tenure, contractual law, and commercial legislation dealing with things of which the simple nomads of the desert had no previous knowledge. Much of this they adopted, indeed such adoption was inevitable, and it henceforth was incorporated in Muslim law. It is true that there are some branches of law which had already been incorporated in Jewish law, and those may have come through a Jewish medium to the Arabs, but it is more probable that most of the law dealing with land tenure, contract, usufruct, inheritance, and certain other matters came direct from the customary law already prevalent in Syria and Egypt when the Arabs conquered those lands, and that established law which they found there was the Roman law.

In the parallel case of theology it may be noted,

(i) One of the earliest theological problems faced by the Muslims was that of the eternity of the Quran. The older doctrine was that it was eternal, co-eternal with God. Then the problem arose, if this were so, then God is not the one source and creator of all things, for there must have been an uncreated Quran, like a second god, side by side with the One. This was hotly debated. The sect of the Mu'tazilites held that the Quran was created by God and, as the author must precede the work produced, the Quran must be less eternal than God. The orthodox maintained that the Quran is co-eternal with God, though the words in which it is expressed, like the paper on which it is written, may be created and so not eternal with God. Ultimately the orthodox opinion prevailed and the Mu'tazilites became extinct, for those who now call themselves by that name in India are modernists of recent date, in no way connected with the old Mu'tazilites. The point is that in the discussions between the Mu'tazilites and those who adhered to the orthodox theory very much the same arguments are used as were employed in the Arjan controversy in the Christian Church, much of this repeated in the writings of St. John of Damascus. In Christian theology the term " Word " was used as a mystical name for Christ, as it was used by St. John in the fourth gospel, whilst the Muslims used the same term to denote the written word in the Quran, but in general the arguments are the same. It is difficult to avoid the conclusion that the problem involved was suggested to the Muslims by Christian theology, the teaching of St. John of Damascus, or some other.

(2) Another early problem concerned the freedom of the will. If God is almighty, then everything is overruled and directed by him. Therefore man has no freedom. But Greek ethics assumes that man is responsible only when he has free choice, and the Quran gives commands and prohibitions in such a way as to imply that man has such a choice. The Mu'tazilites argued that as God is just, he will only punish men when they have been free to choose and have chosen wrong. From this and the preceding point the Mu'tazilites called themselves " the People of Unity and Justice ", of unity because admitting only One Creator, One Source, and so asserting that the Qur'an is created, and of justice as defending the freedom of the will as necessary for man's responsibility.

(3) A third problem concerns the qualities of God. God as the sole source of all that is must be a unity, not compounded : so God has no qualities or accidents, he is himself essence. The only attributes that can be predicated of God are negative, that he is eternal or having no beginning or end, that he is infinite as having no limitations, and so on. This, however, seems to be contrary to the Quran which does apply qualificative adjectives to God. The orthodox opinion is that these attributes given in the Quran may be applied to God because they are so applied, but they do not convey the same meaning

as they would if applied to men, nor do we know what they imply. This was already taught by Plotinus and other neo-Platonists, and it would seem that the problem and its solution was borrowed by the Arabs from them.

At first sight it seems that these traces of Greek influence on Arab thought most likely connect with Syria where Arabs and Christians had very free intercourse ; but the first traces of that influence appear in Mesopotamia towards the middle of the eighth century. Greek influence may have been applied at more than one point, or may have spread from one area to another. It must be admitted that we have very little evidence of philosophical or theological speculation in Syria under the Umayyad dynasty, the dynasty which began with Mu'awiya : such matters seem to have made little appeal to Arab interest at that period. The beginnings of speculative thought in philosophy and theology and of interest in scientific research arose in Mesopotamia, and more especially in Basra, to a less degree in Kufa. These two cities were in the area where were the ancient cities of Hira and Jundi-Shapur, and it is quite possible that a general influence due to intercourse between Muslims and Christians had been engendered before the direct transmission of Greek science from Jundi-Shapur to the Muslim community had commenced.

After their first outspread and contact with the Roman and Persian armies, the Arabs set themselves to learn the methods of warfare used by the Romans, realizing that something different was now required from the rapid raids and retreats which had sufficed for desert warfare. The Byzantine writer, the Emperor Leo Tacticus, describes the Arabs as imitating the order and discipline of the Roman army in all details. And that was natural, for the most influential Arabs under the Umayyads were those of the Syrian border who had been trained as auxiliary Roman forces. At the same time it must be admitted that the Persians also had already endeavoured to copy Roman military methods. One of the new forms of warfare was the use of engineering for besieging fortified cities and for constructing fortifications for their own defence. For this latter purpose they imitated the rectangular fortified camp characteristic of Roman military methods. In each conquered area they planted such camp cities, often on ill-chosen sites. In Palestine the chief such camp city was Jabia, in Egypt it was Fustat, in Ifriqiya, Qairawan. But none of these were of so great importance as the two camp cities in Iraq—Basra founded by 'Utba ibn 'Azwan in 635 or 637, and Kufa founded by Sa'd ibn Waqqas a little later. These played a very leading part in the history of Islam.

When the Umayyads seemed to be secularized and indifferent to religion, and their laxity spread, as it did, to Medina and Mecca, many of the stricter Muslims were greatly discouraged and removed from those places such as Medina and went out to one or other of the Iraqian camp cities, which thereby became the homes of orthodoxy and incidentally of resistance to a khalifate commonly regarded as disloyal to religion.

The intellectual life and interests of Basra and Kufa were directed by religion and centred in Quran study and theological sciences more or less connected with the Quran. At first these sciences were chiefly those concerned with the Quran text and that especially meant grammar and lexicography, but later on opened out so as to include jurisprudence, tradition, and philosophy, all to a great extent directed and tinctured by ideas gained from Greek studies. Greek authorities were not used or read, but there are clear indications that their substance had filtered through and at Basra and Kufa impinged on Arabic culture far more than was the case in Damascus. It must not be overlooked that Hira, the great Nestorian stronghold, was not far from Basra and a good deal of its population drifted to the camp city.

Grammatical and literary studies began at Basra with Abu l-Aswad ad-Du'ali, the friend and confidant of the Prophet's son-in-law, 'Ali. It naturally happened that many of the people of Iraq who had learned Arabic only late in life when they were converted to Islam committed many solecisms in reading the text of the Quran, and these errors distressed Ali. So he appealed to ad-Du'ali to draw up some rules for the guidance of those who were not well used to the use of the only language permitted for prayer and reading the revealed word. But ad-Du'ali was prevented from carrying out this command by 'Ali's murder on 21st January, 661, and he was reluctant to take any steps to assist the governor Ziyad ibn Abihi whom he regarded with disapproval because he, after serving Ali, had transferred his services to the Umayyad usurper Mu'awiya. Though Ziyad renewed Ali's request ad-Du'ali held back and did nothing. Then one day he heard a reader mispronounce two vowels in the text of Qur., 9, 3, so as to pervert the sense from " God is free from (the covenant of) the idolaters, and His Apostle (also is free) " into " God is free from (the covenant of) the idolaters and (from the covenant of) His Apostle ", and this misrepresentation of the inspired word so shocked him that he forthwith began to devise methods to prevent similar errors. For this purpose he introduced vowel points into the hitherto unpointed Arabic text and began giving instruction in the grammar and vocabulary of the Arabic language. Incidentally in doing this he seems to have been to some extent influenced by Aristotle's logic, not by any of the Greek grammarians.

From Abu 1-Aswad ad-Du'ali came a regular succession of grammatical students and teachers in Basra. Nearly a century later similar grammatical lectures were commenced at Kufa by Abu Muslim Mu'adh ibn Muslim al-Harra (d. 723 or 727), who at one time was tutor to the sons of the khalif 'Abd al-Malik. These two centres developed rival schools which agreed in theory, but differed in practice. As yet the works of the ancient poets, valuable in illustrating and explaining the older usages of the language, were not collected in written Diwans, but transmitted by word of mouth, often altered and interpolated in their transmission. Aware of this the Basra school carefully criticized the poetry heard and rejected that which did not fit in with accepted standards, whilst the Kufans accepted all that was heard and are said to have used a good deal of forged material. At first sight it seems that the Basri method was better, but against that it must be noted that by that method the examples were made to fit the rules drawn up, whilst the Kufi grammarians had to adapt their rules to meet the spoken use, which is sounder.

The line of oral transmission of the two schools formed a grammatical pedigree which led down to the great Basri grammarian Abu 1-Hasan (or Bishr) 'Amr ibn 'Uthman al-Harithi, commonly known as Sibawaih (d. between 783 and 816) who, it must be noted, was not an Arab himself but a Persian and compiled his grammar under the early Abbasids.

At Basra arose the first indications of Mu'tazilite thought, with evidence of the solvent effect of Greek philosophical speculation on Arab theology, and in Iraq round about Basra were the first traces of juristic theory showing evident traces of Roman law and the philosophical theories adopted by Roman lawyers. Obviously the results of Greek influence began to appear, not in Syria where the ruling Muslims were in such close contact with Christian theology and its philosophical speculation, but in Basra, though we have no direct evidence of intercourse with Greek and Christian elements there. Damascus and its court were given over to sports and politics, and theological speculation could not have sunk very deep. Basra, on the other hand, kept alive a scholarly tradition and must have been impressed by Greek teaching, possibly through Hira, more probably through Jundi-Shapur, and so shows the first traces of Arab Hellenization.

The Abbasid Revolution

Mu'awiya had assumed the khalifate at Jerusalem in 661, but at once removed to Damascus, where he had already spent several years as Governor of Syria. At his accession began the rule of what is known as the Umayyad dynasty, which ruled Islam until 749. That dynasty suffered a break in 684 when it passed from one family to another, but the new family, descended from Marwan, was a branch of the Umayyad clan, so the monarchy remained in Umayyad hands, and that was the case until 744, when a second Marwan, not of Umayyad blood, assumed power by military force. The court and administration were settled at Damascus until 724 when the khalif Hisham removed to a country residence, and after that the khalifs went to Damascus only to be installed, and then retired to reside elsewhere, but the administration remained at the Syrian capital until the accession of Marwan II in 744. The court necessarily accompanied the khalif, but in 744 not only the court but also the administration were removed to Harran, which thus became the capital, and Damascus sank to the level of a provincial town, a change greatly resented by the Arabs of Syria.

Under the Umayyad dynasty the khalifate was a purely Arab state. Its intellectual output consisted entirely of poetry, largely of the old desert type, some of it so far modified as to reflect the tone of the courts of Hira and of the B. Ghassan, all in the spirit of the Jihiliya or " times of ignorance " before the coming of Islam. Its poets praised their patrons, derided their rivals and enemies, pictured the perils of the desert life, or sang the echoes of ancient tribal wars. The culture and science of the Greek world found no place in their compositions and apparently meant nothing to them.

Under Marwan II the Syrian army was disaffected, the Kharijites of Iraq revolted and entrenched themselves in Mosul. Marwan was unable to march against them, his hold on Syria was too insecure and he had to send an army down into Arabia where there was another Kharijite revolt.

His more serious trouble, however, threatened from Khurasan in East Persia. The Persians were dissatisfied : they felt that the Arab conquest of Persia had been due to a series of accidents, to domestic revolution which undermined their military organization and to the rash conduct of their youthful king. They longed for an opportunity to try issue again with those whom they regarded as half-civilized nomads. In such conditions it was inevitable for conspiracies to flourish, indeed the whole Umayyad period shows the community of Islam seething with dissatisfaction and ready for revolt, partly on racial grounds, resentment at the way in which the Arabs domineered over them even after they had embraced Islam, partly on religious grounds, regarding the Umayyads as lax in religious observance. Amongst the Persians were many adherents of the house of Ali, and these regarded all the khalifs, except Ali himself, as usurpers. They recognized the leadership only of those descended from Ali. The extremer Alids even preferred Ali to Muhammad himself. All these Shi'ites, as they were called, were divided amongst themselves into many sects, but all agreed in disapproving the Arabs. At length a revolutionary outbreak took form, its centre in Khurasan, but its propaganda spread by secret agents who circulated everywhere through the world of Islam, except in Spain where Muslims had their own troubles. The identity of the person who was to be set upon the throne after Marwan was deposed was kept secret until the revolution had reached a successful end, then it was disclosed that the one selected as khalif was Abu 1-'Abbas of the Hashimite clan of the

Quraysh tribe, the same tribe as that to which the Umayyads belonged. The throne merely passed from one Arab family to another.

Abu 1-'Abbas was invested with the khalifate in the great mosque of Kufa on 28th November, 749, and made it his first task to exterminate the surviving Umayyads and their adherents, and this he did so drastically as to earn for himself the surname of af-$a/ah "the butcher". Of the deposed dynasty only one young man escaped and, after incredible dangers and hardships, reached distant Spain where he became head of an independent state, and later on his descendants assumed the title of khalif in opposition to the dynasty of Abu l-'Abbas. There are stories of other Umayyads who found refuge in the remoter parts of Africa, but these seem, to have been adherents of the dynasty, not themselves of Umayyad stock.

The downfall of the Umayyads was a definite turning-point in the history of Islam. The Abbasid khalifs were no less Arab than the Umayyads, but they had gained their throne largely by Persian help. Their chief ministers were Persians more often than Arabs. The heirs of several of the earlier Abbasid khalifs were educated in Persian surroundings and had Persian blood as the result of intermarriages. Persian ideas and Persian interests rivalled, in many cases displaced, Arab ideas and interests, and so to a certain extent Islam became Persianized. For all that the khalifate and its subject must still be classed as Arab : they were commanded by a ruling dynasty which was Arab, they used the Arabic language, professed an Arab religion, and held in unbroken continuity from the desert men who had conquered the near East.

At first the Abbasid khalifs. lived at al-Anbar on the Euphrates. They had no desire to go to Syria where prevailing feeling was strongly pro-Umayyad. But the second ruler of the Abbasid line, Abu 1-'Abbas' brother al-Mansur was determined to found a new capital. After considering various sites he at length decided to build at Baghdad, a town of considerable antiquity which had been known in Babylonian times as Bag-Da-Du, a name of unknown origin. By a play upon words later Persian writers gave this name a fanciful Persian derivation and made it mean " the Garden of God ".

In making this choice he was guided by the advice of his minister, the Persian Khalid ibn Barmak, and having re^olved on building he called in the services of two astrologers to lay out the foundations and select a propitious hour for setting the first stone in position. The astrologers chosen for that purpose were an-Nawbakht, who was a Persian, and Mashallah ibn Athari, a Persian Jew, of Marw.

Guided by these astrologers al-Mansur laid the first stone of his new capital towards the end of the year 762, and three years later the building was sufficiently advanced for occupation to commence. Many of the inhabitants came from the neighbouring camp cities of Basra and Kufa, both hotbeds of sedition and always restless and fanatical. The presence of these new citizens helps to explain why from the outset Baghdad showed a turbulent and troublesome atmosphere. One suburb of the city known as Karkh, which had already existed as a Persian village, was given over to Persians.

Al-Mansur desired to make his capital a city whose fame should radiate through all Islam, and for this purpose he invited to it a number of distinguished scholars, Quran readers and preachers, grammarians and traditionalists from the two neighbouring camp cities which had already become recognized centres of Muslim scholarship, as yet restricted to Quranic and theological studies. Such men of learning were then beginning to form a respected middle class which later rose by court favour to high offices in the State, but was entirely distinct from the older aristocracy of the Arab tribal chieftains of noble pedigree who had dominated Islam under the Umayyads. The learned men of Kufa and Basra, many already famous, formed a kind of academic aristocracy which tended to act as a check on the arrogant pretensions of the hereditary nobility who had proved a source of danger in the court of Damascus and were still disaffected towards the Abbasid dynasty which they regarded as semi-Persian. Unfortunately al-Mansur suffered from the unprincely vice of avarice, and the rewards he offered were so moderate and were paid so grudgingly that he earned the nickname Abu d-Dawaniq " father of sixpences ".

In 765 al-Mansur was taken seriously ill with some gastric disorder and was advised to send for the Nestorian physician Jirjis ibn Bukhtyishu, head of the academy and hospital at Jundi-Shapur. This was the first contact of the court at Baghdad with the family of

Bukhtyishu which afterwards played an important part in the cultural education of the Arabs. Nothing is known of the Bukhtyishu who was the father of this Jirjis, but as the name occurs several times in the course of the history of Baghdad it is convenient to classify him as Bukhtyishu I.

Of all the East Persians who had helped the Abbasid revolution and afterwards came west to share the prosperity of the new dynasty, the most distinguished belonged to the wealthy and well-born family of the Barmakids, originally of Balkh in Bactria, but afterwards settled at Marw. This family was descended from the Barmaks or hereditary abbots of the Buddhist monastery of Nawbahar in Balkh, but had conformed to the Mazdean religion some time probably not long before the Muslim conquest, and then embraced Islam. Khalid ibn Barmak, the head of the family, was minister of finance under as-Saffah, and was made governor of Mesopotamia by al-Mansur. His son Yahya, at one time governor of Armenia, was entrusted by al-Mahdi with the education of his son who afterwards became khalif as Harun ar-Rashid, and he appointed Yahya wazir of the whole empire and entrusted him with unlimited power. In this office Yahya showed himself a wise and just administrator, and under his guidance the empire prospered. Of Yahya's three sons Fazl was governor of Khurasan, then of Egypt, and Ja'far succeeded Yahya as Wazir. But the family, after being the first in wealth, power, and honour in Islam, fell from its high estate in 803 for reasons which were a mystery to contemporaries and never have been adequately explained. Yahya died in prison in 806, Ja'far in 909. Other sons seem to have been set at liberty after Yahya's death. At the accession of al-Amin in 808 all surviving members of the Barmakid family were set free and had property and honours restored to them.

The Barmakids were keenly interested in Greek science, which was then the subject of much attention at Marw, and brought with them this taste, finding a kindred spirit already existing in the Nestorian academy of Jundi-Shapur.

Jirjis ibn Bukhtyishu, who had come from Jundi-Shapur to attend al-Mansur, remained in Baghdad as court physician until advancing years caused him to ask to be released and he retired full of honours to Jundi-Shapur where he died in 769. In 785 al-Hadi, mindful of Jirjis' excellent services, invited his son Bukhtyishu II, who had succeeded his father as head of the academy and hospital to go to Baghdad, but at court he had to face such determined opposition from Abu Quraysh the Queen's physician that for the sake of peace he was sent back to Jundi-Shapur. Under Harun ar-Rashid he was again summoned to court to treat the khalif for severe headaches, and later his son Jibra'il was brought to court and remained there until his death in 828-29. Whilst he was there the influence of the Barmakid wazir was making itself felt and efforts were being made to introduce to the Arabs the revived scientific learning derived from Greek sources, which was already spreading amongst the Syriac-speaking Christians. The Barmakid Yahya was an enthusiastic supporter of this revival of science with which he had been in touch in Marw, and was warmly supported by the Nestorian scholars of Jundi-Shapur.

Harun ar-Rashid became khalif in 786. He had been educated in Persia and under Persian influence at the hands of Yahya the Barmakid and throughout his reign showed strongly pro-Persian sympathies. He took great interest in science and literature, far beyond any of his predecessors, and the Hellenistic movement in Islam matured under his auspices. His reign was afterwards looked back upon as a golden age, but the khalifate had already begun to show signs of decay : in 800 he consented to the practical independence of the Aglabid governor of Qairawan in Libya, the beginning of a process of devolution which finally brought about the disintegration of the empire. Neither he nor any other of the Abbasid khalifs were able to extend their rule over Andalus, which had been a province under the Umayyads.

Influenced by his Barmakid minister Harun gave active support to the scholars who studied and translated Greek scientific works, sending out agents to purchase Greek manuscripts in the Roman Empire, a generous policy which brought a good deal of important material to Baghdad, and this was supplemented by similar generosity on the part of private persons who spent freely on manuscripts and translators. A good deal of the material thus obtained was medical and so appealed to the physicians of Jundi-Shapur, and this was rendered into Syriac as had been the case in former times, but before long Arabic versions made their appearance, at first translated from the Syriac, later directly from the Greek originals. The works of

Aristotle were familiar in Syriac translations, and with them were commentaries and summaries, some composed in Syriac, others translated from the Greek. But at first the Aristotelian material was confined to the logical treatises. It was not until some time after the death of Harun ar-Rashid that a serious and direct examination of Aristotelian philosophy was undertaken by Arab scholars. Derived through Syriac versions and commentaries the teaching of Aristotle was strongly tinctured with neo-Platonism, and that type of thought continued to colour Arabic philosophy to quite later times.

There seems reason to suppose that some of the earliest direct translations from the Greek was concerned with astronomy and mathematics. At an early date the *Sindhind*, an Indian treatise on astronomy and connected mathematics, based on Alexandrian teaching, was translated into Arabic, perhaps by means of a Persian version. It is said that the translators into Arabic were Ibrahim al-Fazari and Ya'qub ibn Tariq. Of the former of these Mas'udi says, " I will also cite the astronomer Ibrahim al-Fazari, author of the celebrated poem on the stars, astrology, and the study of the skies" (Mas'udi, Muruj, viii, 290), and then goes on to name him as one of al-Mansur's personal friends. The celebrated poem on the stars is not extant. He is said also to have been the first Arab to make an astrolabe. The son of this Ibrahim was Muhammad (d. between 769 and 806), who is sometimes mentioned as having been the translator. The date of a translation which is ascribed sometimes to the father, sometimes to the son, must be regarded as uncertain. Ya'qub ibn Tariq was a distinguished mathematician who is said to have been the author of a treatise on the sphere and another on the karaja or arc of 225 , following the tradition of Archimedes who divided the circle into 96 degrees, and also to have drawn up astronomical tables. That the Sindhind was translated so early as al-Mansur is doubtful, but obviously the translation was well known to Abdallah Muhammad ibn Musa al-Khwarizmi, who made it the basis of his astronomical tables, but his work came some fifty years later, and the tables are now lost, but are cited and incorporated in later work by Maslama al-Majriti. When tables are only known to us by being cited or incorporated in later work, we can never be sure how they have been touched up or improved, and how much remains of the original.

In order to understand and use the *Sindhind* it was found necessary to make translations of the Almajest of Ptolemy and Euclid's Elements, and these seem to have been translated directly from the Greek and to have been the earliest translation thus made. It is stated that it was made from a Syriac version, and this is not disproved by the absence of any such version surviving : Syriac literature is not rich in mathematical works. In favour of an early rendering from the Greek we have only the presumption that reference must have been made to the original to get an accurate rendering of the technical terms, a matter of the utmost importance in mathematical work. The Arabic versions were several times revised and corrected by comparison with the Greek text, so the earliest may have been made before Harun ar-Rashid, or in the early part of his reign. There is a tradition that the translations of Euclid and the Almajest were made at the suggestion of Ja'far the Barmakid, which would put them before 803, when the Barmakids fell into disgrace. If the observatory at Jundi-Shapur was in use before the time of an-Nahawandi (813-833), of which we cannot be certain, no doubt the necessary equipment in mathematics was available there and would be in Syriac. It is of course quite possible that the necessary mathematics were obtained from Indian works, not from Euclid or Ptolemy. The " Sons of Musa " had an observatory in Baghdad, but that would be after the time of Harun ar-Rashid.

Not much can be learned from the two astrologers who assisted al-Mansur in laying the foundations of Baghdad, though both of these are said to have produced mathematical, astronomical, or astrological works. One of these, an-Nawbakht (d. 776-7), is described as a convert from the Zoroastrian religion and a favourite of al-Mansur. He is said to have been the author of a work on judicial astrology and to have compiled astronomical tables, but of these works nothing survives. His son Abu Sahl al-Fadl an-Nawbakht (d. circ. 815) was Harun ar-Rashid's librarian and made translations from the Persian. The other astrologer, Mashallah, is said to have been a Jew of Marw whose name had originally been Misha, short for Manasseh (Fihrist, i, 273). Several of his works survive in Hebrew or Latin translations. Amongst these was a popular work on astronomy, not astrology.

It seems fairly certain that medical material came through a Syriac medium, direct translation from the Greek coming later. This may have been the case also with astronomical and mathematical material, but extant Syriac translations seem to be contemporaneous with the Arabic versions, not earlier, most indeed the work of Hunayn ibn Ishaq or his school. It may be that mathematics and astronomy came through Indian authorities, not translations from the Greek but based upon Greek teaching, and translation from Greek into Syriac and Arabic came later when efforts were made to check and correct the available material. Certainly the earliest Arab mathematicians, such as al-Khwarizmi, knew a great deal which does not appear in the Greek authors and much of which (but not all) can be traced to Indian workers. There are gaps in the chain of transmission which it is not easy to fill up.

Translations into Arabic

Baghdad was founded in 762. Harun ar-Rashid became khalif in 786 and in his reign Baghdad became the centre of a movement which aimed at translating Greek scientific material into Arabic. In the twenty-four years intervening between the foundation of the city and the accession of Harun ar-Rashid influences must have been at work to prompt this undertaking. Of such influences two were obvious, one radiating from Marw far away in Khurasan in the east, the other from Jundi-Shapur near at hand. Marw in Khurasan was indeed distant, but it had a great deal to do with early Baghdad. The Abbasids had been set upon the throne by a rebellion which had its source in Khurasan and which drew its chief support from that province. The Marw family of the Barmakids supplied the all-powerful ministers who guided and to a great extent controlled the Abbasid government. Many Persians, especially those of Khurasan, had flocked west to share in the triumph of the revolution and claim their share in its spoils. At the Abbasid court Persian influence very much thrust the Arab element into the background. The Persians were not modest about this : the Arabs had been arrogant, now the Persians repaid them with greater arrogance, deriding the Arabs as semi-barbarous-nomads of the desert, parvenus without a history behind them, devoid of culture. This anti-Arab demonstration, open and plainly expressed, went by the name of the Shu'ubiya, an organized, virulent, and outspoken expression of anti-Arab feeling.

A typical figure of the times was Abu Muhammad ibn al-Muqaffa, a Persian who entered the service of Isa ibn 'Ali, uncle of the first two Abbasid khalifs, and became a convert to Islam, though many regarded his conversion as insincere. He translated from Pahlawi or Old Persian the book known as *Kalilag wa-Dimnag*, itself a translation of a Buddhist work brought from India by the Christian periodeutes Budh who had been sent to India to procure drugs, and with the drugs brought back this book and the game of chess. Ibn al-Muqaffa' produced a translation which is regarded as a model of classical Arabic, and as such is still studied in schools. He also made a translation of the Persian *Khudai-nama*, a biographical history of the Persian kings, calling his Arabic version Siyar muluk al-Ajam. This work no longer exists, but it formed the basis of Firdawsi's *Shah-nama* and many long extracts are given in Ibn Qutaiba's '*Uyun al-akhbar*. In Arabic he composed a treatise " on obedience due to kings " (ad-durra al-yatima fi ta'at a'-mulk, printed Cairo, 1893 and 1326, 1331 a.h.). He also wrote several short treatises on "*Adab*", etiquette, duties of civil servants, and good manners, a favourite subject in Old Persian literature. Living in Basra and feeling secure in the protection of noble patrons he permitted himself many impertinences towards Sufyan ibn Mu'awiya al-Muhallibi, the city governor, jeering at him as " Ibn al-mughialina " (son of the lascivious female), all of which Sufyan endured in silence. After the rebellion of 'Abdallah against his nephew al-Mansur the khalif agreed to pardon his uncle and Ibn al-Muqaffa' was directed to draw up a formal letter of pardon for the khalif to sign. In this letter he inserted " if at any time the Commander of the Faithful act perfidiously towards his uncle 'Abdallah ibn 'Ali, his wives shall be divorced from him, his horses confiscated to the service of God, his slaves set free, and Muslims absolved from allegiance to him". Al-Mansur read this draft and asked who had composed it. On hearing that it was drawn up by Ibn al-Muqaffa' he said nothing, but sent a letter to Sufyan telling him that he might deal with the secretary as he saw fit. Various accounts are given of the way in which the governor gratified his resentment towards Ibn al-Muqaffa' by putting him to death, all of them extremely cruel. This took place in 757-8 (Ibn Khallihan, i, 432-3).

The cradle of the Shu'ubiya was Khurasan and its capital Marw. Harun ar-Rashid himself was educated at Marw and had strongly pro-Persian leanings. The astronomical records kept under the Sasanid kings of Persia were continued under the Arabs and were continued in Persian, not in Arabic, until much later. From Marw came some of the earliest translators of astronomical works, and it would seem that Khurasan was the channel through which astronomical and mathematical material came to Baghdad, for which very probably the Barmakid ministers, natives of Marw, were the agents. There was, it is true, an observatory at Jundi-Shapur, but we know little of its activity before the time of Ahmad an-Nahawandi (813-833), who made observations there some years after Harun's death. Some of the astronomical and mathematical material seems to have been obtained from India, derived from a Greek source in the first place, but probably it was transmitted to the Arabs through a Persian medium, though the actual Persian works whereby it was transmitted are no longer extant.

Jundi-Shapur was near Baghdad and under the Abbasid khalifs distinguished physicians were summoned thence to court. Successful in their professional work they remained in Baghdad as court physicians and became men of wealth and influence. Their success inspired other physicians to follow them and they, with scholars from Marw, formed a group under court patronage which became something very like an academy, a society of scholars rather than a teaching body. The men of Jundi-Shapur were accustomed to study Greek science in Syriac translations : gradually these Syriac versions were supplemented by Arabic ones, and finally the Arabic versions replaced them.

There is a legend that the Sindhind, the Hindu revised form of Brahmagupta's *Siddhanta*, was translated into Arabic as early as the reign of al-Mansur. It was an early translation, though probably not so early as that. But it proved useless as the Arabs could not understand it. It is related that Ja'far the Barmakid perceived the reason of this to be that the Arabs lacked the preliminary knowledge of geometry and astronomy necessary to follow it, and at his advice Harun ar-

Rashid ordered a translation to be made of Euclid's Elements and Claudius Ptolemy's megale (synaxis)? To this title the Arabs added the article al- and changed the *megale* into *megiste*, deliberately, it would appear, for Ya'qubi writing in 891 explained that "the meaning of *al-majisti* is ' the greatest book' " (Ya'qubim, ed. Houtsma, Leiden, 1883). Thus, the work appears in Arabic as *Kitab al-Majisti*, which in medieval Latin became *magasiti*, presumably an attempted vocalizing of the unpointed *mjsty*. It does not appear that the translations of Euclid and Ptolemy were made until after the reign of Harun ar-Rashid, so the story that they were suggested by Ja'far ibn Barmak is dubious.

The translator of the *al-Majisti* is said to have been al-Hajjaj ibn Yusuf ibn Matar al-Hasib, who finished it about 827, which was well after the fall of the Barmakids and after the death of Harun ar-Rashid. The same translator is said to have made an Arabic version of Euclid's Elements, not including Book X which was later (about 910) translated with Pappus' commentary by Sa'id ad-Dimishqi. The translation of Euclid by al-Hajjaj with the commentary of an-Naziri (d. circ. 923), who also wrote a commentary on the al-Majisti, was published by T. O. Besthorn and J. L. Heiberg, Euclidis elementa ex interpretatione al Hadschdschadschii cum commentario an Nazirii arab. et lot., ed. notisque . . . Copenhagen, 1893. The earliest commentary on Euclid seems to have been that of al-'Abbas al-Jawhari (d. circ. 833). Another tradition represents the translation of the *al-Majisti* was made by Saki ibn Rabban at-Tabari, a native of Marw and a Jew as his name ibn Rabban " the rabbi's son " denotes. Marw, one of the centres of Greek scholarship, had many Jewish neighbours who formed a colony of their own as was the Jewish custom, for they preferred to live in communities where the Jewish law could be observed. On the road between Marw and Balkh lay the city of Maymana which was at one time called al.yahudiya "the Jewish (city)", but that name was changed to Maymana "the auspicious" at the request of its inhabitants who disliked the association with Jewry. This Sahl is described as having gone to Baghdad in the days of Harun ar-Rashid and having made the translation for him. He was a distinguished scholar and teacher of Marw who was known there as Barbun "the surpassing". Some account of him is given by his son Ali ibn Sahl ibn Rabban at-Tabari (d. 850) in his great medical work *Firdaws al-Hikhma* "the Paradise of Wisdom " (ed. I. Siddiqi, Berlin, 1928). Yet another tradition represents the translation of al-Majisti as made by Sahl and revised by al-Hajjaj. This early version of the work was subsequently revised by Hunayn ibn Ishaq (below), later by Thabit ibn Qurra (below), then by Muhammad ibn Jabir ibn Sinan al-Battani (d. 929). Al-Hajjaj's translation of Euclid was revised by Qusta ibn Luqa about 912-13.

The earliest information which the Arabs obtained about Aristotle from Syriac sources was confined to his logical works which had been translated and retranslated into Syriac, and on which several commentaries were accessible. The corpus of Aristotelian logic included the Categories, the Hermeneutics, the Prior Analytics, the Posterior Analytics, the Topics, the Sophistica, the Rhetoric, and the Politics, these last two works classed with the logical treatises by the Arabs. To these was added by Yuhanna (or Yahya) *ibn Batriq* about 815 another work, unfortunately a spurious one, the *Sirr al-asrar* or "secret of secrets", which was accepted as Aristotelian. It is a work of miscellaneous contents, including physiognomy and dietetics.

Not long afterwards, about 835, a Christian of Emessa named 'Abd al-Masih ibn 'Aballah Wa'ima al-Himsi translated another apocryphal work, the so-called *Theology of Aristotle*, really an abridged paraphrase of Plotinus, Enneads, iv—vi (cf. Fr. Dieterici, Die sogennante Theologie des Aristoteles, Leipzig, 1882).

About the same time lived Abu Yahya al-Batriq (d. between 798 and 806), who made an Arabic translation of an astrological work, the Tetrabiblos of Ptolemy. A commentary on this was written by Umar ibn al-Farrukhan (d. circ. 815), and a paraphrase by Muhammad ibn Jabir ibn Sinan al-Battani (d. 929);

Jibra'il I, the son of the otherwise unknown Bukhtyishu' I of Jundi-Shapur had attended al-Mansur, then retired to his own city and there finished his life. His son Bukhtyishu' II for a time acted as court physician to al-Hadi, but had to go back to Jundi-Shapur because of the opposition raised by the Queen's physician. He returned to the court of Baghdad under Harun ar-Rashid and attended both the khalif and his minister Ja'far the Barmakid. Before his death in 801 this Bukhtyishu' recommended his son Jibra'il II to the khalif, and he in due course became court physician. There is no evidence that the first two members of this family did anything to promote Greek science amongst the Arabs, but the second Jibra'il did, and as he acted in conjunction with Ja'far ibn Barmak it is obvious that he held an influential position in Baghdad even before his appointment as court physician. Bukhtyishu' died in 801 and then Jibra'il became the khalif's physician, after Harun's death in 808 continuing to serve his son al-Amin. But this led to his imprisonment when al-Ma'muni became master of Baghdad and all those who had been supporters of his brother al-Amin fell into disgrace. He was set free in 817 to attend the wazir Hasan ibn Sahl and lived without other disturbance until 829. He, no less than Ja'far ibn Barmak, was a patron and encourager of the work of translation from the Greek, a great admirer of Greek medical science, but was not himself responsible for any translation. He was the author of a *Kunnash* or medical compendium in Syriac in which he drew freely from Galen Hippocrates and Paul of Aegina; this manual was long in use amongst Syriac-speaking practitioners and did a good deal to familiarize them with Greek medical teaching. The work is now lost, but some knowledge of it can be obtained from the tenth century Syriac lexicon of Bar Bahoul, who uses it to illustrate technical medical terms (*Bar Bahoul*, edited by R. Duval, Paris 1888-1898). It was largely at his suggestion that Harun ar-Rashid sent into the Roman Empire to obtain manuscripts and commissioned translations from the Greek. He and other contemporary patrons not only provided for Arabic translations but also encouraged the preparation of improved Syriac versions, for it is worth noting that a new and better series of translations into Syriac was being made at the same time that translation into Arabic was commenced. Translation into Syriac went on as long as the Jundi-Shapur academy was in existence.

The general conclusion is that the work of translation of scientific material began under Harun ar-Rashid with the encouragement of the wazir Ja'far ibn Barmak, and that this at first was especially concerned with mathematical and astronomical works, several of them translated by scholars from Ja'far's own city of Marw. The translation of medical works perhaps began a little later, and was associated with Jibra'il II. But there seem to have been some other translators not connected with the semi-official group gathered at court. Medical works came through Syriac versions in the first place and so did at least some of the astronomical and mathematical material, but in this latter direct reference to the Greek originals seems to have taken place earlier. This is as might be expected, for it was in mathematics that absolute accuracy in terminology was most important. Arabic lacked the technical terms used by Greek scientists. Sometimes the Greek terms were simply transliterated, but very often those terms show that they have passed through an Aramaic (Syriac) medium on their way, and this is more obvious in medical works than in mathematical and astronomical. As has been noted, the desire of more accurate scientific knowledge led to the preparation of more careful translations or the revision of existing versions, but it also resulted in the compilation of commentaries as well as original treatises based on the Greek authorities with citations illustrated and explained by original work. The encouragement of science became fashionable under Harun and many of the leading courtiers became patrons and spent freely on their scientific protege's. Not all of these may have been inspired by a pure love of science. When it became a fashion at court it is likely enough that many ambitious of advertising themselves found this a means of doing so. Outside court circles the scientific movement made small appeal. The Arabs generally took little interest in it: their learned men still spent their time in the study of Quran, jurisprudence, and grammar. So far, until the end of the reign of Harun ar-Rashid, no real work was done in the Aristotelian philosophy, Aristotle was treated only as an authority on logic.

Harun ar-Rashid died in 808, leaving the empire to his two sons al-Amin and al-Ma'mun, the former taking the western half with his capital at Baghdad, the other the eastern half with Marw as his capital. This naturally did not work and civil war between the two brothers followed inevitably. Al-Ma'mun's army, led by abler generals, obtained the upper hand, until in 812 under the leadership of Tahir it besieged Baghdad. This siege involved terrible sufferings and al-Amin was compelled to lay heavy requisitions on the citizens. At this the merchants entered into correspondence with Tahir. Discovering that he was betrayed al-Amin tried to escape and was on his way to make his submission to Tahir when he was found and murdered by some Persian freelancers. These tragic events form the subject of an epic poem by al-Khuzaimi, a type of poem rare in Arabic.

At the death of al-Amin the whole empire fell into the hands of al-Ma'mun, but he preferred to remain at Marw and sent Hasan ibn Sahl to Baghdad as his deputy. Hasan's rule lasted six years, a period of tyranny and disorder gradually merging into anarchy, of which al-Ma'mun was kept in complete ignorance. At last the city revolted and elected Mansur ibn Mahdi governor until such time as al-Ma'mun could take over control in person. There was another reason why Baghdad was dissatisfied in addition to the tyrannical misrule of Hasan. Al-Ma'mun had invited the Shi'ite claimant to the throne, Ali ar-Rida, to Marw, received him with exceptional honour, and promised to make him his heir. This caused great offence at Baghdad which had no desire to be under Shi'ite rule.

At length the khalif was made aware of the critical state of affairs and warned that unless he went to Baghdad and took matters in hand for himself the khalifate would pass out of his hands. Thus warned he set out for Baghdad in 819, first disposing of Ali ar-Rida by poison. With him he took an extensive and extravagant court, as well as an army and also a select company of scientists, for he himself was deeply interested in scientific studies. At Baghdad he was welcomed with great rejoicings. He was a man of handsome presence, a thing which counts for much in oriental princes, generous, even lavish to extravagance in his expenditure and generally regarded as prudent, determined, of sound judgment, and clemency. According to the historians he was endowed with every grace and favour of an ideal prince. Educated in Marw in a neo-Hellenistic atmosphere, he applied philosophical principles to Muslim doctrines : no doubt others did the same, some of them men of exemplary piety, but they were careful to preserve external decorum by treating matters of religion with respect. Not so in case of al-Ma'mun. He had a taste for discussing religious problems and this he did with considerable freedom, so that one of his courtiers once addressed him in jest as " Prince of Unbelievers ", a jest which was allowed to pass but its maker was never forgiven. Pro-Persian and anti-Arab, son of a Persian mother and married to a Persian wife, he had little in common with the na.row fanaticism of the typical Baghdadite. Unfortunately he was so far convinced of the Tightness of the Mu'tazilite views that he was determined to force them upon his subjects, selecting as a test point the question whether the Quran was, or was not, created. In 837. He published a decree penalizing any who did not agree that it was created and so not co-eternal with God. This decree was deeply resented as an innovation, for Islam has never recognized the khalif as a religious teacher. The doctrines of religion are defined, not by the State, but by those who are learned in theology. As the penal was not successful, al-Ma'mun reissued it in stricter terms with many peevish complaints about the non-observance of his commands, and established a *mihna* or inquisition before which any person could be brought and examined as to his opinions, suffering punishment if they differed from the officially authorized rationalism. Under this law there were some martyrs and many suffered imprisonment and other punishments, amongst them Ahmad ibn Hanbal, a revered and greatly honoured traditionalist and jurist. All those who suffered were regarded as saints.

Ten years after his arrival in Baghdad al-Ma'mun attempted to repeat the experiment of the Greek geometer Eratosthenes and measure the earth's arc. To do this he assembled a number of scientists in the plain of Sinjar in Mesopotamia, west of Mosul. The leading scientists thus gathered were Abu t-Taiyab Sanad ibn 'Ali (d. after 860), who afterwards directed the erection of the observatory in Baghdad, Yahya ibn Abi Mansur al-Mai'muni, a freed man of al-Ma'mun's family, al-'Abbas ibn Sa'id al-Jawhari (d. after 833), and 'Ali ibn 'Isa al-Asturlabi. He divided these scientists into two parties which moved apart until they saw a change of one degree in the elevation of the pole. The distance travelled was then measured, and it was found that one party had travelled 57 miles, the other 58 miles, each mile reckoned as 4,000 " black cubits ", a measure of length specially devised for this experiment. In 832 the experiment was repeated at Qasian, near Damascus.

When Jibra'il left Jundi-Shapur for Baghdad he was succeeded as head of the academy and hospital there by Abu Zakariah Yahya ibn Masawaih (d. 857), a Nestorian who was the son of a druggist and had received his training as a pupil of 'Isa b. Nun, who became

Nestorian patriarch in 823. At that time medicine was in such great repute that it was regarded as the foremost form of scientific education and consequently it is common to find that Nestorian and Monophysite clergy in Asia often had a medical training rather than one in *litterae humaniores*. But Ibn Masawaih left Jundi-Shapur and went to Baghdad at Jibra'il's suggestion, and was introduced at court as a skilful physician and one learned in Greek medicine. He was the author of a treatise on ophthalmology entitled *Daghal al-ayn* "the disease of the eye", and also a collection of medical aphorisms *An-nawadir at-tibiyya*, which he dedicated to his pupil Hunayn ibn Ishaq. This work attained great popularity and was translated into Latin, but wrongly ascribed to St. John Damascene. In later times Ibn Masawaih's treatise on the eye was so greatly esteemed that it was selected as one of the set books for the examination established by the Khalif al-Qahir (932-34) for the licence to practise medicine, an examination at first under the direction of Sinan ibn Thabit. There is also an "Instruction for the examination of oculists" which is ascribed to him, but it is simply a cram book based on the *Daghal al-ayn* probably a later compilation made for the use of examination candidates. The *Daghal al-ayn* "is the earliest treatise on ophthalmology, the Greek, Syriac, and other special textbooks being lost. It is written in bad Arabic, with many Greek, Syriac, and Persian technical terms, a rather confusing compilation without system, and doubtless intermixed with later interpolations. One complete MS. is extant in Taimur Pasha's library (Cairo), another in Leningrad " (M. Meyerhof, *The Book of the Ten Treatises*, Cairo, 1928, ix-x). Analysis and extracts of this work in German by M. Meyerhof and C. Preufer, Die Augenheilkun.de des Juhanna ibn Masawaih, in Der Islam, vi, 1915, pp. 217-56.

The most celebrated of all translators of Greek scientific works into Arabic was Hunayn ibn Ishaq al-'Abadi (d. 873 or 877). The outline of his life and work are well known from his autobiography written in the form of letters to 'Ali ibn Yahya in 875. (Text from two manuscripts in the Aya Sofia Mosque at Stambul, ed. with translation by G. Bergestrasser, Leipzig, 1925.) He was a native of Hira, the son of a Christian (Nestorian) druggist. In later life he learned Arabic, so presumably he did not belong to the ruling class of Hira which was

Arabic-speaking, and this is endorsed by his name 'Abadi, which shows that he belonged to the subject people of Hira. As a young man he attended the lectures of Ibn Masawaih (above) at Jundi-Shapur, and so far carried the approval of his teacher that he was made his dispenser. But later he annoyed Ibn Masawaih by asking too many questions in class, and at last his teacher lost patience and said : "What have the people of Hira to do with medicine ?—go and change money in the streets," and drove him out weeping (Ibn al-Qifti, 174). Expelled from the academy Hunayn went away to "the land of the Greeks " and there obtained a sound knowledge of the Greek language and familiarity with textual criticism, such as had been developed in Alexandria. In due course he returned and settled for a time at Basra where he studied Arabic under Khalid ibn Ahmad then, some time before 826, proceeded to Baghdad where he obtained the patronage of Jibra'il and for him prepared translations of some of Galen's works. Harun ar-Rashid died in 808 and al-Ma'mun succeeded in 813, after the brief and stormy reign of al-Amin, so that Hunayn's activities belong to a period later than Harun ar-Rashid. The excellence of his translations, far surpassing any previous work of the sort, greatly impressed Jibra'il who then introduced him to the three "Sons of Musa", wealthy patrons of learning. Their father, Musa ibn Shakir, after a life spent in the lucrative profession of a brigand in Khurasan, had reformed and been pardoned, then settled down to spend his declining years in cultured leisure. He entrusted his sons to the Khalif al-Ma'mun, who appointed Ishaq ibn Ibrahim, and later Yahya ibn Abi Mansur to be their teachers, and from those preceptors they received a training in mathematics. They were not so much interested in medicine, but patronized Hunayn chiefly because of his excellence as a translator. Of these "Sons of Musa" the eldest Muhammad rose to high office under the Khalif al-Motadid (892-932), and distinguished himself in astronomy and geometry, a second son Ahmad excelled in mechanics, and the third son Hasan became a celebrity in geometry. They had a house in Baghdad near the Bab at-Taq, the gate at the eastern end of the main bridge over the Tigris, opening into the great market street of East Baghdad, and there they built an observatory where they made observations during the years 850-870. To them we owe a treatise on plane and spherical geometry, a collection of geometrical problems and a manual of geometry which was translated into Latin by Gerhard of Cremona (d. 1187) as " Liber Trium Fratrum de geometria " (ed. M. Curtze in Nova Acta d. Kais. Leap. Carol, deustscen Akad. Naturforscher, xlix, 109-167), which long held its own as an introduction to geometry. They were generous patrons of scientific research and according to Ibn Abi Usaibi'a spent at one time an average of 500 dinars (say £200) a month on their scientific proteges.

The " Sons of Musa " introduced Hunayn to the Khalif al-Ma'mun some time before Jibra'ils death in 828-29, and apparently at Jibra'il's suggestion the khalif founded an academy which he called the "House of Wisdom" (Dar al-hikhma) as an institution where the preparation of translations from Greek scientists would be made and circulated amongst the Arabs, placing Hunayn in charge. From that time forwards the work of translation went on steadily, and before long Arab students found themselves equipped with the greater part of the works of Galen, Hippocrates, Ptolemy, Euclid, Aristotle, and various other Greek authorities. The work of translation was twofold, versions were made in Arabic and also in Syriac, these were later to replace the defective translations already in use. Ibn Masawaih, the teacher who had expelled Hunayn from Jundi-Shapur, was reconciled to him and became his warm supporter. Hunayn had many other friends and clients, mostly physicians of Jundi-Shapur and those who had removed to Baghdad and used the Arabic language, like Salmawaih ibn Bunan an alumnus of' Jundi-Shapur who became court physician to al-Mu'tasim in 832. All these were better translations than had been known in the past and were made from good Greek manuscripts, many of them procured by agents of the khalif who were sent into the Roman Empire and empowered to spend considerable sums on the purchase of the best codices.

Altogether Hunayn translated into Syriac twenty books of Galen, two for Bukhtyishu' Jibra'il's son, two for Salmawaih ibn Bunan, one for Jibra'il, and one for Ibn Masawaih, and also revised the sixteen translations made by Sergius of Rashayn. He translated fourteen treatises into Arabic, three for Muhammad, one for Ahmad, sons of Musa. He and his assistants produced versions both in Syriac and Arabic, though no doubt some of his staff excelled in one language rather than the other. Most of the translators of the next generation received their training from Hunayn or his pupils, so that he stands out as the leading translator of the better type, though some of his versions were afterwards revised by later writers.

The complete curriculum, of the medical school of Alexandria was thus made available for Arab students. This included a select series of the treatises of Galen which was :—

1. De seeds. 2. Ars medica. 3. De pulsibus ad tirones. 4. Ad Glauconem de medendi methodo. 5. De ossibus ad tirones. 6. De musculorum dissectione. 7. De nervorum dissectione. 8. De venarum arteriumque dissectione. 9. De elementis secundum Hippocratem. 10. De temperamentis. 11. De facultatibus naturalibus. 12. De causis et symptomatibus. 13. De locis affectis. 14. De pulsibus (four treatises). 15. De typis (febrium). 16. De crisibus. 17. De diebus decretoriis. 18. Methodus medendi.

The range and method' of Hunayn's work is known to us from his autobiography, the *Risalat Hunayn ibn Ishaq*, letters written to 'Ali ibn Yahya in 865, of which the text with translation has been published from two manuscripts in the Aya Sophia Mosque at Stamboul, by G. Bergestrasser, Leipzig, 1925, a work which has been analysed by Dr. Meyerhof in Isis, viii (1926), 685-724.

Al-Ma'mun's reign came to an end in 833 and he was succeeded by his son al-Mu'tasim (833-842), who found it difficult to control the populace of Baghdad and formed a guard of Turkish slave-soldiers. But this body-guard, holding a privileged position, soon became insubordinate and many complaints were made about their conduct. At last al-Mu'tasim in 836 removed himself and his court to Samana, and there the khalifs reigned until 892. These disorders affected scholarship adversely and the "House of Wisdom" fell into decay which was not checked during the brief reign of Wathiq (842-47).

As Wathiq's son was too young to occupy the throne his brother Mutawakkil (847-861) was invested with the khalifate. His accession made a great change. The previous khalifs had been tolerant in religion, al-Ma'mun was generally regarded as a free-thinker. But Mutawakkil was of the strictest orthodoxy and fanatical in his orthodoxy, possibly afraid of the disaffected attitude of the Syrian

Christians. He was of sadistic temperament, mischievous and capriciously cruel. Though not himself a scholar like al-Ma'mun, he was a patron of science and scholarship and reopened the Dar al-Hikhma, granting it fresh endowments. The best work of translation was done during his reign, as the training of the staff and experience were bearing fruit.

Mutawakkil's personal relations with Hunayn were chequered. It is related that the khalif told him to prepare poison for his enemies and, on Hunayn's refusal to do so, cast him into prison. Not long afterwards he was released and Mutawakkil explained that he had only desired to test his loyalty to the traditional standards of medical practice. Then a Nestorian physician named Isra'il ibn Zakariya at-Taifuri, or else his friend Bukhtyishu', denounced him as a heretic, that is a heretic from the Nestorian standard, for Hunayn had never conformed to Islam. The Nestorian Church, like other tolerated religious communities, was self-governing in its private affairs and could punish heretics and other offenders, though the khalif quite gratuitously comes into the story. It is said that Mutawakkil ordered Hunayn to spit on a picture of the Holy Theotokos and on his refusal handed him over to the Nestorian Catholicos Theodosius who imprisoned and scourged him. The implication seems to be that the khalif invited him to repudiate Christianity, and when he refused to do so handed him over to the Nestorian Catholicos for punishment. Just possibly this vague and confused story contains an echo of the iconoclastic controversy which at that time was disturbing the Eastern Church. Mutawakkil further confiscated Hunayn's property, including his library, a loss which he felt sorely. After four months he was set free because of a remarkable cure following his treatment of a court dignitary, and his goods and library were restored. The whole matter sounds very much like an intrigue amongst the court physicians, as on his release the other court physicians had to pay him 10,000 dirhams compensation.

After his release he lived another twenty years, which he employed in making translations and correcting those made by others. In 861 Mutawakkil was murdered by his Turkish guards at his son's instigation. Hunayn enjoyed the favour of that son Montasir (861-62), and of his successors Mosta'in (862-66), Mo'tazz (866-69),

Muhtadi (869-70), and Mu'tamid (870-92), and was engaged in making a translation of Galen's De constitutione artis medicae at the time of his death, which took place in 873 according to the Fihrist, or in 877 according to Ibn Abi Usaibi'a, who is often inaccurate in his chronology. According to I.A.U., Hunayn was the author of more than a hundred original works, but only a few of these are extant. Hunayn, the greatest of the translators, must be reckoned to the credit of Jundi-Shapur, although his fuller and more accurate knowledge was gained by his studies in the " land of the Greeks ", for those travels and studies were prompted and directed by what he had learned at Jundi-Shapur under Ibn Masawaih.

Although Mutawakkil was bigoted, fanatical, and sadistic, he was a generous patron of scientific research and is generally reckoned as having re-endowed the " House of Wisdom ", which probably means that it was reopened after the disturbed period which followed al-Ma'mun's death and its endowments restored to it. The best work of this academy was done under Mutawakkil, for by that time experience told and Hunayn was surrounded by well-trained pupils.

Amongst those who worked with Hunayn must be noted his son Ishaq, who died in November, 919 or 911, and his nephew Hubaysh ibn al-Hasan, who was at work in the days of Mutawakkil. He translated Greek texts of Hippocrates and the botanical work of Dioscorides which became the basis of the Arab pharmacopoeia (infra). It is noteworthy that most of the names of planys in Arabic show that they have passed through an Aramaic (Syriac) medium (cf. Loew, Aramaische Pflanzennamen, 1881).

Another noteworthy pupil was 'Isa ibn Yahya ibn Ibrahim who was a translator of Greek medical works into Arabic. Almost all the leading scientists of the succeeding generation were pupils of Hunayn.

Although Hubaysh is given as the translator of *Dioscorides*, the current Arabic version is more commonly ascribed to Hunayn's pupil Staphanos ibn Basilos, who translated the work into Syriac, and this Syriac version was then translated into Arabic by Hunayn himself (or Hubaysh) for Muhammad, one of the "Sons of Musa". But another independent version of *Dioscorides* was afterwards made in Spain (cf. below).

About 908 the Christian priest Yusuf al-Kkuri al-Qass translated

Archimedes' (lost) work on triangles from a Syriac version, and this was afterwards revised by Thabit ibn Qurra. He also made an Arabic translation of Galen's *De simplicibus temperamentis et facultatibus*, which was afterwards revised by Hunayn ibn Ishaq.

About the same time lived Qusta ibn Luqa al-Ba'lbakki (3. 912-13), a Syrian Christian who translated *Hypsicles*, afterwards revised by al-Kindi, Theodosius' *Sphaerica*, which was afterwards revised by Thabit ibn Qurra, Heron's *Mechanics*, Autolycus, Theophrastus' *Meteora*, Galen's catalogue of his books, John Philoponus on the Physics of Aristotle and several other works, and also revised the existing translation of Euclid.

Abu Bishr Malta ibn Yunus al-Qanna'i (d. 940) was responsible for a translation of the Poetica of Aristotle.

Medical and logical works were translated also by the Monophysite Abu Zakariya Yahya ibn Adi al-Mantiqi "the logician" (d. 974), amongst them the Prolegomena of Ammonius, an introduction to Porphyry's Isagoge.

To these may be added the late translator Al-Hunayn ibn Ibrahim ibn al-Hasan ibn Khurshid at-Tabari an-Natili (d. 990) also the Monophysite Abu 'Ali 'Isa ibn Ishaq ibn Zer'a (d. 16th April, 1008), who prepared versions of medical and philosophical works. With these the series of translators in Asia comes to an end. After this the work changes to commentary and exposition, occasionaly revising earlier translations,

A final phase of translation appears in Andalus, the Muslim occupied Spain. There the fugitive 'Umayyad prince 'Abdarrahman had established an independent kingdom in 755. The eighth prince of that Andalusian state 'Abdarrahman III in 929 adopted the title Khalif and so from 929 to 978 there were khalifs of Cordova, usually with strained relations with the 'Abbasids in the east, but friendly with the Emperor of Byzantium who was their enemy. In 949 the Byzantine Emperor Constantine VII sent an embassy to Cordova and amongst the presents he sent to 'Abdarrahman was a copy of *Dioscorides* in Greek with painted pictures of the many plants described in the text. This book attracted much attention, but no one in Cordova could read Greek, so the Khalif in thanking the Emperor begged him to send someone who could translate and explain the work. In 951 the Emperor sent a monk named Nicolas, who was able to speak Arabic, and he not only made translations of *Dioscorides* and other Greek works, but began teaching the Greek language, his lectures arousing great enthusiasm and being attended by many court officials, including Hasdai ibn Shaprut, the Jewish wazir. Translations of *Dioscorides* already existed, that of Hunayn ibn Ishaq from the Syriac version of his pupil Stephenos ibn Basilos, and the version made by an-Natali for the Prince Abu 'Ali as-Sanjuri. But Nicolas made an improved translation in which pains were taken to identify the plants described, thus laying the foundation of a serious study of botany which very quickly bore fruit in the work of Abu Dawud Sulaiman ibn Juljul (circ. 1000), physician to 'Abdarrahman's successor Hisham II, who wrote a supplement to Dioscorides describing a number of plants found in Spain, a land peculiarly rich and varied in its flora, but not known to the Greek author. Although there was a very productive cultural harvest in Andalus and the reign of'Abdarrahman III was the golden age of Andalusian culture, there does not appear to have been any further output of translations from the Greek there. The Andalusian version of Dioscorides as made by Nicolas exists in a Bodleian manuscript. Apparently the older version prepared by Hunayn ibn Ishaq or an-Natali was quite unknown in Spain.

Thabit ibn Qurra is prominent amongst those who revised and corrected Arabic translations of mathematical and astronomical works, and introduces a new source of pro-Greek interest. He was a native of the town of Harran, the ancient Charrae, where men adhered steadfastly to their ancient paganism, although the deities worshipped there bore names borrowed from the Greek pantheon. It was in the midst of Syriac Christian culture, between Edessa and Rashayn, situated on the Bellas, a minor tributary of the Upper Euphrates. It was famous for the purity of the Aramaic spoken there, and this was sometimes attributed to its comparative freedom from Jewish or Christian influences, though in fact there was a Christian bishop and presumably there was a Christian congregation there. It seems to have been in touch with the renaissance of Greek learning which affected both the Nestorian and Monophysite churches and its thought was strongly tinctured with neo-Platonism.

Our knowledge of the ancient religion of Harran is chiefly gleaned from the observations of ad-Dimishqi, who died in a.d. 1327, long after the city had passed into obscurity and who could only have had traditional information about its religion. His information is summarized in Chwolson's Die Ssabier und der Ssabismus, ii, 280-411. From that we learn that the Harranians had five great temples dedicated respectively to the First Cause, the First Reason, the Ruler of the World, Form, and Soul. There were seven other temples dedicated to the seven planets. It was an anomaly for a pagan city to enjoy religious freedom under Muslim rule and noninterference was not due to the city being obscure as it was the capital of the province of Diyar Mudar and under the last 'Umayyad khalif Marwan II it was the residence of the court and government administration. The Fihrist relates a story that al-Ma'mun towards the end of his reign passed by Harran on a military expedition, and he and his officers were astonished at the strange and uncouth appearance of the townsmen. He asked who they were, and was shocked to learn that they were pagans. This implies that Harran was unknown to Muslims generally and a remote isolated district, which is not true. Al-Ma'mun ordered the people to adopt one of the recognized religions, Islam, Judaism, Christianity, or Mazdeanism, before he came back that way. He never did come back, but the people were alarmed at his threats and many of them conformed to Islam or Christianity : Mazdeanism seems to have ceased to make converts by then ; but others adhered to their paganism and sought a way to escape the Khalif's anger. A certain lawyer offered to show them a possible way of doing so for a consideration, and when they had paid him his fee he advised them to claim to be Sabaeans (Sabi'a), as those are mentioned in the Quran as one of the "peoples of the Book" (Qur., 2, 59; 22, 17; 5, 73), and no one knew who the Sabaeans were. The story is obviously apocryphal : the Harranites could not have been so little known in the days of al-Ma'mun as his father Harun ar-Rashid had already put pressure on them as heretics and their city had been the seat of government under Marwan II. The story is an attempt to explain how the Harranites came to be called Sabaeans, a name which we now recognize as not belonging to them. The real Sabaeans were a people of South Arabia, with whom Harran had no concern. But the Mandaeans of the Lower Euphrates, the Haemerobaptists of the Christian fathers and the rabbinical writers who earned the title of "baptists" from their frequent and punctilious ablutions, were in Aramaic called Saba'in from the root SB' "ummerse". Those Mandaeans were Gnostics who inclined to astrological beliefs, possibly actual star-worshippers. The people of Harran were not Gnostics, but they had temples dedicated to the planets, which gave some colour to the confusion between them and the Mandaeans. Harranite neo-Platonism might possibly be confused with Gnostic beliefs. It is characteristic that the Harranites claimed that their religion had come to them from Hermes. It is an interesting instance, though not a unique one, of the way in which the Muslim law was sometimes evaded.

Thabit ibn Qurra (d. 901) " was originally a money-changer in the market of Harran, and when he turned to philosophy he made wonderful progress and became expert in three languages, Greek, Syriac, and Arabic. ... In Arabic he composed about 150 works on logic, mathematics, astronomy, and medicine, and in Syriac he wrote another fifteen books " (Bar Hebraeus, Chron., x, 176). About 872 he was excommunicated by the High Priest of Harran, unfortunately we know nothing about the ecclesiastical discipline of Harran— and sent to Kafartutha, near Dara, but he remained staunch to his religion. "Our fathers," he said, " by the help of God stood firm and spoke boldly, so this favoured town never was polluted by the error of Nazareth (Christianity), and we are their heirs and transmitters of paganism in these days : fortunate is he who bears his burden in hope strengthened by paganism (ibid.). He maintained that it was the pagans who first cultivated the land, founded cities, made ports, and discovered science (ibid.)." After wanderings in various lands he met Muhammad, one of the " Sons of Musa", who recognized his scholarship and took him to Baghdad where he did most of his work. He made translations of Apollonius, Archimedes, Euclid, Ptolemy, and Theodosius, or revised existing translations. He also composed several works on astronomy and mathematics. It has been supposed that he was responsible for the extremely mechanical form in which Ptolemy's cosmography was presented to the Arabs, but that hardly seems justified. In mathematics he introduced the theory of "amicable numbers", a Chinese idea. Such numbers are those in which one is the sum of the factors in the other. Thus, if $p = 3.2^n - I$, $q = 3.^{2n-1} - I$, and $r = 9.2^{2n-1} - I$, assuming that n is a whole number, then $a = 2^n pq$, and $b = 2^n r$ are amicable numbers. Suppose $n = 2$, then $p = 3.2^n - i - II$: $q = 3.2^{n-1} - I = 5$: $r = 9.2^{2n-1} - I = 71$: so the amicable numbers are $a = 320$, $b = 284$. Nothing very much results from this investigation, but it was continued by Maslama al-Majriti and a few other Arab mathematicians.

Thabit had a son Abu Sa'id who became physician to the Khalif al-Qahir. He also was a pagan, but the khalif tried to convert him to Islam and fell into the habit of using the most bloodthirsty threats to force him to do whatever he wanted, until the unhappy physician fled to Khurasan and remained there until al-Qahir was dead. Then he returned to Baghdad and lived there until his own death in 943. Thabit had many pupils, one of whom a Christian named 'Isa ibn Asd translated into Arabic various works which Thabit had composed in Syriac.

About 932-34 the city of Harran was destroyed either by the 'Alids, as Hamawi says, or by Egyptian invaders as Dimishqi asserts. The contemporary historian, John of Antioch, describes this destruction.

In 975 Abu Ishaq ibn Hilal, secretary to the khalifs Muti' and Ta'i', obtained a decree granting religious toleration to the Sabaeans of Harran, of whom there were many in Baghdad— some were still there in the eleventh century—one of whom the most distinguished were the mathematician Abu Ja'far al-Khazin, a convert to Islam, and Ibn al-Wahshiya, author of a work known as "the Nabataean Agriculture" (*Kitab al-falaha an-nabatiya*), which pretended to be a translation from ancient Babylonian. This work was finished in 904 : it is a collection of popular beliefs, superstitions, and legends. It gives no real botanical information but simply aims at proving that the ancient Babylonian civilization existed ages before the rise of the Arabs whose culture was a comparatively recent and inferior one. In fact it is an example of the strong anti-Arab animus characteristic of the early 'Abbasid period. The work had no influence on the development of intellectual culture amongst the Muslim Arabs.

After its destruction in 932-34 Harran was rebuilt, but destroyed again in 1032 when only the great Temple of the Moon was left standing. After these misfortunes it still lingered on and was visited by Ibn Jubayr in 1184, but in 1332 Abu I-Feda found only a decaying village on its site.

Bibliography

Ahudemmeh. "*Life*," ed. F. Nau in PO., iii fasc. I, Paris, 1906.

Allman, G. J. *Greek Geometry from Thales to Euclid*, Dublin, 1889.

Ammianus Marcellinus. Tauchnitz edit., *Leipzig*, 1876.

Arnold, T. W. *Preaching of Islam*, 2nd edit., London, 1913.

Assemani, J. S. *Bibliotheca Orientalis*, i-iii, Rome, 1719-1728.

Bar Hebraeus. *Chronicon Ecclesiasticum*, ed. J. B. Abbeloos et T. J. Lamy, Louvain, 1872-7.

Baumstark, A. *Ceschichte der syrischen Literatur*, Bonn, 1922.

El-Beladhuri. *Kitab futuh al-buldan, Liber expugnationis regionum*, ed. J. de Goeje, Leiden, 1868.

Bergestrasser, G. *Risalat Hunayn ibn Isltaq*, Leipzig, 1925. (Analysis by Meyerhof in Isis, viii (1926), 685-724.)

Bevan, E. R. *House of Seleucus*, 2 vols., London, 1902.

Boer, T. J. *Geschichte der Philosophie im Islam*, Stuttgart, 1901. (Inadequate but the best available.)

Bouyges, A. M. *Sur le de scientiis d'Alfarabi*, Beyrouth, 1924.

Brockelmann, C. *Geschichte d. arabisch. Literatur*, 2 vols. 1. Weimar, 1898; II. Berlin, 1902. Supplementary fasciciles, 1937, etc.

Brooks, E. W. *Vitae virorum apud Monophysitas celeberrimorurn*, in CSCO., ii, 25. Paris, 1907.

Browne, E. G. *History of Arabian Medicine*, Cambridge, 1921.

Caetani, L. *Annali dell' Islam*, vols. i, ii., Milano, 1905-7. (Best account of rise and spread of Islam, but in several details corrected by Musil q.v.)

Cajori, F. A *History of Mathematics*, New York, 1924.

Cambridge History of India, Cambridge, 1922.

Cantor, M. *Vorlesungen uber Gesch. der Mathematik*, Leipzig, I907.

Carra De Vaux. *Penseurs d' Islam*, 5 vols., Paris, 1921-8.

Chabot, J. B. *L'Pcole de Nisibe*, in JA., 1896.

Christensen, *L'empire des Sasanids* in Jour. Iran. Assoc., viii, 434.
Chwolson, D. *Die Ssabier und der Ssabismus*, 2 vols., St. Petersburg, 1856.
Crum, W. E. *Severe d'Antioche an Egypte*, in *Rev. Orient. Chert.*, iii (192-3), 92-104.
Csco., *Corpus Scriptrum Christianorum Orientalium*, Paris.
Cumont. L., *Egypte des astrologues*, Bruxelles, 1937
Darmestster, *Lettre de Tansar au roi de Tabaristan*, in *JA*., 144, 186.
Denha, *Histoire de Marouta*, in PO., III, 52-96, Diehi, Justinien, Paris, 1901.
Dieterici, F. *Alfarabi's philosophische Abhandlungen*, Leiden, 1890.
Doughty, C.M. *Travels in Arabia Deserta*, 2 vols., London, 1923.
Drfyer, J. L. E. *History of the Planetary Systems*, Cambridge, 1903.
Droysen, J. G. *Gesch. de Hellenismus*, 3 Vols., 2nd edit., Gotha, 1877-9.
Duchesne, L. *Early History of the Christian Church*, Eng. trs. of 4th edit., London, 1914.
Dulsem, P. *La systeme du monde*, Paris, 1915.
Dutt, Nalinaksha, *Early Monastic Buddhism*, i, Calcutta, 1941.
Elias of Nisibis, Opus chronologicum, ed. E. W. Brooks and J-B. Chabot, in *CSCO*., iii, vols. 7, 8, Paris, 1909-11.
Goldziher, J. *Muhammedanische Studien*, 2 vols., Halle, 1889-90.
Goodspefd, *Athanasius (of Antioch), Conflict of Severus,* in *PO*., iv, 333-590.
Hankel, H., *Zur Geschichte der Mathematik*, Leipzig, 1874.
Harnack, A., *Lehrbuch der Dogmengeschichte*, 3 vols., Freiburg, 1894.
Haskins, C.H., *Arabic Science in Western Europe*, in *Isis*, vii (1925), 478-486.
Hauser, *Ueber das Kitab al-hijar*, Erlangen, 1922. (Account of the "Sons of Musa", etc.)
Heath, T. L., *Aristarchus of Samos*, Oxford, 1913.
Hffele, C, J., *History of the Christian Church Councils*, English transl., 4 vols., Edinburgh, 1871-83.
Heurtley, C. A., *De fide et symbolo*, Oxford, 1887.
Hirschberg, J., *Geschichte d. Augenheilkunde*, Leipzig, 1899-1918.
Hoffmann, J. G. E., *De Hermeneuticis apud Syros Aristotelis* (Syriac), Leipzig, 1873.

Hogarth, D. G., *The Nearer East*, London, 1905.

Houtsma, T. and others, ed., *Encyclopaedia of Islam*, Leiden, 1906-34.

Huart, C., *Histoire des Arabes*, Paris, 1911-12.

Inge, R. *Philosophy of Plotinus*, London, 1918.

Inostranzev. *Iranian influences on Moslem literature*, Bombay, 1918.

Iorga, N. *Relations entre l'Orient et l'Occident au moyen age*, Paris, 1923.

Janus, "*Zeitschrift fur Geschichte und Litt. des Medizin*," Leiden, 1924.

John of Aphthonia. *Life of Severus*, ed. trs. M. A. Kugener, in PO., II, iii, Paris, 1905.

John, D., In *Migne Patrologia Graeca*, xciv and xcvi.

Joshua The Stylite. *The Chronicle of Joshua the Stylite*, ed. W. Wright, Cambridge, 1882.

Jras., *Journal of the Royal Asiatic Society*, periodical, London.

Karpinski, L.C. Robert of Chester's Latin Translation of the *Algebra of al-Khwarizmi*, New York, 1915.

King, L.W., and Thompson, H.R. *Sculptures and Inscriptions of Darius the Great on the Rock of Behistan*, London, 1907.

Kohl, K. *Ueber den Aufbau der Welt nach Ibn al-Haitham*, in *Sitzb. D. phys. Med. Soc.*, Erlangen, 1925.

Labourt, J., *Le Christianisme dans l'Empire Perse*, Paris, 1904.

Lammens, H., *Le Chantre des Omiades*, Paris, 1895.

Land, J.P.N., *Anecdota Syriaca*, Leiden, 1862.

Landerbg, Graf Von. *Etudes*, Leipzig, 1909.

Leclerc, L. *Histoire de la medicine arabe*, 2 Vols., Paris, 1876.

Le Strange E. *Palestine under the Moslem* (550-1500), London, 1890.

Loew, Aramaische *Pflanzennamen*, 1881.

Lyde, L.W. *The Continent of Asia*, London, 1923.

MacDonald, D.B. *Development of Muslim Theology*, London, 1903.

McCrindle, J.W. *Topography of Cosmas*, Hakluyt Society, 1897.

Maneckji Nusservanji D., *Zoroastrian Civilization*, New York, 1922.

Maspero-Fortescue-Weit, *Histoire des patriarches d'Alexandrie depuis la mort de l'empereur Anastase jusqu'a la reconciliation des eglises jacobites*, Paris 1923.

Mas'udi. *Muruj adh-Dhab*, text trs. B. de Maynard et P. de Courteille, Paris 1861-71.

Merivale, C. *History of the Romans under the Empire*, 8 vols., London, 1896.

Meyer, E. Von. *Gesch. der Botanik*,Leipzig, 1856.

Meherhof, H., *New Light on Hunayn ibn Ishaq*, in *Isis*, viii (1926), 685-724.

Mieli, A., *Pagine di storia della Chimica*, Roma, 1922.

Mommsen, T. *Provinces of the Roman Empire*, Eng. trans., Vol. 2, London, 1909.

Muir, Sir William. *The Caliphate, its Rise, Decline, and Fall*. London, 1891.

Muller, A. Der *Islam im Morgen-und Abehnland*, 2 vols., Berlin, 1885-7.

Muller, M. *Die Quaestiones naturales des Abelardus von Bath*, Munster, 1934.

Musil, A. *The Manners and Customs of the Rwala Bedounis*, New York, 1928.

Nau, F., *Documents pour servir a Phistoire de l'Eglise Nestorienne*, in *PO*., xiii, fasc. 2, Paris.

Neuberger, M. Gesch. *Der Medizin*, Stuttgart, 1908. Engl. trans., Oxford, 1925.

Nicholson, R.A. *Literary History of the Arabs*, 4th Ed., London, 1922.

Noldeke, Th. *Gesch. der Perser und Araber zur Zeit der Sassaniden*, Berlin, 1879.

Pagel. Einfuhrung in *die Gesch. der Medizin*, Berlin, 1898.

Poole, Lane, S. *The Mohammedan Dynasties*, London 1895.

Purgiter. *Ancient Indian Historical Tradition*, 1922.

Pines, S. *Beitrage zur Islamischem Atomenlehre*, Berlin, 1936.

Procopius. Ed. *Dindorf, Corpus Script. Hist. Byzant*., Bonn, 1833-8.

Ray, Sir Praphulla Chandra. *A History of Hindu Chemistry*, 2nd ed., Calcutta, n.d.

Raymond, A. *Histoire des sciences exactes et naturelles*, Paris. 1924.

Schwartz, E. *Concilium universale Chalcedonense*, Berlin, 1932.

Sedillot. *Prolegomenes des tables astronomiques d'Oloug-Beg*, Paris, 1853.

Sewell, A., *Roman Coins found in India*, in *Jras*. (1903), 541 sqq.

Smith, D. E. *History of Mathematics*, 2 vols., New York, 1923-25.

Smith, V.A. *Early History of India*, 3rd ed., Oxford, 1914.

Socrates, *Ecclesiatica Historia*, ed. Oxford, 1844.

Sozoman. *Ecclesiastica Historia*, ed. Migne, PG., lxvii.

Stapleton & Azo-Hussain. Chemistry in *Iraq and Persia in the Tenth Century*, Calcutta, 1927.

Steele, R. *Practical Chemistry in the Twelfth Century* (Rasis de aluminibus et salibus), in *Isis*, xii (1929), 10-96.

Steines, H. *Die Mu'taziliten oder die Freidenker in Islam*, Leipzig, 1865.

Steinschneider, M. *Die europaischem Ubersetz. Dem arabischem bis mitte des* xvii Jahrhund., Wien (Sitz. des Akad.), cxlix, 22-44.

Strzygowski, J. *Der Ursprung des Christlichen Kirchenkunst*, 1919. Eng. trs. Dalton, Origin of Christian Church Art, 1923.

Suter, H. Die *Mathematiker und Astronomen der Araber and ihre Werke*, Leipzig, 1900-4.

Tannery, P. *Recherches sur l'histoire de l'astronomie ancienne*, Paris, 1893.

Tarn, W. W. *The Greeks in Bactria and India*, Cambridge, 1938. (Very useful.)

Thomas, J. *Selections illustrating the History of Greek Mathematics* (Loeb Classical Library), 1941.

Tropeke, J. *Geschichte der Elementar-Mathematik*, 3 vols., Berlin, 1921-22.

Warmington, E. H. *The Commerce between the Roman Empire and India*, 1928.

Weinberg, J. *Die Algebra des Abu Kamil Saga' ben Aslam*, Munich, 1935.

Wiberg, J. *The anatomy of the brain in the works of Galen and 'Ali' Abbas*, in *Janus*, xix (1914), 17-32, 84-104.

Wiedemann, E. *Uber Thabit ibn Qurra, sein Leben und Wirken*, Erlangen, 1922.

Wieleitner, H. *Gesch. der Malhematik*, i, 1921, Berlin.

Winer, L. *Contributions towards a history of Arabico-Gothic Culture*, New York, 1917. (Arguments rash and unproved.)

Woepcke. Sur l'*introduction de l'arithmltique indien en accident*, Paris, 1859.

Wustenfeld, F. *Gesch. der arab. Aertze u. Naturforscher, Gottingen*, 1840.

Index

A

Abbas ibn Sa'id al-Jawahari, 225

Abbasid Court, 217

Abbasid Dynasty, 212

Abbasid, Khalif, 211, 213, 219

Abbasid Revolution, 213

Abd al-Malik, 200, 202, 208

Abd al-Masih ibn 'Aballah, 221

Abdallah ibn 'Ali, 218

Abdarrahaman, 232

Abi Mansur al-Mai'muni, 225

Abraham, Dr., 27

Abu d-Dwamq, 212

Abu I-Feda, 237

Abu Ja'far al-Khazim, 236

Abu l-'Abbas, Khalif, 210, 211

Abu l-Aswad al-Du'ali, 207, 208

Abu l-Hasan, 208

Abu l-Su'ud, 129

Abu Bakr, 125, 199

Abu-Bakr Ibn Zakaria, 67

Abu Dawud, 33

Abu Haraira, 33

Abu Ishaq ibn Hilap, 236

Abu Junus, 23

Abu Malik, Ghiyath, 200

Abu Muslim Mu'adh ibn, 208

Abu Umama Al-Bahili, 56

Abu Yahya al-Batriq, 221

Abu Zakariah Yahya ibn Musawaih, 25

Abu Zayd, 68

Abul-Wafa, 71

Advanced Technology Progress, 102

Afghanistan, 26

Africa, 20, 195

Agriculture and Food Technology, 73

Ahmad an-Nahawandi, 219

Al-Amin, 222, 223

Al-Asma, 68

Al-Batan, 23

Al-Battani, 71

Al-Beruni, 72

Al-Bucasis, 24

Al-Hakam, 19

Al-Hakim's Library, 23

Al-Hassan, 76

Al-Hazan, 23, 24

Al-Hunyan ibn Ibrahim, 232

Al-Khalili, 72
Al Khuzaimi, 224
Al-Khwarizmi, 217
Al-Kindi, 68
Al-Ma'mun, Caliph, 23, 69, 227, 231, 234
Al-Ma'mun's Reign, 229
Al-Mansur, 211-213, 215, 218
Al-Motdid, Khalif, 227
Al-Mu'tasim, 208, 229
Al-Qahir, 226, 236
Al-Yahudiya, 220
Albani's tables, 23
Alessandro Bausani, 76
Alexandria, 202, 227, 229
Ali ar - Rida, 224
Ali ibn Rabban, 221
Ali ibn Yahya, 229
Almajest of Ptolemy, 216
America, 27, 75
Andalusian State, 232
Animal Kingdom, 174, 179
Anti-Arab Demonstration, 217
Antioch, 202
Arab Army, 202
Arab Attack, 202
Arab Conquest, 202
Arab Hellenization, 209
Arab Mathematicians, 236
Arab Pharmacopeia, 231
Arab Religion, 211
Arab Scholars, 215
Arab Scientist, 117
Arab Students, 229
Arab Technology, 209
Arab Thought, 205, 206
Arabia, 26
Arabian Peninsula, 116, 151, 161, 172
Arabian Schools, 18
Arabic Culture, 207
Arabic Culture of Mathematics, 110
Arabic University, 19
Arabic Versions, 219
Arabs of Muhammad's Time, 172
Architectural Engineering, 81
Arculf, Bishop, 200
Aristotle, 76, 163, 221, 232
Asia, 20, 195, 226
Astronomical Tables, 23
Astronomy, 216
Authencity of Quran, 121
Aven Zoor, 24
Averroes, 23
Avicenna, 24

B

Babylonian Civilization, 236
Babylonian Time, 211
Bacon, Roger, 17, 75
Baghdad, 69, 212, 213, 216, 217, 221-224, 227-229, 235, 236
Banu Musa Brothers, 68, 74
Barbun, 220
Barmakid, 216, 221
Barmakid Family, 213, 217, 219
Barmakid Ministers, 219
Barnard Star, 138
Barons and Ladies of Medieval Europe, 21

Basra, 206-209, 212, 227
Battle of Kerbela, 202
Bayt-al-Hikma, 69
Bernard Shaw, 27
Besthorn, T.O., 220
Bible, 116, 119, 127, 141, 146
Biblical Teachings, 141
Birds Behaviour on Divine Order, 182
Bishop of Crete, 202
Blachere, R., 141 154, 180, 194
Biochot, A. Mr., 139
Bonnet, Mr., 121
Boubekeur, Si Hamza, 150
Brahe Tycho, 77
Branches of Science, 30
Buffon, Mr. (Naturalist), 194
Bukhtyishu, 213, 221, 222
Byzantine Government, 200

C

Cairo, 69, 70, 158, 183, 218
Calif's Library, 112
Califs of Baghdad & Cordova, 21
Campbell, Mr., 21
Cardora, 69
Carlyle, Mr. (Philosopher), 27
Carrel Alenis, Dr., 99
Catholic Church, 110
Celestial Organization, 149
Changeis Khan, 57, 93, 96, 121
Charlemagne, Emperor, 17
Chaulukya, King, 41
Chemical Industries, 72, 73
Chemical Science, 48
China, 111
Chisti, Moinuddin, 80
Christ, 26, 120, 122, 141, 182
Christian Countries, 17
Christian Europe, 17
Christian Fanaticism, 16
Christian Monks, 141, 201
Christian Theology, 203
Christianity, 10, 17, 20, 25, 113, 201, 230, 234
Christians, 128, 198
Church, 21
Church Dogmars, 17
Collection of Hadiths, 120, 122, 123
Colonial Dominated Islamic Land, 78
Columbus, 75
Communication Means, 42
Communism, 60
Constituents of Milk, 183
Constitution of Umar, 199
Copernicus (Astronomer), 75, 78, 111
Copernican Theory, 16
Cordoba, 112
Cosmos, 202, 203
Cosmology, 65
Court of B. Ghassam, 210
Court of Hira, 210
Creation of Universe, 30
Crusade, 200

D

Da Vinci, Leonarda, 166
Dagobert, King, 116

Damascus, 69, 201-205, 207, 209, 213, 225
Dar-al-Hikma, 70, 230
Darum (Scientist), 66
Darwin's Principle, 92
Decertes, 163
Divine Omnipotence, 117
Divine Revelation, 12
Divine Wisdom, 180
Diyar Mudar, 234
Donald, R. Hill, 76
Driesch, Hans, 101

E

Earth, 29, 119, 127-131, 134-136, 139, 140, 142, 143, 148, 150, 151, 153, 154, 160, 163, 167, 170-172, 174, 177
Eddington's Position, 94
Egypt, 26, 195, 200, 204, 207, 213
Egyptian Invaders, 236
Einstein, 92
Elchinger, Bishop, 111
England, 75
Environmental Science, 38
Ethical Values, 32
Euphrates, 169, 170, 195, 211, 233, 235
Europe, 126
European Medical Science, 24
Eutychius, 202
Evolution of Land, 170
Explorations of Realm of Nature, 12

F

Faisal, 111, 115
Firdausi's Shahnama, 218
France, 75, 116
French Meterological Office, 167
Freud, 79

G

Gabriel, Archangel, 123, 125
Galen, 76, 232
Galen Hippocrates, 222
Galileo, 78, 111
Galileo's Theory, 98
Garden of God, 211
Geological Science, 39
Germany, 75
Gernada, 69
Gibbon, 27
Giraud, A.K., 192
Glorification of God, 12
Goethe, 27
Gravitational Forces, 137
Gravitational Pull of the Moon, 91
Greek Ethics, 205
Greek influence on Arab, 206
Greek Medical Works, 231
Guerin, P., Mr., 138
Guilliermond, Mr., 177

H

Hadith of Prophet, 111, 112
Hamann, Cecil Boyce, 90
Hamburger, Professor, 182
Hamidullah, Professor, 123, 125, 126, 150, 187
Harran, 237
Harran Religion, 234

Harranite Neo-Platonism, 235
Harun-al-Rashid Khalifa, 23, 69, 215, 220-223, 227
Harvey, 184
Hasan ibn Sahl Wazir, 222, 224
Hadsai ibn Shaprut, 233
Hayyan, Jabir bin, 76
Heavens, 128, 130-133, 135, 139, 142, 143, 155, 158, 160
Hegira, 123
Heiberg, J.L., 220
Heisenberg Uncertainty Principle, 63, 92
Heraclius Emperor, 202
Hindu Philosophy, 17
Hisham, Khalif, 209, 233
Hisham (II), 233
History of Embryology, 191
Human Agency, 103
Hunayn b. Ishaq, 69, 217, 233
Hydrology, 168

I

Ibn Abd Rabbihi, 201
Ibn-al-Haytham, 67
Ibn al-Mughialina, 218
Ibn al-Muqaffa, 218
Ibn al-Wahshiya, 236
Ibn Ihaq, 198
Ibn Jubayr, 237
Ibn Majah, 33
Ibn Masawaih, 226, 227, 231
Ibn Mu'awiya al-Muhallibi, 218
Indonesia, 104
Information on Astronomy from Quran, 144
Intellectual Achievements of Early Muslims, 20
International Centre for Theoretical Physics, 65
Invention of Microscope, 191
Iraq, 209
Iraqian Camp Cities, 207
Isa b. Nun, 225
Isa ibn-Vahga Ibrahim, 231
Islamic Civilization, 67
Islamic Countries, 38
Islamic Culture, 21
Islamic Education, 59
Islamic Empire, 126
Islamic Faith, 9
Islamic Renaissance, 26, 114
Islamic Revelation, 114, 128
Islamic Science, 59, 67, 70, 74
Islamic States, 21
Islamic University, 112
Istanbul, 126
Italy, 75

J

J.N. Sullivan States, 92
J.W.N. Sullivan, 95
Jabir-ibn Hayyan, 23, 67
Ja'far ibn Barmak, 222
Jarir, 201
Jeans, James, Sir, 96
Jerusalem, 203, 209
Jewish Law, 220
Jews, 128, 198
Jibra'il (II), 222, 223
Joad, C.E.M., Dr., 105
John Damascene, St., 226

John, St., 203, 205
Joseph, 182
Judeo-Christian Revelation, 111, 112, 115, 122
Juhanna ibn Masawaih, 226
Julian Colender, 151
Jundi-Shapur, 213, 214, 216, 222, 225, 228, 231
Jundi Shapur Academy, 222
Jupiter, 148

K

Kafartutha, 235
Kant, 88
Kazimirski's Dictionary, 159
Kepler, 18, 78
Khalid ib-Ahmad, 227
Khalid ibn Barmak, 211
Kharijites of Arab, 210
Kharijite Revolt, 210
Khayyam Umar, 67
Khiabar, 56
Khizanat al-Hikma, 69
King of Persia, 198
Kingdom of Persia, 197
Khudainama, 218
Khurasan, 27, 210, 213, 219, 227, 236
Khuwarizmi, 71
Kufa, 206, 207, 211, 212

L

Law of Nature, 88
Leotacticus Emperor, 206
Libya, 214
Lorenz, 180
Lowest Heaven, 149
Lunar Calender, 151

M

Madina, 123, 125, 201, 207
Makka, 56,111, 123, 124, 158, 159, 161, 201, 207
Mandaeans of Lower Eupherates, 235
Mangenot, Mr., 177
Marcus Vitruvius Polio, 163
Marine Engineering, 41
Marioltee, E., 164
Mars, 148
Mathew's Gospel, 120, 121
Martin Luther, 21
Marw, 217, 220, 223, 224
Marw City, 222
Marwan, 209, 210
Marx, 79
Maxwell's Demonstration, 93
Maymana, 220
Mazdean Religion, 213
Mazdeanism, 234
Means of Communication, 181
Medieval Period, 112
Medical Schools, 70
Medical Science, 30, 38, 49
Medieval Europe, 16, 21
Mercury, 148
Mesopotamia, 195, 206, 225
Meteorology, 42
Meton, Mr., 151
Metonic Cycle, 151
Meyerhef, M., 226
Middle Age, 9, 16, 112, 117, 184, 191

Middle East, 166
Military Technology, 73
Mining and metallurgy, 74
Mississipi, 170
Modern Astronomy, 152, 157
Modern Embryology, 119
Modern Geologists, 171
Modern Science, 9, 75, 136, 149, 153
Modern Scientific Order, 135
Monophysite Christian, 200
Montasir, 230
Moon, 119, 144-147, 149-154, 156, 160, 162
Maslama-al-Majriti, 215
Mosul, 225
Mount Wilson Telescope, 136
Muhammad, Prophet, 27, 54-58, 67, 71, 120-126, 141, 164, 174, 184, 196-199, 215, 227, 231
Muhammedanism, 27
Mu'luzilite Thought, 209
Muntakah, Mr., 187
Musa, 227, 228, 231
Musa, al-Khwarizmi, 215, 235
Muslim al-Harra, 208
Muslim Arabs, 200, 236
Muslim Astronomers, 23, 71, 75
Muslim Authors, 116
Muslim Contribution to Engineering, 73
Muslim Culture, 20
Muslim Discoveries, 24
Muslim Doctrines, 224
Muslim Empire, 24, 25
Muslim Europe, 23
Muslim Institutions, 75
Muslim Invaders, 200
Muslim Jurists, 203
Muslim Law, 235
Muslim Occupation in Spain, 19
Muslim Occupied Spain, 232
Muslim Physicist, 119
Muslim Physics, 72
Muslim Polymaths, 68
Muslim Rituals, 203
Muslim Research, 24
Muslim Rulers, 69, 200
Muslim Scientists, 67, 68, 70, 71, 74, 121
Muslim Spain, 17, 21
Muslim Teachers, 17
Muslim University, 17
Mutawakkil, 229-231

N

Nabateam Agriculture, 236
Nahawandi, 216
Nasiruddin, Tusi, 23
National School of Agronomy, 166
Naturalists, 181
Nawbakt, 216
Neo-Platonism, 233
Neptune, 148
Nestorian Academy, 213
Nestorian Catholics, 230
Nestorian Church, 230
New Testament, 121
Newton, 18, 75, 78,143
Nietsche, 88
Nile River, 169

Nishapur, 69
Non-Arab World, 197
Non-Christian Affairs, 111
North-East Africa, 195

O

Ocean, 175
Oceanography, 30, 38
Old Testament, 120-122, 141, 143
Omar, 125
Orbital Movement of Sun, 152, 153

P

Palissy, Bernard, 164, 166
Parthia, 198
Pascal, 78
Paul (VI), Pope, 111
Perrault, P., 164
Persia, 26, 214
Persian Armies, 206
Persian Territory, 196
Persian Writers, 211
Physical Laws, 50
Physiological Studies, 103
Pilgrims of Makka, 194
Plank, Max, Prof., 98
Planetary System, 138, 143
Planets, 147
Plato, 163
Pluarality System, 138
Pluto, 134, 148, 163
Policy of Earlier Caliphs, 198
Portugal, 75
Pre-Christian Era, 122
Pre-Islamic Civilization, 75
Pre-Islamic Religions, 25
Pre-Muslim Days, 201
Preufer, C., 226
Primitive Civilization, 195
Primitive Society, 195
Problem of Contraception, 193
Prophet of Islam, 12, 15, 26
Ptolemy, 216
Ptolemy's Cosmography, 235
Ptolemy's Time, 150
Pythogoras, 76

Q

Quran, 134, 135, 139-164, 166-194, 199, 204, 205, 207, 212, 234
Quranic Instructions, 38, 116, 132, 143
Quranic Revelation, 117, 122, 123, 141, 142, 150, 161, 163, 184, 185, 191

R

Rasulullah, 66
Rationalist Movements, 17
Red Fort, 81
Red Sea, 195
Rennaissance, 166
Respiratory System, 104
Rights of Private Property, 195
River Valley Culture of Mesopotamia, 195
Rockfeller Institute, 99
Rogers, 17
Roman Army, 206
Roman Catholic Church Inquisition Court, 80
Roman Emperor, 198, 222

Roman Empire, 214, 228
Roman Government, 202
Roman Law, 199, 204
Roman Military Method, 206
Roman Territory, 196
Rome, 163, 198, 204

S

Sabaeans of Harran, 236
Sa'd ibn Waqqar, 207
Saki ibn Robban al-Tabari, 220
Salt ibn Tariqa al-Akhtal, 200
Saturn, 148
Saudi Arabia, 111, 115
Scientific Obligations to Mohammedans, 10
Sergius, St., 20
Sex Education, 192
Sexual Area of Man, 192
Sexual Relations, 193
Shapley, Mr., 152
Sheik Si Boubakeur Hamza, 180
Ships and Navigation, 73
Siddhanta Brahmagupta's, 219
Sinam ibn Tabit, 226
Social Evolution, 195
Social System, 23, 135, 137, 148, 149, 151, 155
Solomon, 54
Solomon , David, 182
South Arabia, 234
Spain, 233
Spanish Republic, 19
Spanish Saracen, 18
Species of Bird, 182
Spherical Trigonometry, 24
Stars, 147, 156
Stephenos, ibn Basilos, 233
Sun, 29, 119, 136-138, 145, 146, 148, 150-153, 155-157, 173
Supremacy of God, 60
Supreme Council of Islamic Affairs, 158, 183, 188
Surface Distribution of Continents and Oceans, 171
Syria, 195, 198-200, 202, 204, 206, 211
Syriac, 217
Syriac Christian Culture, 233
Syriac Translations, 217
Syriac Versions, 219
Syrian Army, 210
Syrian Christian, 229, 232

T

Tabit ibn Ihaq, 232
Tabit ibn Qurra, 233, 235
Tabri, Mr., 150
Taghlib Clan of Jusham ibn Bakr Tribe, 200
Taimur Pasha's Library, 226
Taj Mahal, 81
Tariqa-al-Akhtal, 200
Tashkent, 126
Technical Education, 53
Temple of Moon, 237
Temple of Solomon, 54
Test of Faith, 13
Textile Industries, 73
Thales of Miletus, 163
Theodorus, Abucara, 203
Theory of Evolution of Darwin, 79

Theory of Relativity by Einstein, 62
Theory of Seeds, 191
Thermonuclear Reactions, 137
Tigris, 169, 195
Tinbergen, 180
Transformation of Embryo, 193
Trieste Research Institute, 65
Tripoli, 203
Turkey, 26

U

Uddain, Nizam, 80
Uisham, 203
Ulema Grand, 111
Ulugh Beg, 70
Umar (II), 201
Umar ibn Farrukhan, 221
Umayyads, 201, 210, 211, 212
Umayyad Dynasty, 209
Umyyad Khalifate Period, 200
United States, 112, 136
Universal Laws of Gravitation by Newton, 63
Universsalis Encyclopaedia, 107, 166, 167
Universalism, 27
Universe, 132, 134, 136, 139, 140, 142, 155, 157, 158, 175
Uranus, 148
Utba ibn 'Azwan, 207
Uthman, 126, 208
Uyun, al-Akhbar, 218

V

Vegetable Kingdom, 175, 178, 180
Venus, 148
Veterinary Science, 46, 47
Volger, O., 164
Von Frisch, 180

W

Walid (I), 201
Walids's Reign, 201
Water Cycle and Seas, 163, 175
Wathiq, 229
Western Asia, 195, 198
Widowhood, 194
Wilson, John, 91

Y

Yahya, 213, 214
Yahya ibn Ali Mansur, 227
Yangtze River, 170
Yazid, 20, 201
Yazid (T), 201
Yusuf Ali, 124, 129, 153

Z

Zaid Ibn, Tabit, 124, 125
Zakariya at-Taifuri, 230
Zayd, 198
Ziyad, ibn Abihi, 207, 208
Zoological Science, 47
Zoroastrian Religion, 216

❑❑❑